IMAGES
*of America*

# GREEKS IN PHOENIX

**ON THE COVER:** The groundbreaking ceremony of the Hellenic Community House, which was to be used for church services until the church was built in 1947, was held on October 31, 1930. (Courtesy Holy Trinity Greek Historical Committee Archives.)

IMAGES of America

# GREEKS IN PHOENIX

Holy Trinity Greek Historical Committee

Arizona Historical Foundation

ARCADIA PUBLISHING

ISBN 978-0-7385-5634-5

Published by Arcadia Publishing
Charleston SC, Chicago IL, Portsmouth NH, San Francisco CA

Printed in the United States of America

Library of Congress Catalog Card Number: 2007941885

For all general information contact Arcadia Publishing at:
Telephone 843-853-2070
Fax 843-853-0044
E-mail sales@arcadiapublishing.com
For customer service and orders:
Toll-Free 1-888-313-2665

Visit us on the Internet at www.arcadiapublishing.com

*This book is dedicated to all those who preceded us in the Greek community and church. Our hope is that their memory will live on through this book to help future generations recognize their Greek legacy.*

# Contents

# ACKNOWLEDGMENTS

We want to thank the many people who helped us prepare this book, all of whom gave generously of their time and shared their photograph collections, treasured memories, and other historical information. In doing so, we rediscovered our history.

A special thank you goes to Helen Stamatis Glitsos for her extensive collection of photographs and newspaper articles and for identifying individuals among the early pioneers. Also, a special thank you goes to Bessie Johnson Demos for her contribution of historical information of the beginning of our community.

Unless the photograph is credited otherwise, all the photographs in this book are from the Holy Trinity Greek Historical Committee Archives. A special thanks to the following individuals: John Katsenes, Zella Zannis, Helen Metsopolos Moschovitis, Stella Ladas Glitsos, Tassie Ladas, Art Haritos, George Mallas, Fred Xalis, Connie Xalis Loomis, Georgia Hotis Poulos, Deanne Poulos, Helen Kostopoulos Williams, John Gannis, Fannie Gannis Pappas, Ange Poulakidas Pappas, George Papadopoulos, Mary Annos Floor, Dora Contos Tsantilas, Vaso Sanichas Hepler, Florence Sanichas Peters, Patty Valesquez Davis, Georgana Kimmell Frieh, Rev. Chrysostom and Presbytera Penny Selimos, Rev. James and Presbytera Catherine Tavlarides, Rev. Anthony Pentikis, Bebe Speros, Aspacia Stevens, Steve Fotinos, Maria Fakonas, Mae Ducas, Tina Papagalos Zannis, Gabriel and Helen Papagalos, Christine Stamatis, Debbie Doukakis, Melanie and John Ioannou, Gordon and Angie Thomas Yates, Mary Falkedes Scarla, Dean and Stella Tsantilas, Jim Thomas, Andrea Contos Nicoluzakis, Irene Bafaloukos Goad, and Leonard Bafaloukos; without them, this book would not have been possible.

Our sincere thanks go to Jared S. Jackson, the Southwest acquisitions editor at Arcadia Publishing, for his patience and guidance. He was always supportive and accommodating when called upon.

# INTRODUCTION

This book represents dedication and a tremendous effort by a relatively small group of historians committed to documenting for posterity the history of the Greek community in Phoenix, Arizona.

In these pages, you will learn through detailed documents, verbal accounts, and photographic images how a handful of emigrants from Greece settled in Phoenix in the early 1900s, bringing with them an ethic of hard work, a love for family, and a deep belief in their Orthodox faith.

Any written accounts of the Greeks in Phoenix from 1912 to 1922 are either altogether nonexistent or have been lost. We do know, of course, that such monumental world events as the Great War (1914–1918) in Europe and elsewhere shaped the course of the American nation and its people for generations to come. What impact the war may have had on the Greek families at the time in Phoenix can only determined by speculation.

On May 17, 1923, the articles of incorporation were signed by the officers and board of trustees of the new nonprofit church organization. The Phoenix founders of the Holy Trinity community purchased real estate for their church and school. The Bennett property at Third Avenue and Van Buren Street was purchased, but the property was not large enough for its intended purpose, and the decision was made to sell the lot to the First Presbyterian Church.

The next site considered was at Fifth Street and Willetta Street, known as the Los Olivos property, but the neighbors objected to the construction of a church and school because they considered it a residential area.

On October 19, 1930, the minutes of the Holy Trinity Board of Trustees indicate that funds were loaned to the church in the amount of $2,500 by a Mr. Zambaras, who would hold the deed to a property known as the Evergreen Addition. The exact street address is unknown.

In the fall of 1929, the first general assembly meeting took action by the members and the newly elected board of directors to finalize the site for the church and school. The meeting agenda considered the purchase of a sizable property, which was an unpaved street on the perimeter of the city. The general assembly approved the purchase and granted the construction contract to build the church and adjoining community hall.

The project experienced some delays and difficulties along the way, occurring less than a year after the 1929 U.S. stock market crash, the enormous event that triggered what would come to be called the Great Depression.

Father Sardounis from Los Angeles celebrated the completion of the Holy Trinity Greek Orthodox Church in 1931 with the first Divine Liturgy. After two decades, the religious and social center for Greek American families became a reality.

In the sprawling, ever-growing modern metropolis of today's Phoenix and surrounding municipalities, it may be difficult to envision a sparsely settled Salt River Valley, just barely distant in time from its rough and tumble frontier era. At the beginning of the 20th century, electric power, telephones, and motorized transportation were just beginning to transform the Old West into a more civilized society. It would take a dozen years into the 20th century before Arizona would leave its territory status behind and enter the Union as the 48th state on February 14, 1912.

It is against this backdrop that Greek-speaking pioneers first began to arrive in Phoenix (and a few other Arizona communities). They learned the English language, secured employment or started their own businesses, purchased homes for their families, advanced formal education for their children, and eventually fulfilled their desire to have their own religious and social center.

While this is a story that has essentially been repeated in the United States by other ethnic groups, what is unique here is that the early Greek immigrants were generally so few in number, and fewer yet were those who ventured West to such young cities as Phoenix. Once here, their innate industriousness and determination bore the fruits of success, and it is upon this early foundation that the very few made it possible for the now very many to enjoy the modern continuation of an extraordinary culture, a glorious history, and an eternal spiritual faith.

We have gone to great lengths in our research to be as accurate as humanly possible regarding the names, dates, places, and occasions that comprise the specific history of the people represented in this book. This has been a labor of love, though it may not be without its flaws. In time, critical observation may reveal some errors, omissions, or inaccuracies, and for such unintended defects, we ask for your forbearance.

Most of all, to our children, grandchildren, and beyond, we hope you enjoy this step back in time and gain an appreciation for those hearty and resolute men and women who pioneered the Greek community in Phoenix. This is part of your legacy, and we are pleased to have had the privilege of preserving it for you in these pages.

—Alexandra (Tsokatos) Anagnopoulos
Helen (Stamatis) Glitsos
Bessie (Theodoropoulos) Hotis
Emily (Gannis) Kimmell
Andrew A. Limber
Mary Louise (Gannis) Theodoropoulos

# *One*

# The First Families

The early Greeks of Phoenix were part of a large wave of European immigrants who came to America in search of a better life in the 1880s. Most from Greece were men from small villages that were affixed to an agrarian society, so the majority of them had no marketable trade when they arrived on the shores of the New World.

Consequently, with no formal skills and without knowledge of the English language, the first Greeks in America worked as day laborers, bootblacks, fruit and vegetable peddlers, candy and tobacco vendors, or as railroad section hands during the great expansion of the nation's railroads to the West. Many would later gravitate toward the food service and hospitality business, finding an especially comfortable and profitable niche working in and owning restaurants.

The first Greeks listed in the 1908 Phoenix City Directory were two brothers, Charles Sanichas and Chris Sanichas. Upon emigrating from Greece, the two brothers went to Chicago in 1907 and soon thereafter came to Phoenix. Charles opened a fruit and confectionery store at 44 West Washington Street, while Chris established the Sanichas Confectionery Store at 320 East Van Buren Street. He and his family would later have an important role in the founding of the Greek community in Phoenix.

By 1912, the year of Arizona statehood, the list of Greek names in the city directory had grown to nine families. One of these was the Georgouses family, consisting of five brothers: Anthony, James, John, Nicholas, and Peter. Anthony and Peter owned an ice cream wagon, and James and Nicholas were bootblacks. By 1931, they were joined by many more families who migrated to Phoenix.

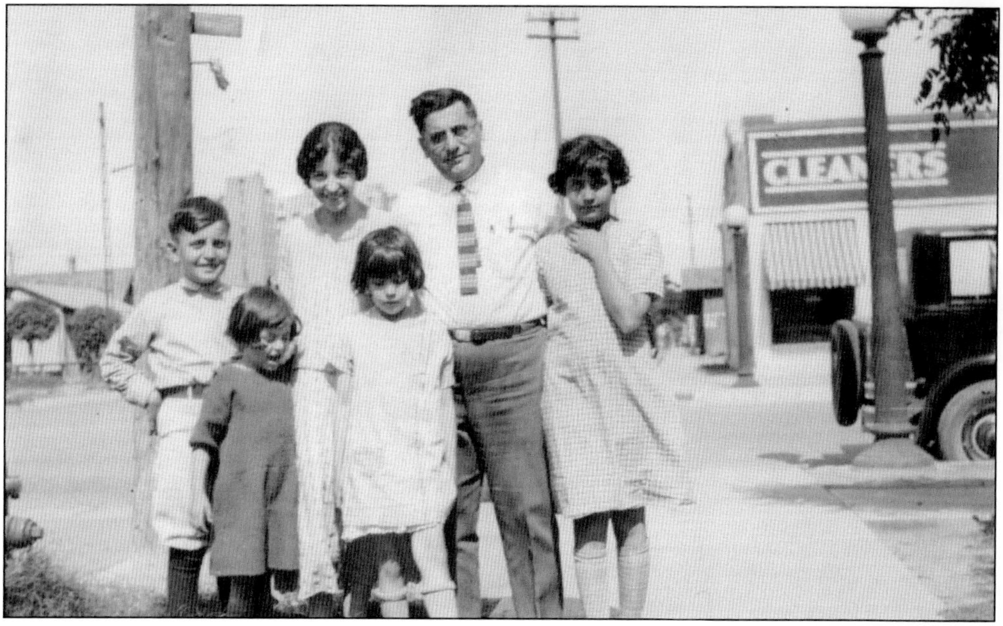

In 1908, Chris and Anna Sanichas settled in Phoenix. They had four children: Vaso, Georgia, Florence, and John. Chris was the owner of the Sanichas Candy Company. They manufactured and sold candy, employing many of the early Greek settlers. He was instrumental in the founding of the Holy Trinity community.

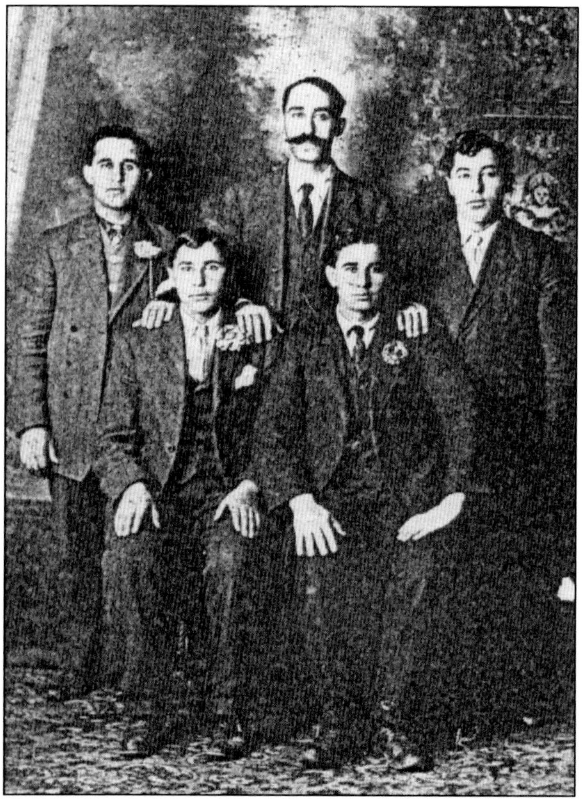

In 1909, the five Georgouses brothers arrived in Phoenix. They established various businesses, including shoe shining, hat cleaning, ice cream vendors, restaurants, and real estate. They served in various positions in the founding of the Holy Trinity community.

Dimetri (James) Georgouses moved to Phoenix around 1910 along with his four brothers. Dimetri married Matina Vrahos in the 1920s. Having no children of their own, they adopted Frances Georgouses, who was the daughter of Tom Georgouses (deceased) and Angela Georgouses.

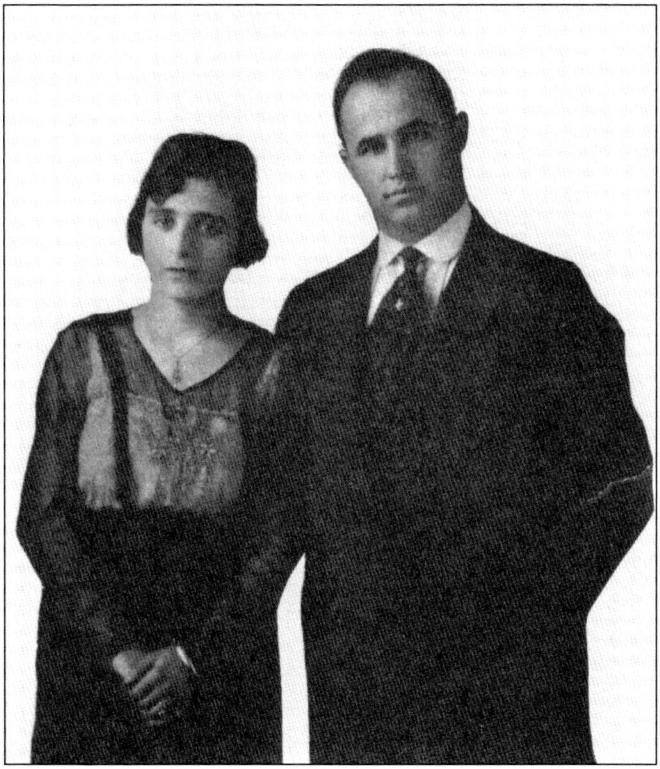

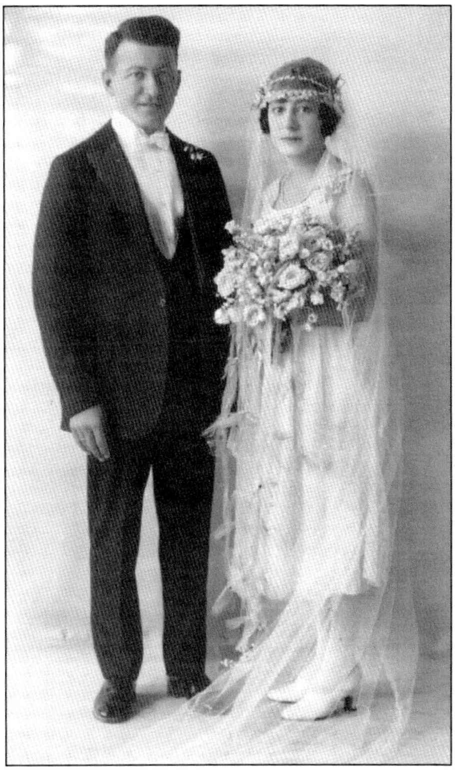

In 1912, Nicholas John Gannis came to Phoenix to live with his sister and brother-in-law, Anna and Chris Sanichas. He worked for the Sanichas Candy Company. In the 1930s, he opened the Southwest Candy Company. Nicholas married Meropy Laskari in 1925 in Phoenix. They had four children: John, Emily, Fannie, and Mary Louise.

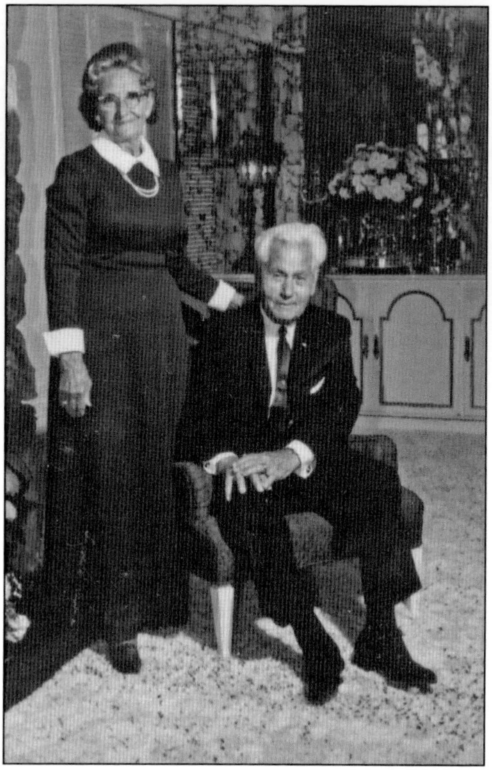

Panagiota (Spiropoulos) Georgouses came to Phoenix in 1910. She married Nick Georgouses, and they had three sons: Chris, Pete, and Jim. After the early death of Nick, Panagiota married Chris Petoumenos. Together they raised her three sons.

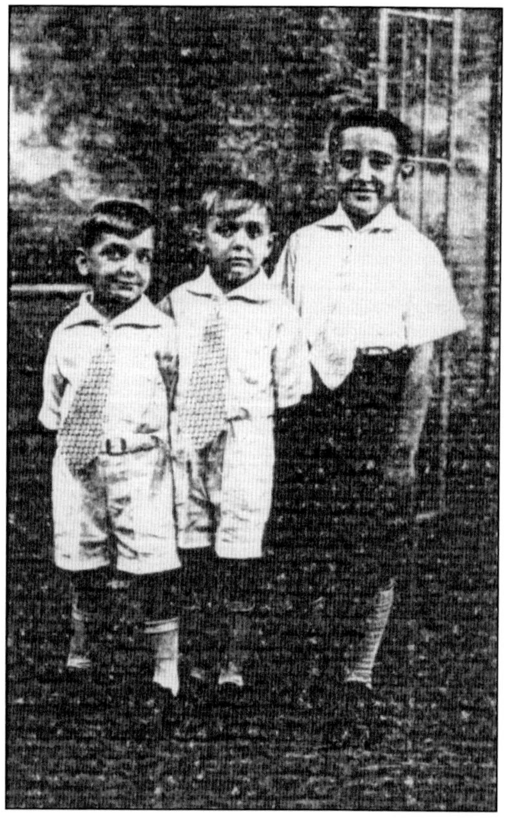

In 1910, John B. Anagnopoulos (at right) came to Phoenix to live with his cousins at 37 West Washington Street. He then brought his brother, Tom (Anagnopoulos) Annos, over in 1911. John left Phoenix to fight in the Balkan War, intending to return, but was captured and held prisoner for years. Tom founded the Nogales Café in 1941 (below). The Nogales was in operation until the City of Phoenix purchased the property in 1983. He married Mercedes in the 1920s, and they had three children: Katherine, Pete, and William.

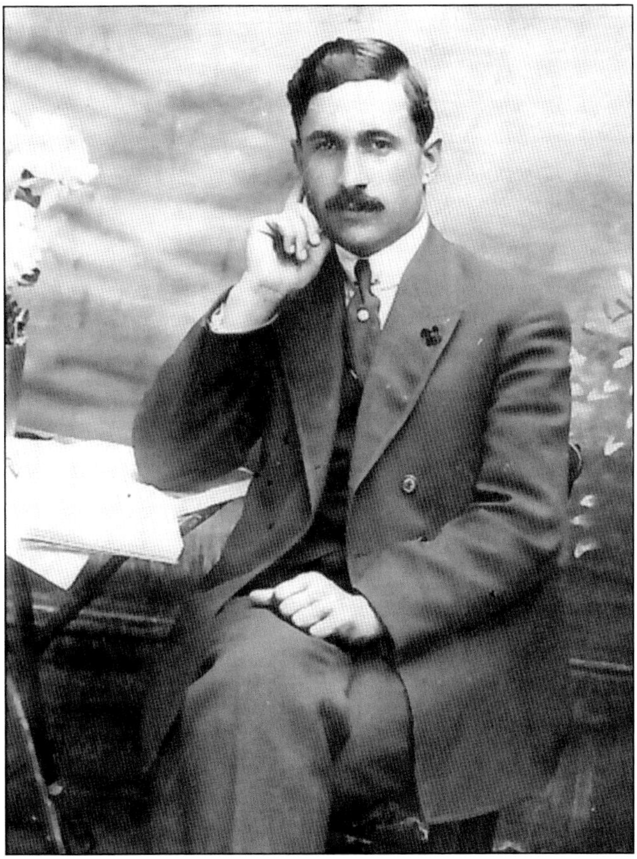

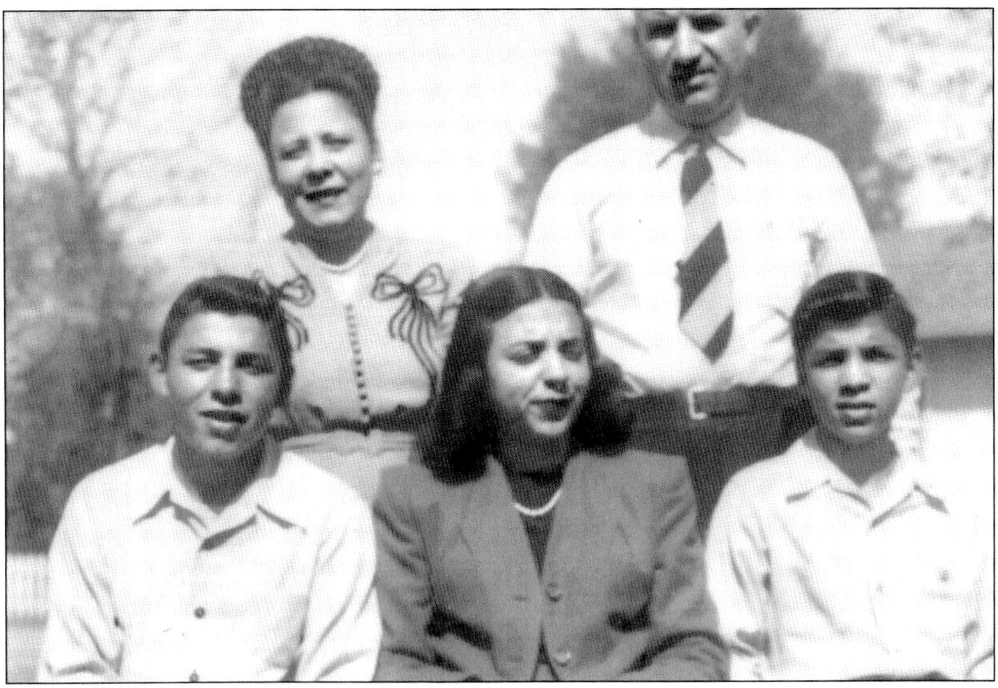

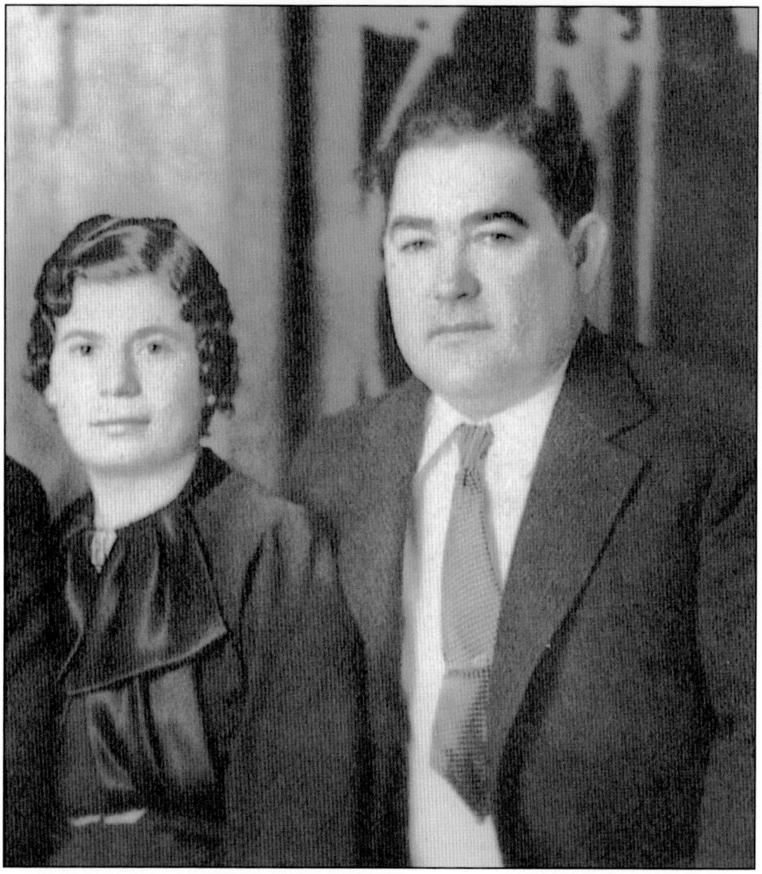

In 1912, John Pappas came to Phoenix. He returned to Greece in the early 1930s, at which time he married Katina Chotras. They had three children: Jenny, Alex, and Tommy. He was a partner in the Busy Bee Café. John never drove a car and was a well-known figure in downtown Phoenix, riding his bike to and from work until the time of his death in 1956.

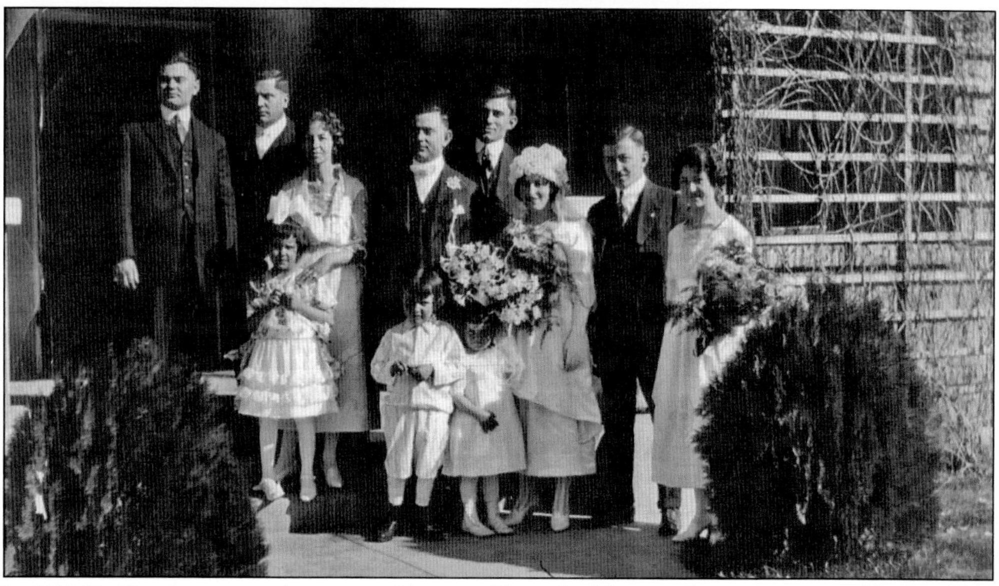

In 1913, Basilios Anagnopoulos came to Phoenix. He worked for a produce company and for Sanichas Confectionery. He married Komna Gannis in 1914. They had three children: Pauline, Georgia, and Rosemary. Basilios was involved in the founding of the Hellenic Community House.

Nick (Anagnopoulos) Annos arrived in Phoenix in 1914. Nick and Garifalia Sakellario were married in 1925. Nick was in the candy and sundries business in the Phoenix area. They had four children, George, Pauline, Mary, and Antoinette. Nick also was a president of the Holy Trinity board of directors in 1935.

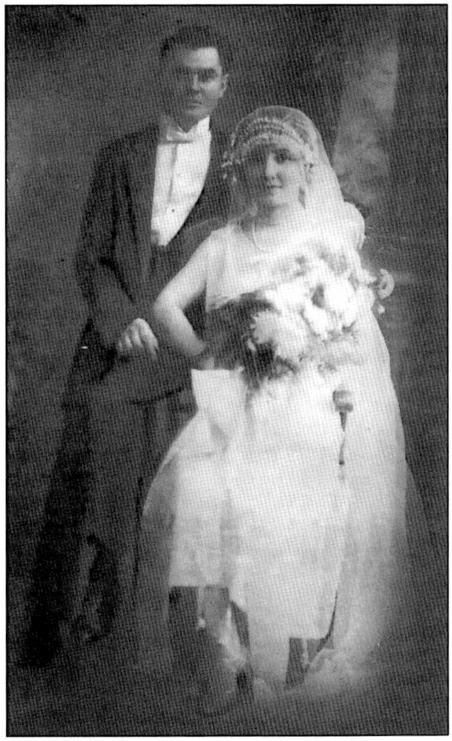

Costantina (Gouzounis) Tamaras traveled to the United States with her aunt Aspacia Georgouses. Costantina was orphaned at an early age and was raised by her aunt Aspacia. Pete Tamaras and Costantina were married in Phoenix. As their families grew, they moved to what was known as "the Farma," the Tamaras farm. They had four children: Tom, Lula, Mary, and George.

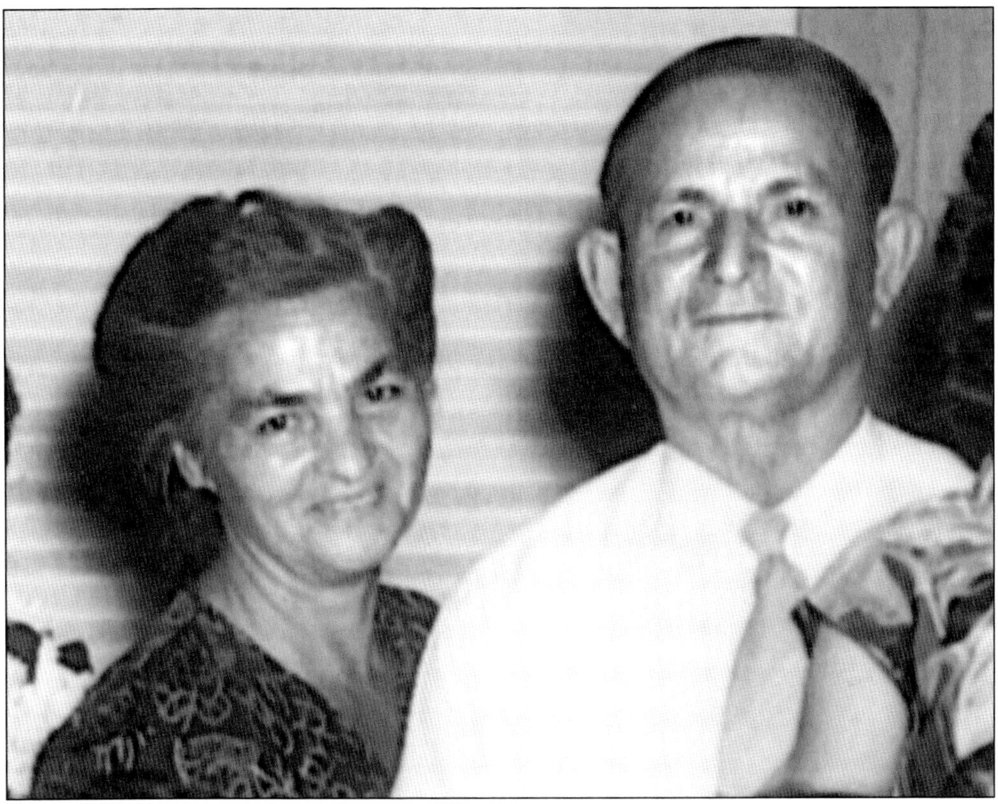

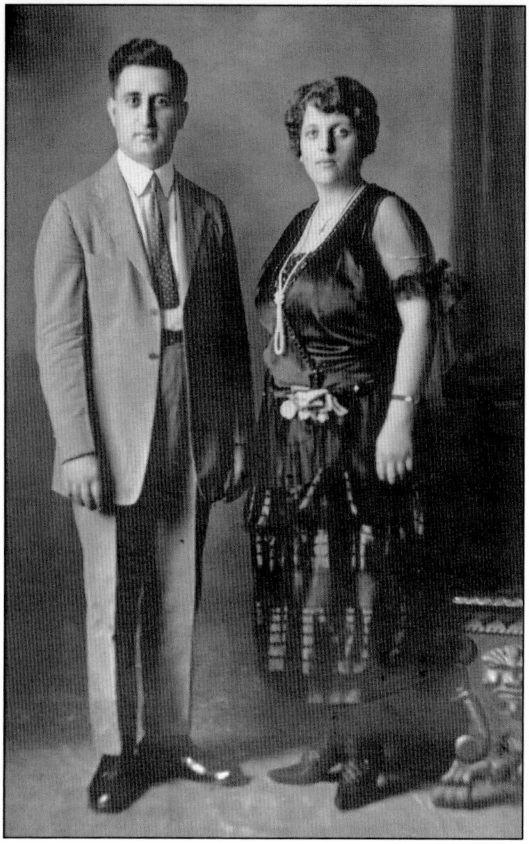

Milton and Chrysanthe Stamatis came to Phoenix in 1917 with their four children: Helen, Milton (Pete), Sam, and James. Milton Stamatis was a prominent member of the Phoenix community, where he established various businesses. He was one of the founders of the Holy Trinity community and was elected as the first president in 1923.

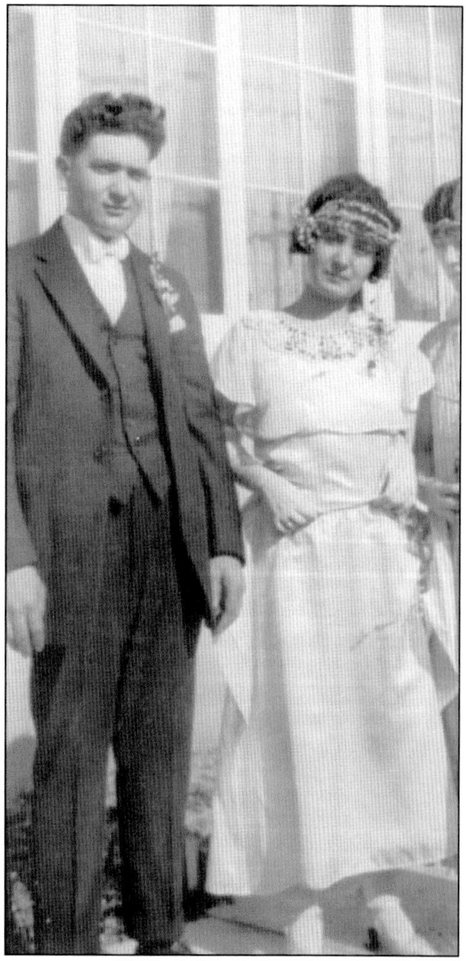

Chris and Maria Mitchell came to Phoenix in the late 1910s. Chris owned Mitchell's Sweet Shop. He developed and manufactured Cactus Candy. Maria Mitchell sang professionally and was involved in many church activities. They had two children: Alice and Helen. Chris was one of the founders of Holy Trinity.

John and Olga Thomas came to Phoenix in the 1920s. They had four children: George, Tony, Nick, and Angie. John Thomas established various shoe shine and repair shops. Tony's Shoe Repair (with three locations) was very well known in the city of Phoenix.

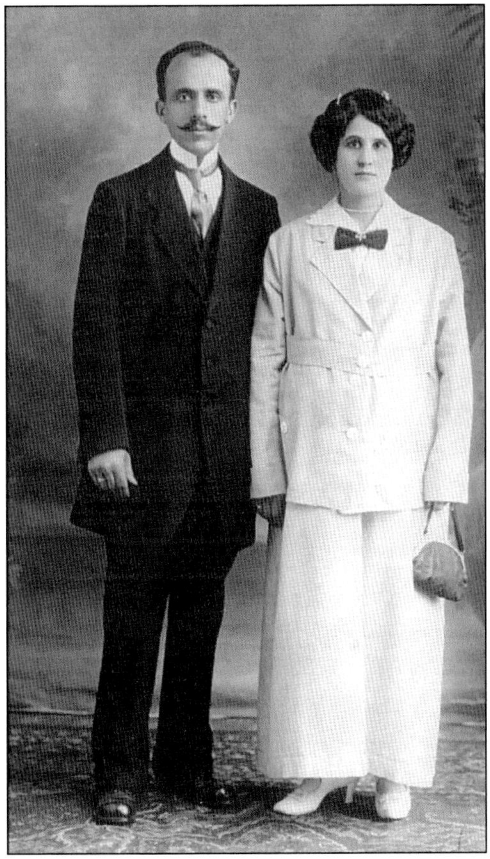

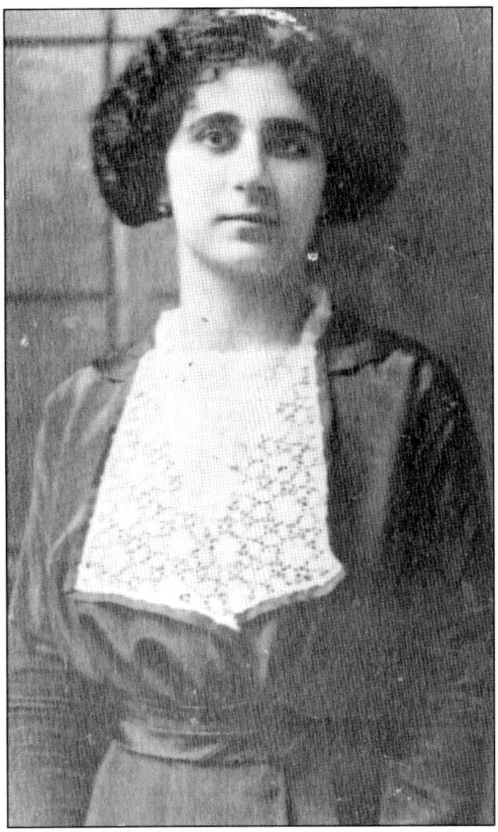

George Falkedes married Katherine Glitsos in 1919 in St. Louis, Missouri. They moved to Phoenix in 1921. He was the owner of the Athens Hat Works. Their three children were Jenny, Mary, and Angelo.

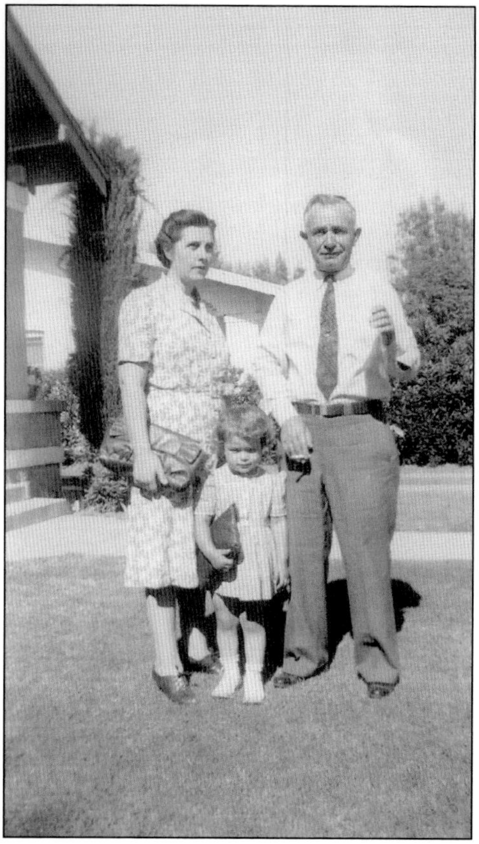

Chris Pallas came to Phoenix in the 1920s and opened two restaurants. In 1941, he married Christina Tountas. Together they raised her two sons, Chris and Nick Tountas. Chris Pallas was very well known in the community and was a big supporter of the Holy Trinity church.

Gust Metsopoulos came to Phoenix in 1923. He owned and operated a business selling fruits and sandwiches. He later opened a restaurant known as Gust's Chili Parlor. Gust and Mary married in 1929 and had three children: Jimmy, George, and Helen. He was always involved in the Holy Trinity church and later became one of its presidents.

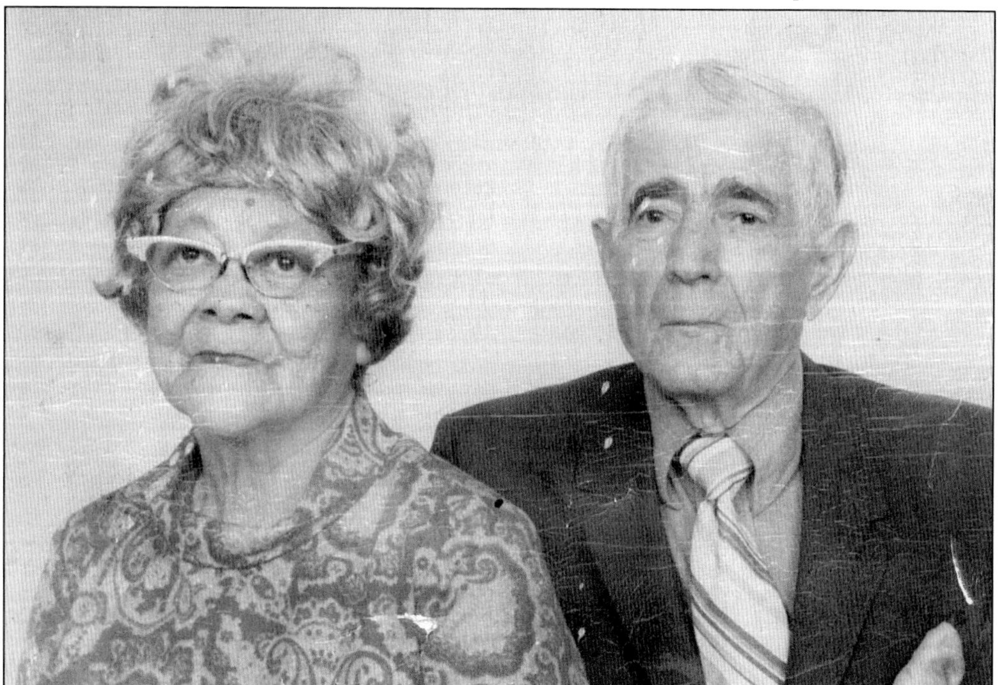

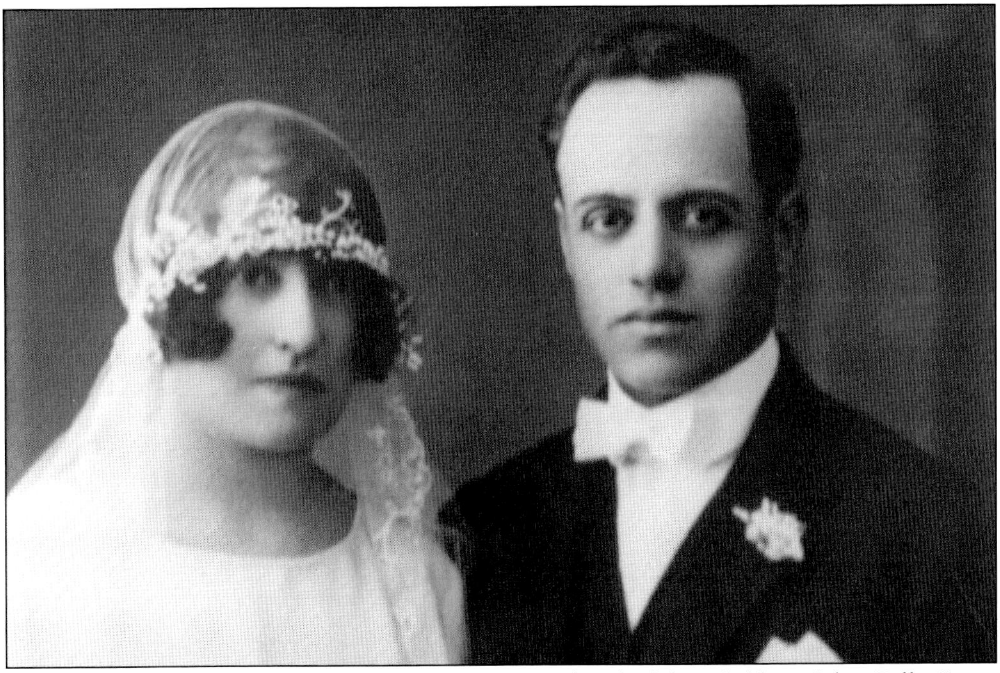

Michael and Joan Zannis came to Phoenix in 1925. They had four children: John, Zella, Peter, and Helen. Michael Zannis was part owner of the Saratoga Café until 1928; he then left Phoenix for Los Angeles, returning in 1935. Upon his return, he worked at the Grand Café until opening his own business in 1947.

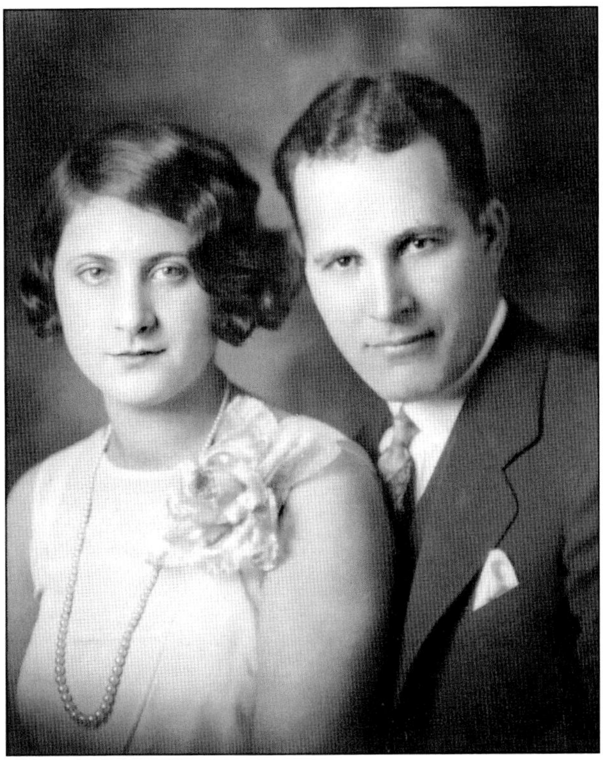

Tom Katsenes came to Phoenix in 1925. He was a salesman for the New York Life Insurance Company. He married Fannie Ladas on October 31, 1926, in Douglas, Arizona. They had four children: John, Katherine, Paul, and Chris. The family was very active in the Holy Trinity community.

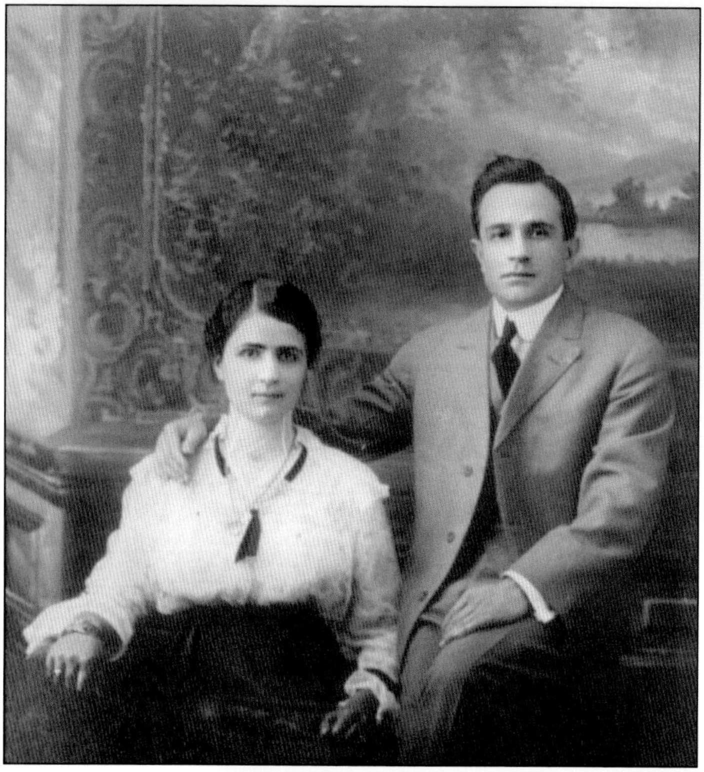

James and Fotinie (Rogokos) Xalis married in 1914 in Chicago. They had seven children: George, Nick, Connie, Alexandra, John, Catherine, and Fred. Before he was married, James settled in Douglas, Arizona, where he opened a movie theater; he would later own a chain of movie theaters in southern Arizona. In 1926, Fotinie passed away at the age of 35, and James moved his family to Phoenix. He owned 10 acres on Central Avenue and Camelback Road. In 1955, this property, where Uptown Plaza was built, was leased to Del Webb. It was the first major shopping center in Arizona.

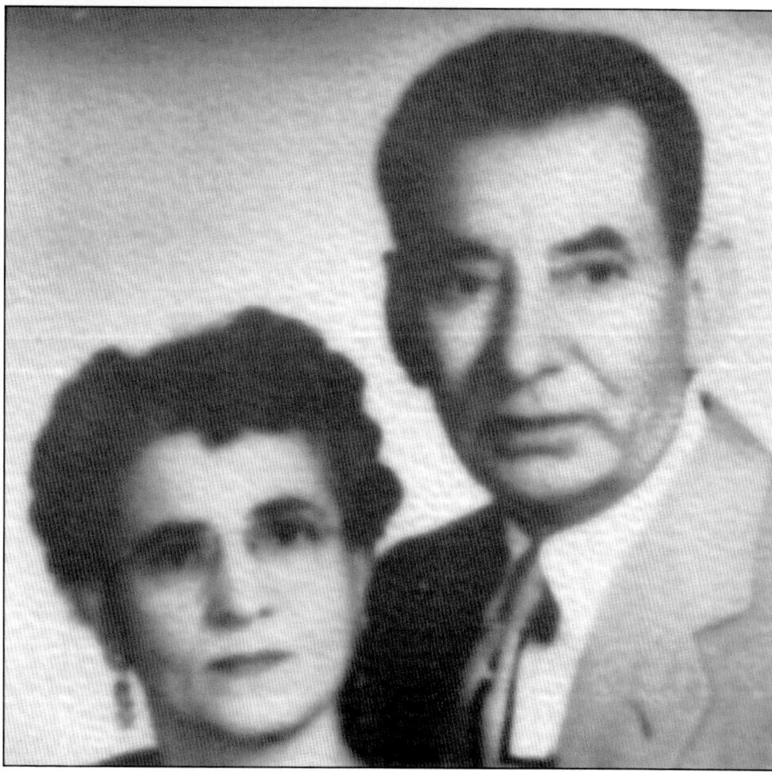

Peter and Rozalia Manos moved to Phoenix in 1929. He opened several businesses, including a market, café, and bar. They had three children: Harriett, Jim, and George.

Tony and Anna Fotinos came to Phoenix in 1927. He was a cook and later became a partner in the Saratoga Café. They had no children.

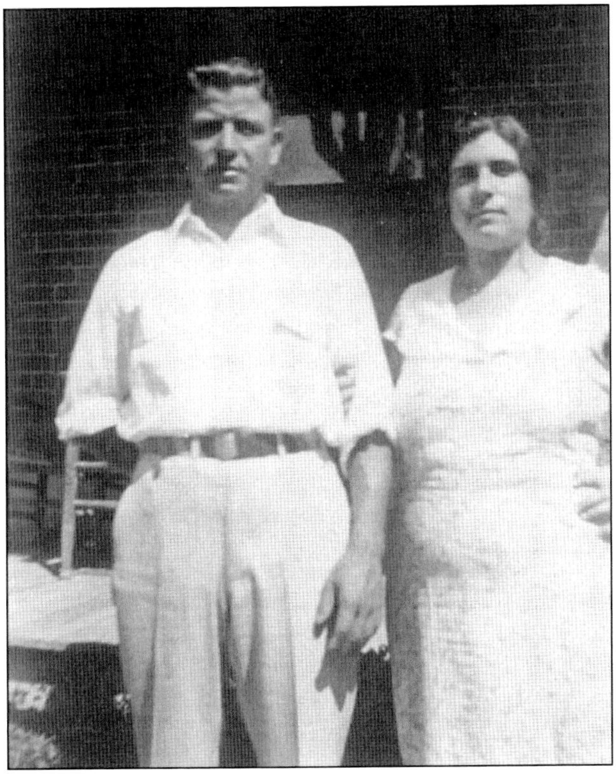

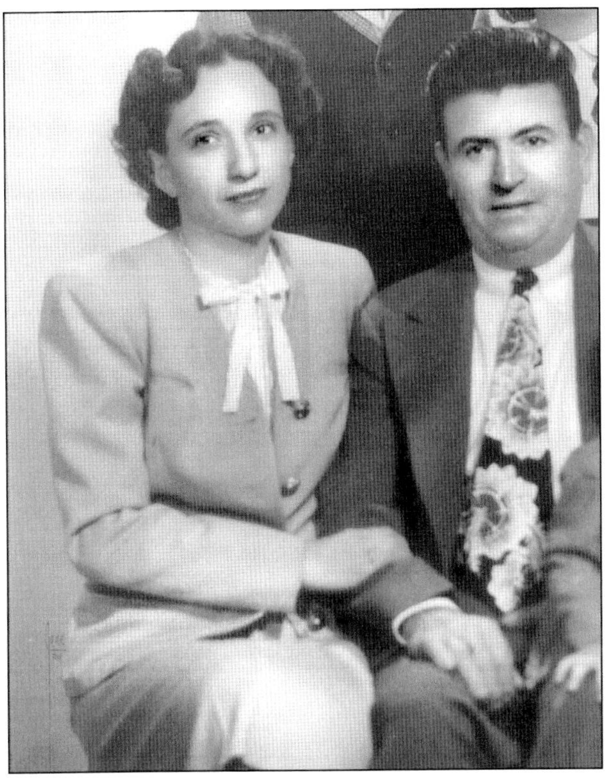

Chris Fotinos came to Phoenix in 1928. He worked as a cook at the Saratoga Café. In 1920, he became a partner. On May 10, 1936, he married Dimetra Tsegouris. They had four children: Steve, Irene, Tony, and Nick.

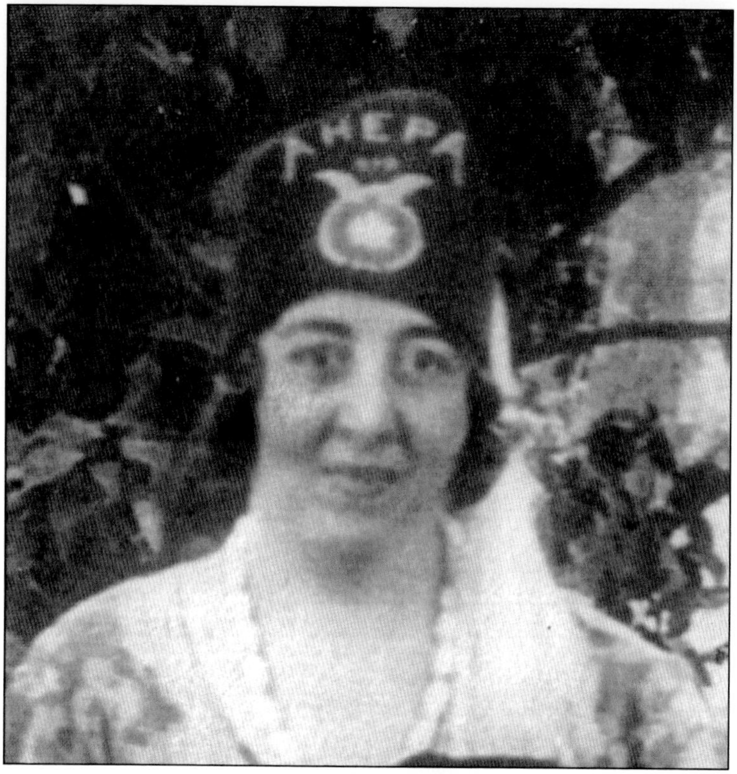


Floros and Eftihia Mitchell came to Phoenix in the 1920s. Floros opened a confectionery store at 133 North First Avenue in 1926; he was president of the Holy Trinity board of directors in 1935. No photograph of Floros Mitchell is available.

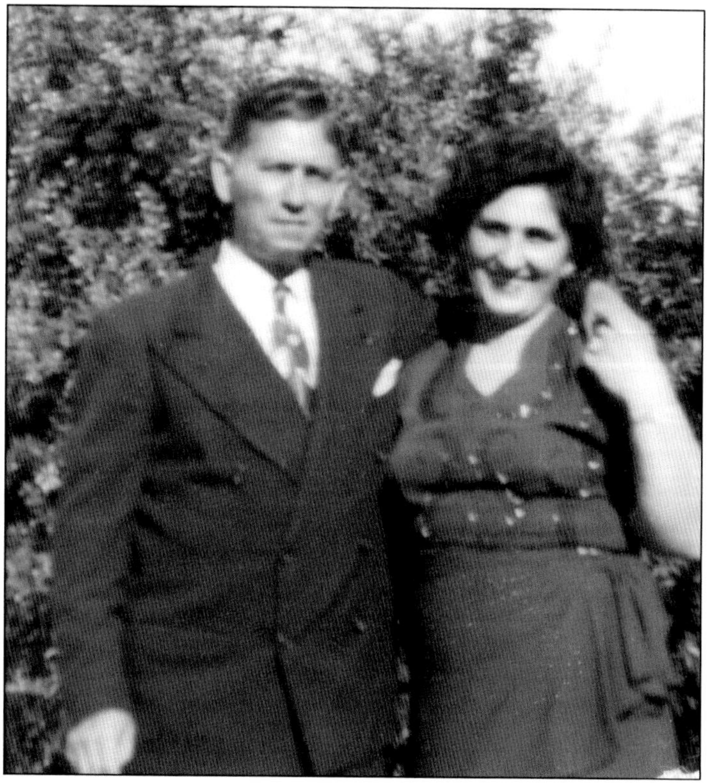

Harry Johnson first came to the United States in 1912. He served in the army supply company stationed in France. He came to Phoenix in the early 1920s. He married Paraskevi Koutsoukos on August 25, 1929. They had four children: Bessie, George, Katherine, and Nick. He eventually became a partner in the Farmers Produce Company.

## *Two*

# Birth of the Greek Community

The pivotal year of 1923 is well documented. On March 29, at 9:00 p.m., nine men gathered at the Phoenix home of John Georgouses, 340 East Roosevelt Street, to initiate the process securing incorporation papers from the State of Arizona to organize a new church: Holy Trinity Hellenic Orthodox Church. Each of the nine men—Milton Stamatis, Gus Loomis, Chris Sanichas, Tom Morris, Jim George, John Thomas, George Zambaras, Floros Mitchell, and John Georgouses—donated $50 toward this matter.

The articles of incorporation were signed on May 17, 1923, and named the following as officers and the board of trustees of the new nonprofit church organization: Milton Stamatis, president; John Georgouses, vice-president; Floros Mitchell, treasurer; and John Marakas, secretary. The board members were Gus Loomis, Chris Sanichas, Tom Morris, John Thomas, D. Gotsis, Pete Tamaras, William Anagnostopoulos, and John Efstathew.

With the legal framework set, the next step for the Phoenix founders of the Holy Trinity community was to plant the roots for a tangible structure. Between 1923 and 1928, three locations were considered and/or purchased: first at Third Avenue and Van Buren Street; then at Fifth and Willetta Streets; and third at the Evergreen Addition.

Although there is some dovetailing in the time frame leading to the finalization of a site for the church and school, the first general assembly meeting in the fall of 1929 clarifies subsequent actions by the members and the newly elected board of directors: Harry Johnson, president; George Zambaras, vice-president; Chris Mitchell, secretary; and Jim Jarvis, treasurer. Board members were Tony Georgouses, Gus Georgantos, and Jim Konomos.

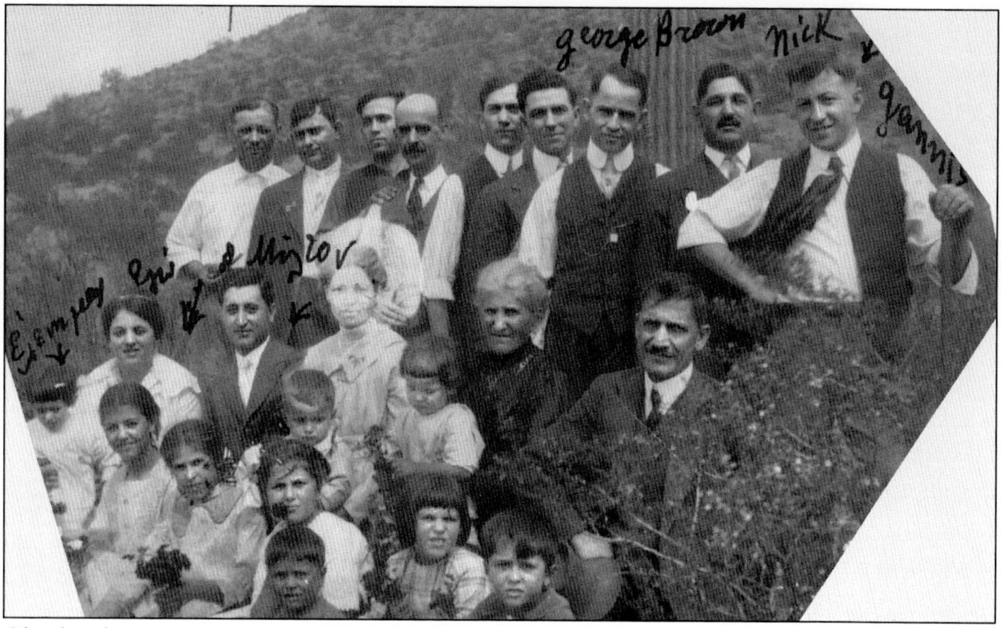


Oh what fun it is to go on a picnic in the desert in 1917, all dressed up in one's Sunday best. From left to right are (first row) two unidentified boys (second row) H. Gannis, V. Loomis, J. Sanichas, V. Sanichas, and L. Loomis; (third row) C. Stamatis, M. Stamatis, A. Sanichas, unidentified child on lap, Yiayia (which means grandmother) Sanichas, unidentified child on lap, and unidentified; (fourth row) five unidentified, G. Brown, two unidentified, and N. Gannis. These were the pioneers of the Greek community.

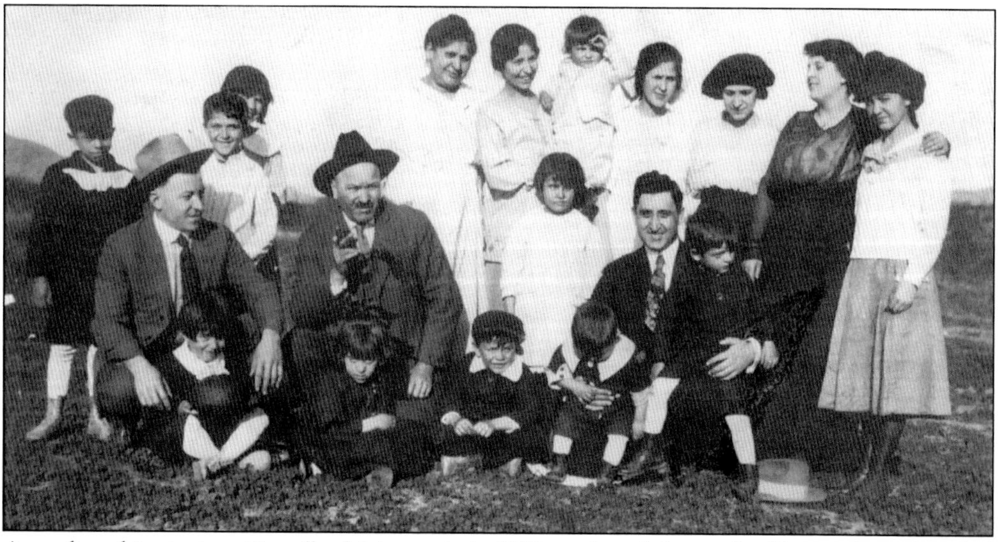

Attending this picnic at Camelback Mountain in 1917 are, from left to right, (first row) unidentified child, Helen Stamatis, John Sanichas, and Efthimios "Sammy" Stamatis; (second row) Nick Gannis, Kostandinos Loomis, Vaso Sanichas, Milton Stamatis, and Jimmy Stamatis; (third row) John Loomis, Jimmy Loomis, Lilli Loomis, Mrs. Loomis, Anna Sanichas, Georgia Sanichas, Venetia Loomis, Alice Loomis, Chrysanthe Stamatis, and Helen Gannis.

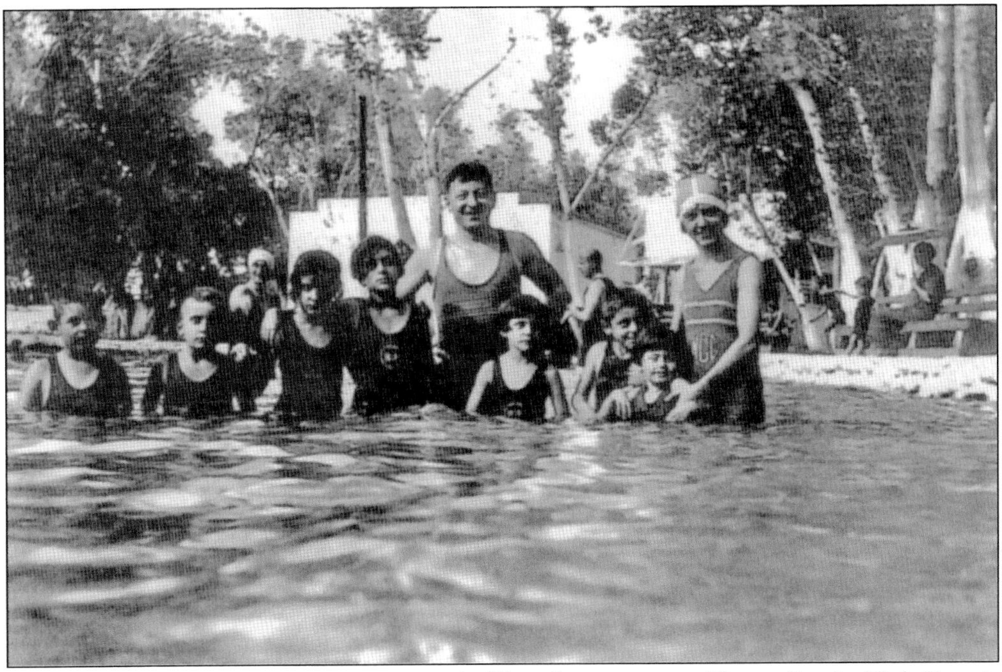

In the 1920s, there were no swimming pools. The place to go was Tempe Beach. Nick Gannis and his sister, Helen Gannis, took their nieces and nephews for an outing.

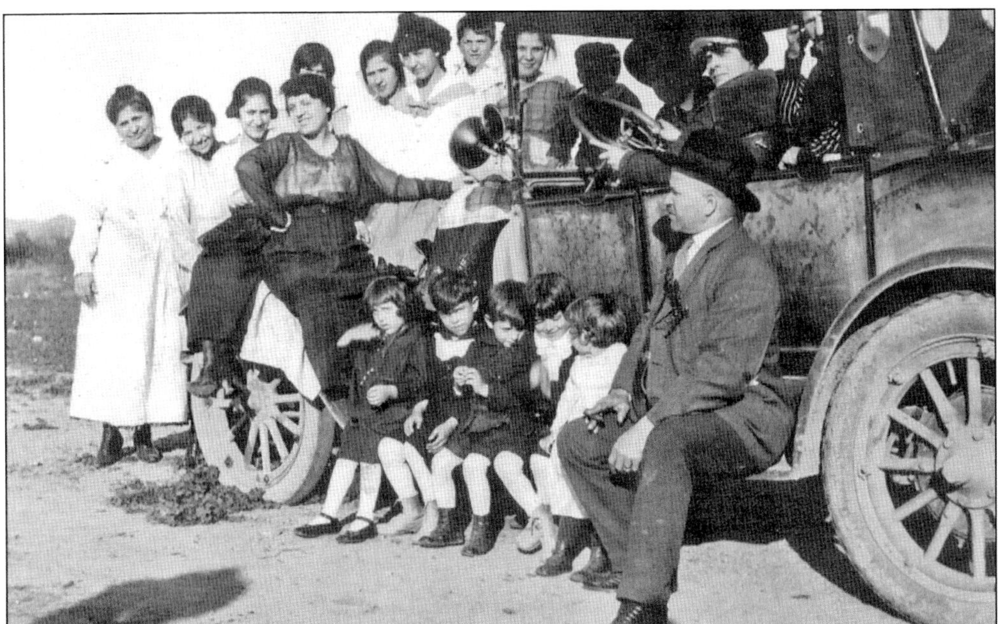

This group is on its way to another picnic in a Model T. It looks like it will be a tight fit. They are all dressed in their finest and ready to be on their way.

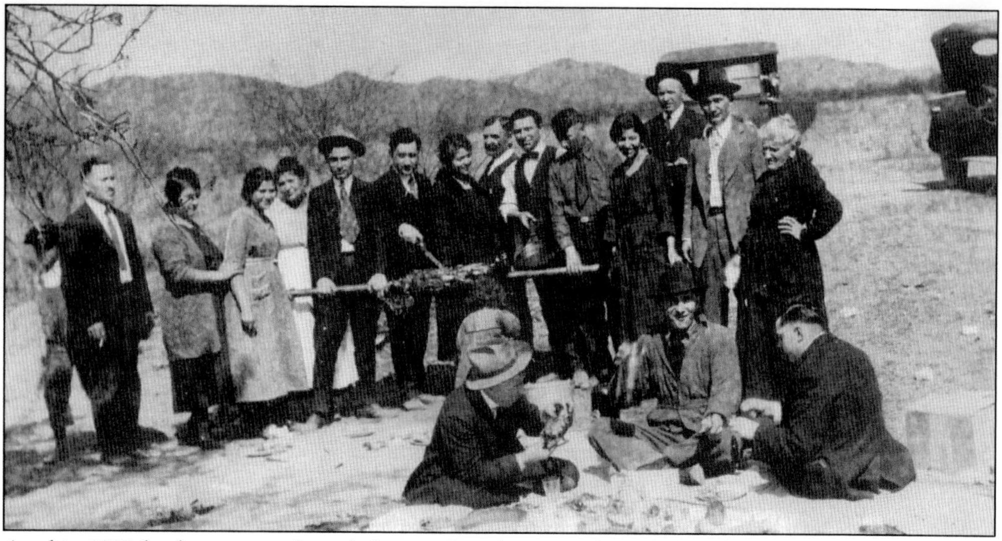

At this 1921 barbecue are, from left to right, three unidentified, Alexandra Loomis, Venetia Loomis, unidentified, Milton Stamatis, Chrysanthe Stamatis, Angelo Pelonis, George Brown, unidentified, Helen Gannis, Gus Loomis, unidentified, and Chris Sanichas. The men seated are unidentified.

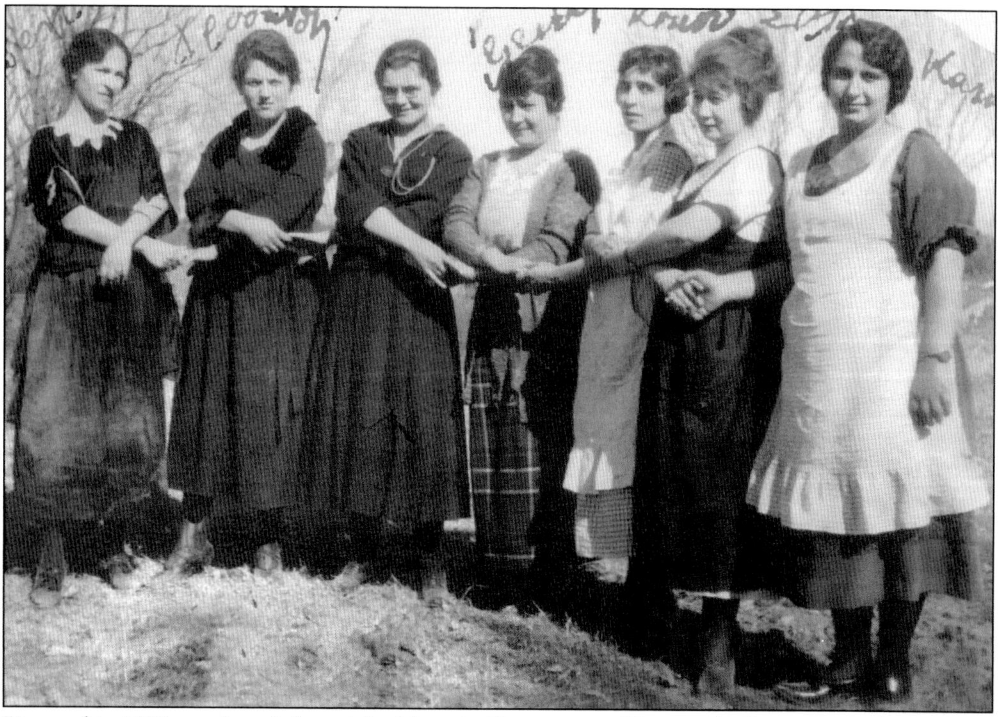

Pictured in 1922 are, from left to right, Venetia Georgantos, Chrysanthe Stamatis, Helen Brown, Eleftheria Pelonis, Mrs. Kokow, Stella Mitchell, and Katina Falkedes.

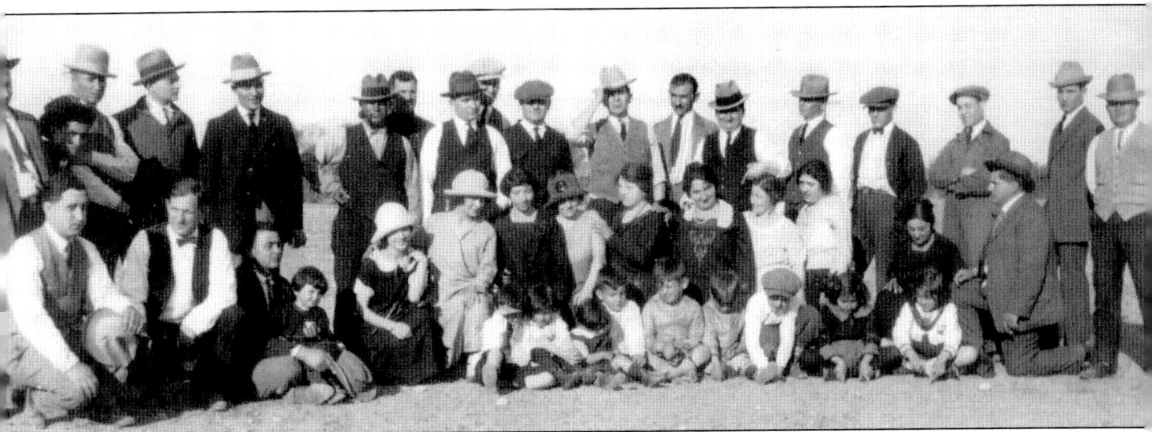

In 1923, a meeting was held to form a church. It is reasonable to presume that many of the individuals at this 1923 picnic and their families were the founders of the church.

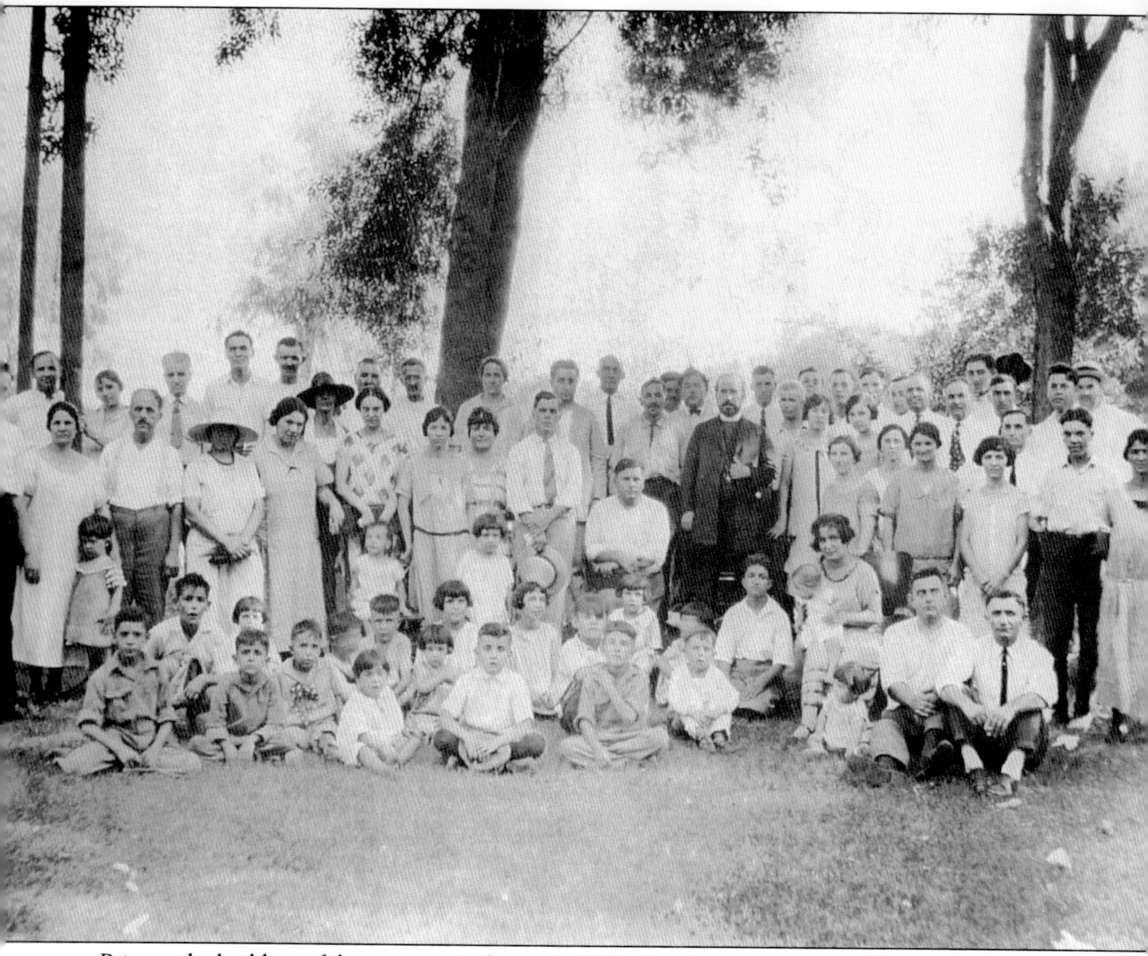

Prior to the building of the community house in 1931, church services were held at various locations. In the mid-1920s, a visiting priest would come to Phoenix to hold church services, weddings, and baptisms. This is a service held on the Tamaras farm on Third Avenue and Osborn Road. The Tamaras farm was considered way out in the country.

# *Three*

# HOLY TRINITY CHURCH

The purchase of a sizable property at 333 East Virginia Avenue—an unpaved street on the perimeter of the city—was on the agenda of a crucial meeting in 1930. Approval for the purchase was granted by the general assembly, and a subsequent construction contract for $15,900 was awarded to a local contractor on October 7, 1930, to build a church and adjoining community hall. The cornerstone-laying ceremonies were conducted on October 31.

On March 25, 1931, the first Divine Liturgy was celebrated by visiting Los Angeles priest, Reverend Sardounis, in the newly completed Hellenic Community House (used as Holy Trinity Greek Orthodox Church until 1947). Rev. Ieronimos Koutroulis celebrated the first Easter service in April 1931 and became its first resident priest, serving until his retirement in 1949.

The long-held dream of a religious and social center for the American families of Greek ancestry in Phoenix that had been in the making for over two decades had finally, in 1931, become a reality.

The 1930s in America were marked by the economic distress of the Great Depression. Consequently, the Holy Trinity community in Phoenix was faced with what was then a substantial debt nearing $20,000. In 1935, board president Floros Mitchell, vice president James Jarvis, and succeeding presidents Nick Annos in 1935 and Michael Zannis in 1936 presided over numerous meetings focusing on the debt of the church.

The years 1937 to 1941 were dark times of financial instability for the Holy Trinity community. The church was lost in 1937 and reacquired in 1941, when they resumed their spiritual, social, and educational activities at 333 East Virginia Avenue.

The presidents of the community during those founding years were as follows: Milton Stamatis (1923, 1934–1935, and 1937–1939); John Georgouses (exact years unknown); Chris Sanichas (1929 and 1940); Harry Johnson (1930–1933); John Georgouses (1933–1934); Floros Mitchell (1935); Nick G. Anagnopoulos (1935–1936); Michael Zannis (1936–1937); and Chris Pallas (1940–1944).

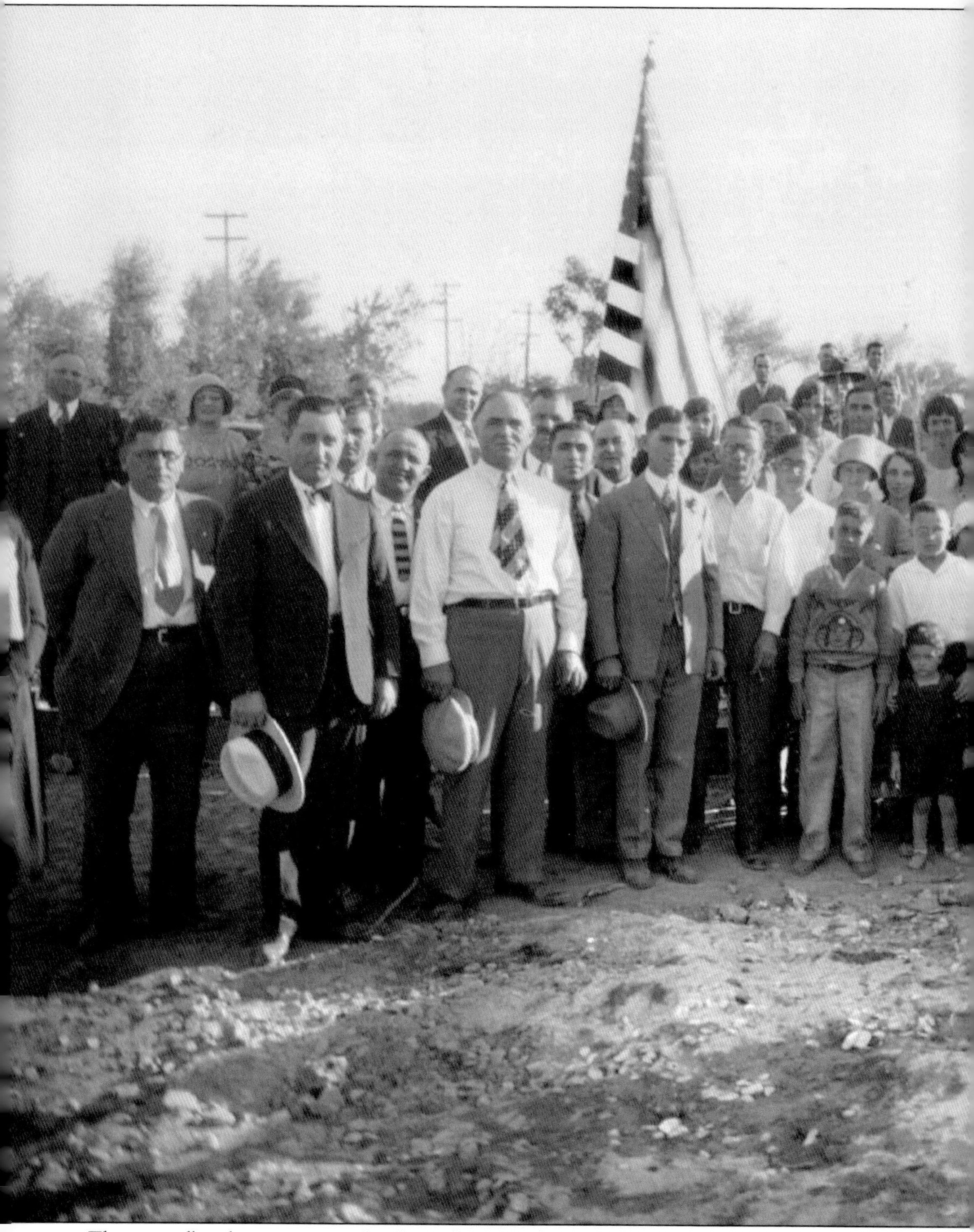

The groundbreaking ceremony for the Hellenic Orthodox Church Community House was held on October 31, 1930. The cornerstone sits on the table in the center of the picture. A visiting priest officiated. Some of the individuals that the authors were able to identify are listed, not

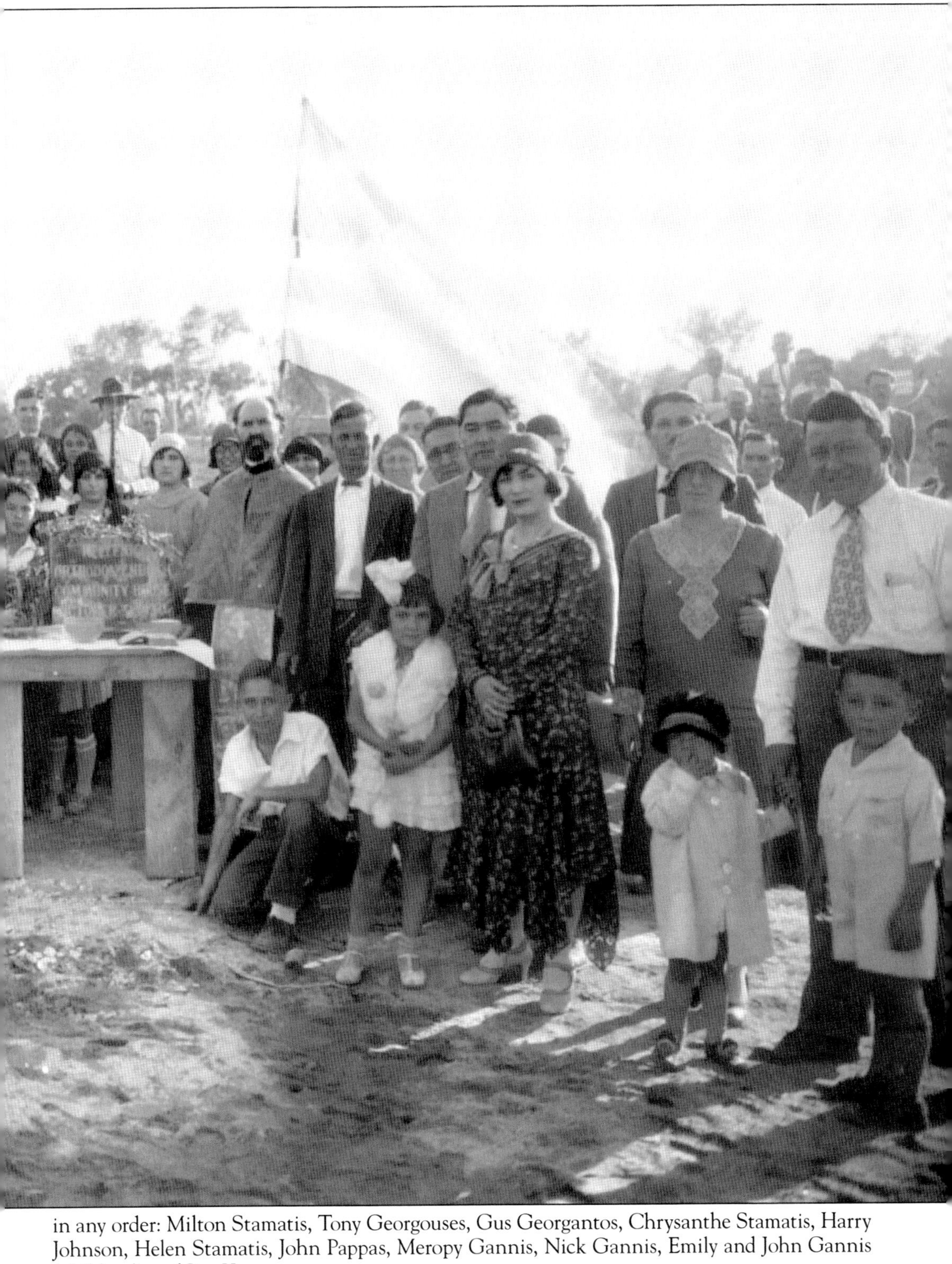

in any order: Milton Stamatis, Tony Georgouses, Gus Georgantos, Chrysanthe Stamatis, Harry Johnson, Helen Stamatis, John Pappas, Meropy Gannis, Nick Gannis, Emily and John Gannis (children), and Jim Konomos.

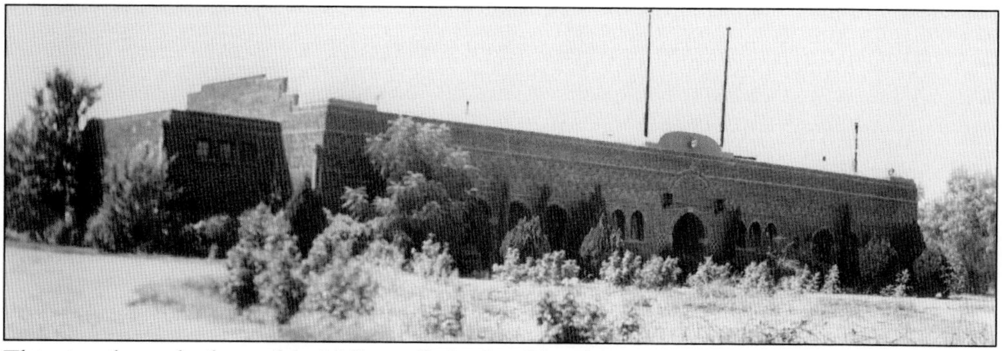

This view shows the front of the Hellenic Orthodox Church Community House at 333 East Virginia Avenue. The first church service was held in March 25, 1931, with visiting priest Reverend Sardounis. The first Easter was celebrated in April 1931 with Rev. Ieronimos Koutroulis officiating.

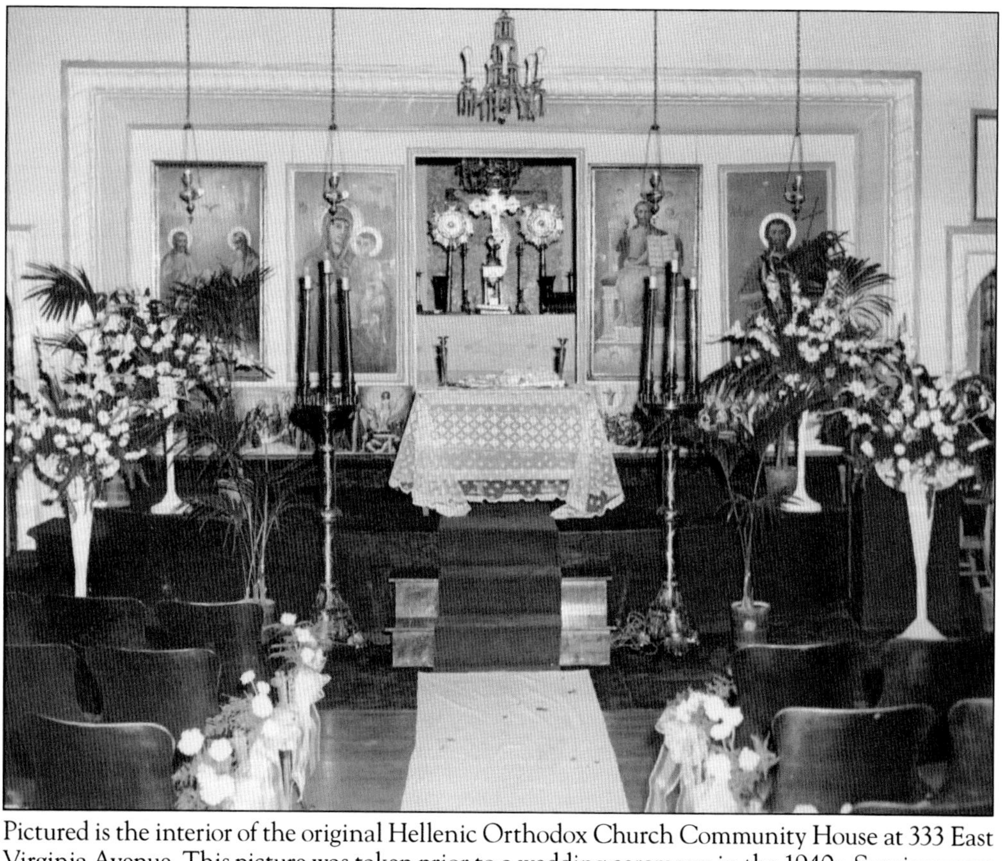

Pictured is the interior of the original Hellenic Orthodox Church Community House at 333 East Virginia Avenue. This picture was taken prior to a wedding ceremony in the 1940s. Services were held in this building until 1947, when the new church was built.

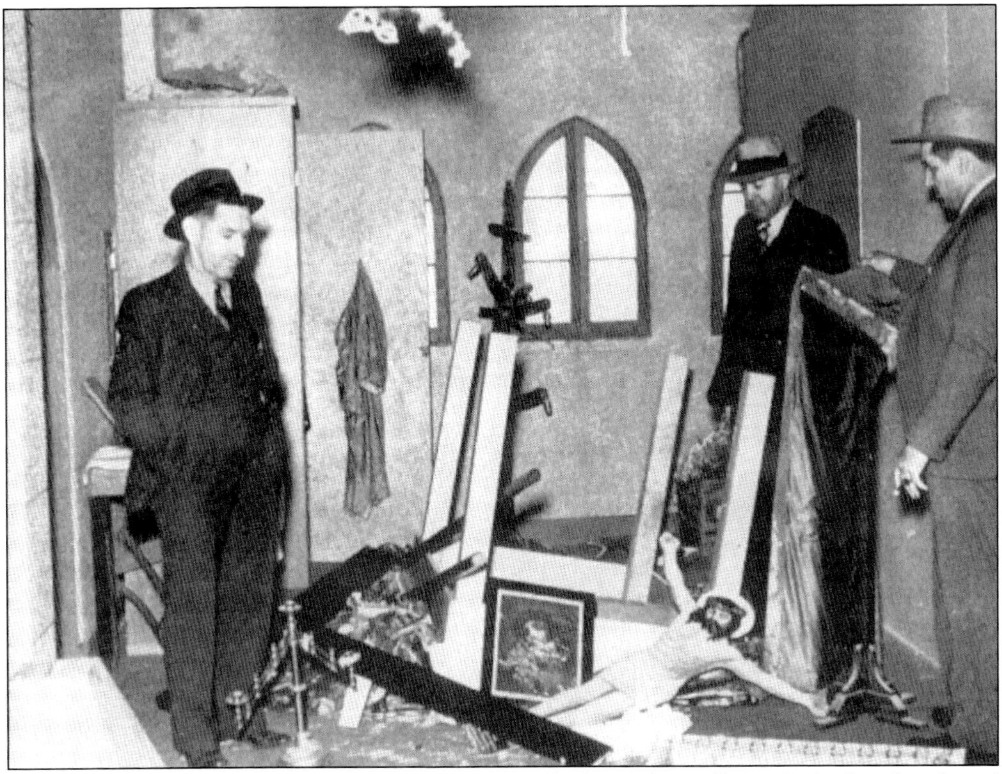

A few days before Christmas 1937, Chris Johnson walked into the Hellenic Orthodox church and found the interior in shambles. The destructive work was accomplished by two 7-year-old boys. They broke into the church building and spent an afternoon wreaking havoc room by room, smashing everything they could.

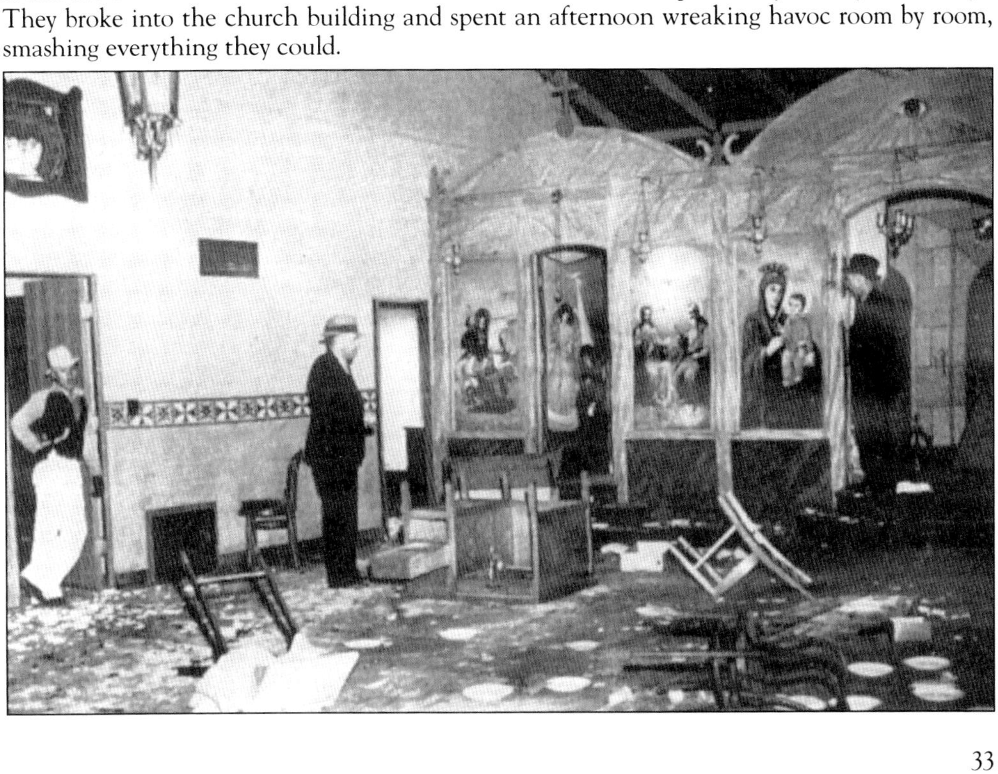

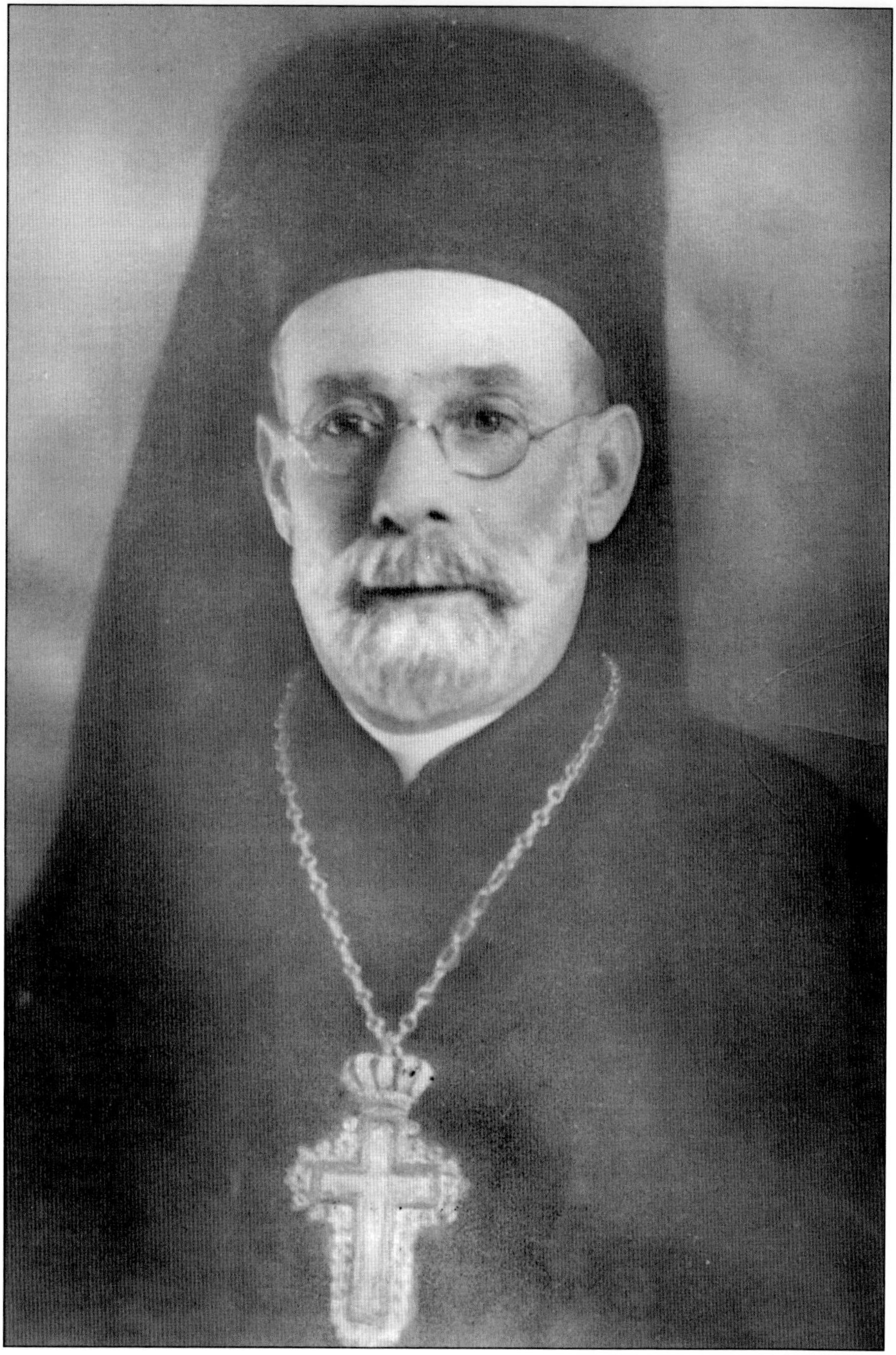

In 1931, Rev. Ieronimos "John" Koutroulis arrived in Phoenix to become the first resident priest. He was transferred to Sacramento, California, in 1933. Rev. Elias Tsaouses served from 1933 to 1935, and Rev. Kostantinos Polechrones was here from 1935 to 1937. Reverend Koutroulis returned in 1937, serving until his retirement in 1949. From the time the church was lost in 1937 until it was reacquired in 1941, church services were held in various other churches, mainly the Trinity Cathedral, located at 100 West Roosevelt Street.

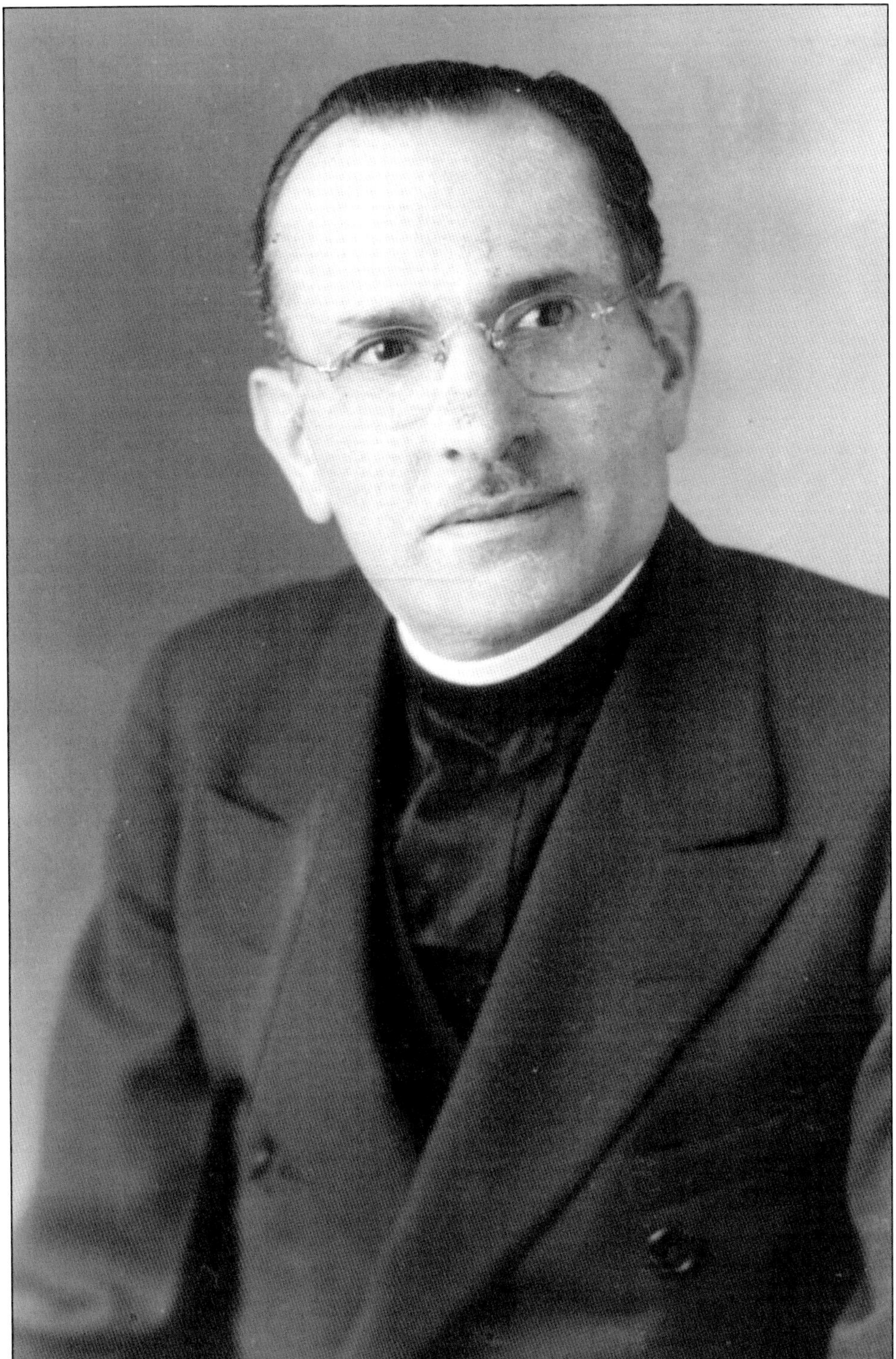

Rev. Elias Tsaouses served from 1933 to 1935. Following him was Rev. Kostandinós Polechrones from 1935 to 1937.

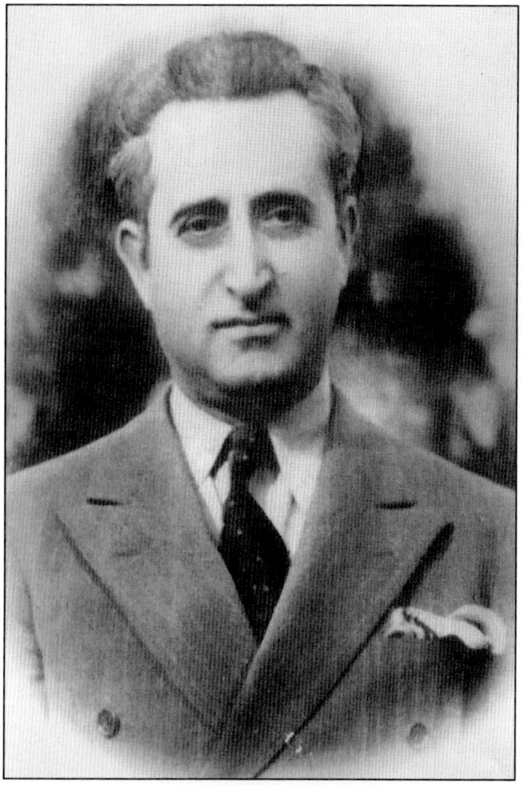

Milton Stamatis served as the first president of the community in 1923. He also served from 1934 to 1935 and from 1937 to 1939.

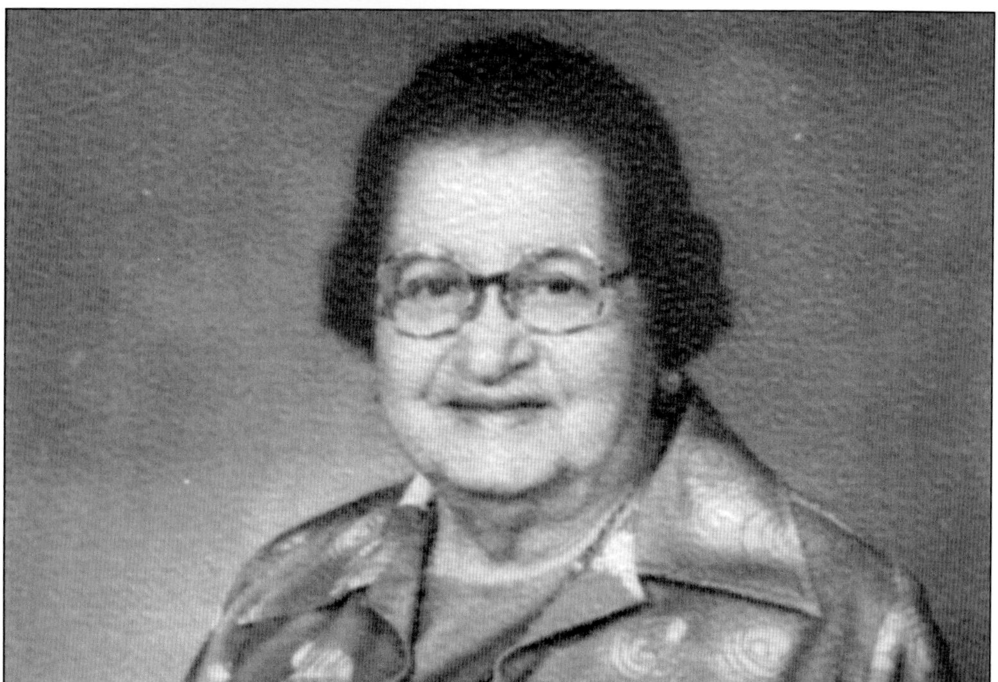

Antigone Wells was the first Greek schoolteacher of Holy Trinity in the 1930s. Parents were adamant that their children learn the language of their heritage.

## *Four*

# The Latter Years

From 1945 to 1949, Harry Johnson was president of the Holy Trinity parish council and Chris Pallas was vice president. During this administration, the leaders and members of the community joined forces to build a new church, which was attached to the west end of the existing building with its main entrance facing Virginia Avenue. The space that had been the church proper since 1931 was converted back to the community house, known as the "big hall" and "little hall."

The new Hellenic Orthodox Church of Phoenix was larger and more accommodating than the old one and provided for numerous weddings, baptisms, and funerals, in addition to the weekly Divine Liturgy and holiday services. In later years, Chris Montague and Sam Colachis emphasized education, spearheading the effort to build a separate classroom building on the church property.

Noted architect Al Beadle designed the new single-story modernistic building, which was completed in 1962. The dedication ceremony that spring had as its keystone speaker U.S. senator Barry M. Goldwater, a longtime friend of the Greek population, who would in 1964 be the Republican Party nominee for president of the United States.

Four years later in 1966, with the election of former Chicago resident and business entrepreneur George Kokalis as president of the parish council, a new era would blossom.

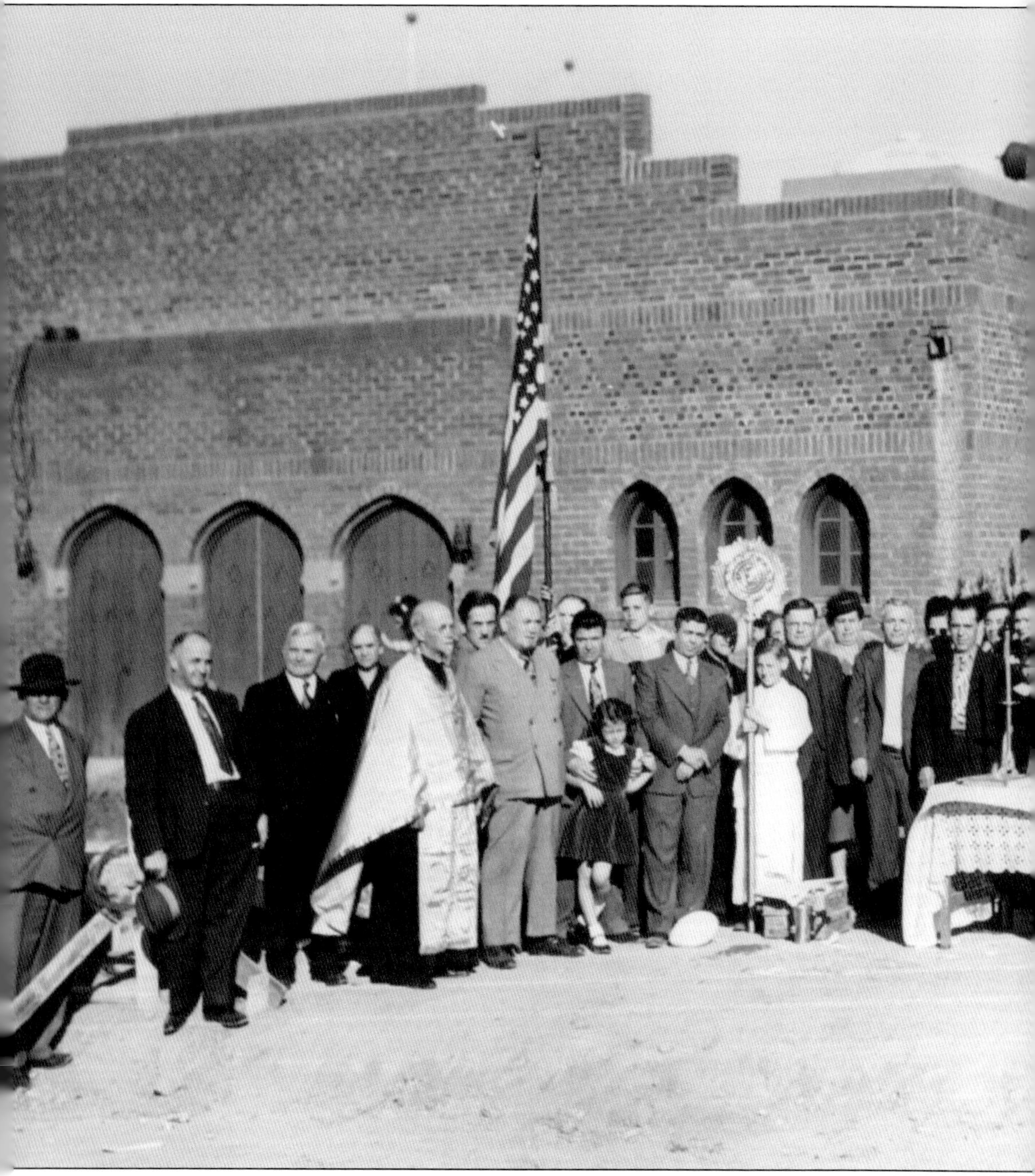

This 1947 photograph shows the ground-breaking for the Hellenic Orthodox church built adjacent to the community house. Services were held at the church until 1973, when the parish moved to their new church at 1973 East Maryland Avenue. Included in this image are Jim Georgouses, Pitsa Ladas, altar boy Andy Limber, James Poulos, Despo Poulos, Evangeline Diamos, Chris Mitchell, Harry Johnson, Theodore Theodoropoulos, Nick Gannis, Meropy

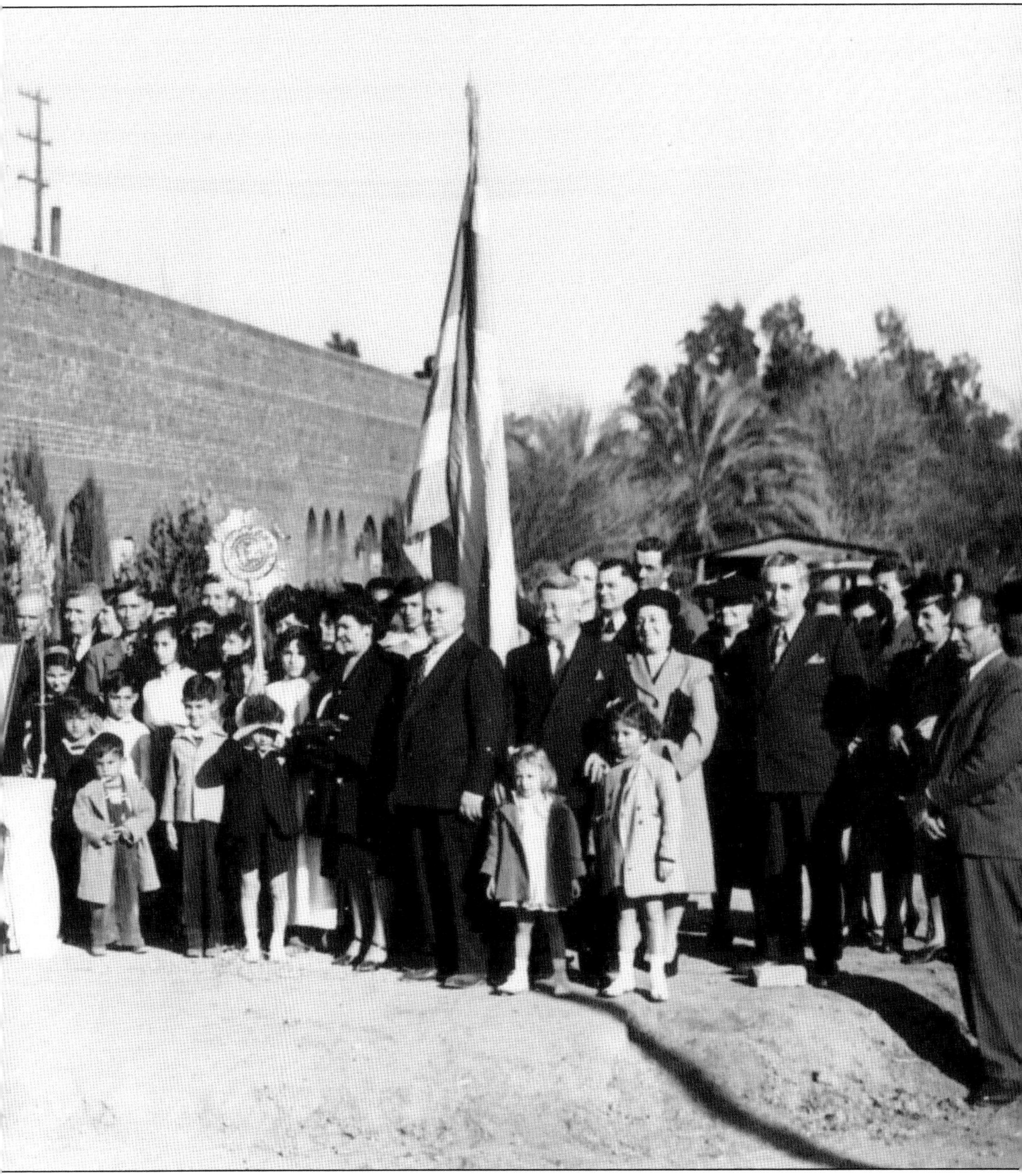

Gannis, Tom Katsenes, Irene Fotinos, Nick Johnson, Rev. Ieronimos Koutroulis, Tony Fotinos, Gust Metsopoulos, Chris Pallas, Christina Pallas, John Dagres, Katina Diamos, Katherine Johnson, George Manos, Alexandria Theodoropoulos, Nick Anagnopoulos, Harry Ladas, Milton Stamatis, Zoe Contos, Gus Theodoropoulos, Mary Louise Gannis, and Alexandra Tsokatos.

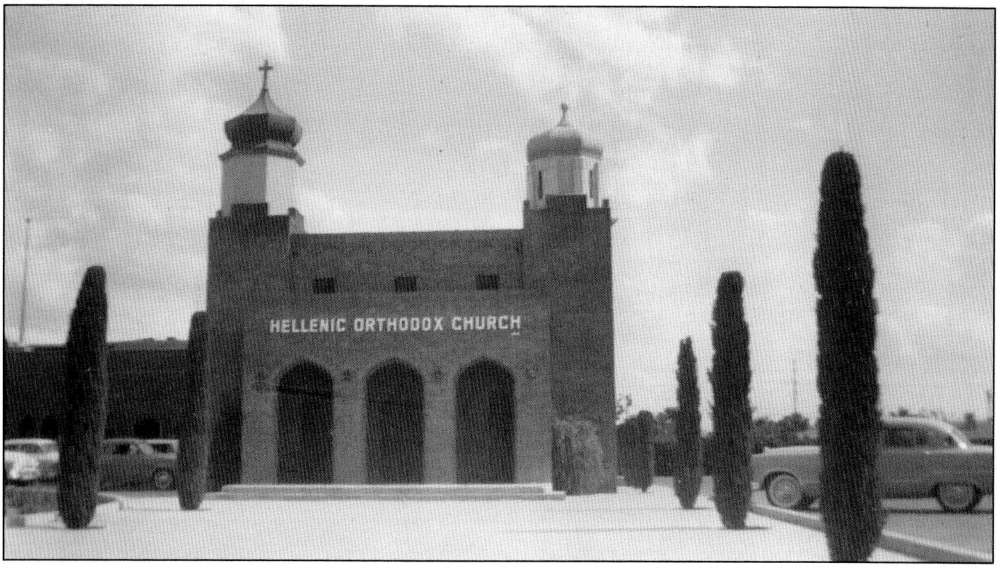


This is the new church at 333 East Virginia Avenue, built next to the community house in 1947.

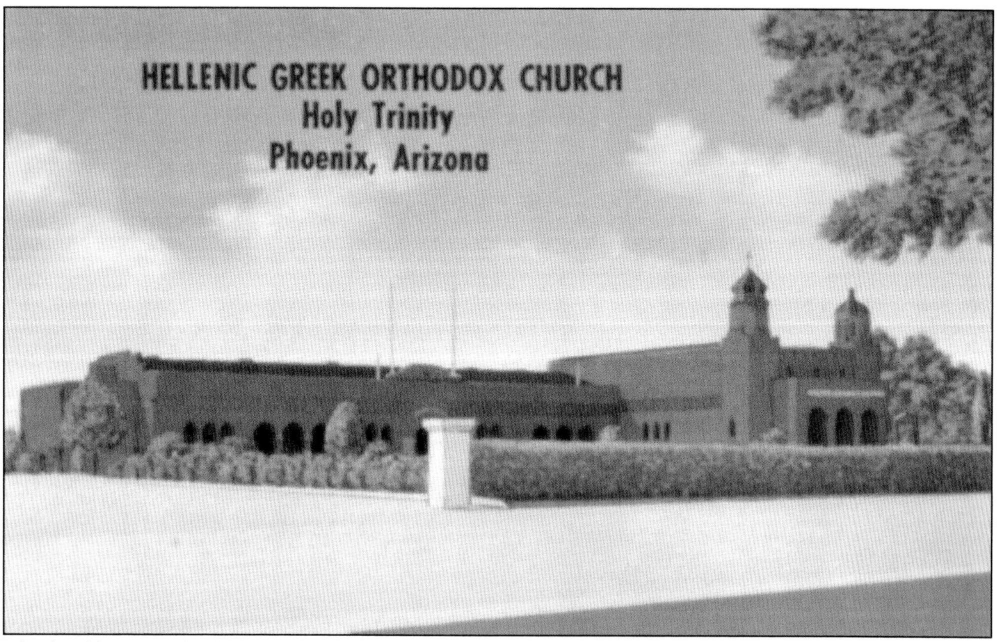


The building on the left was constructed in 1930 as the community house, where church services were held. The building on the right was the new Hellenic Orthodox Church of Phoenix, built in 1947. The building on the left was then used as a community center for receptions and Greek school programs.

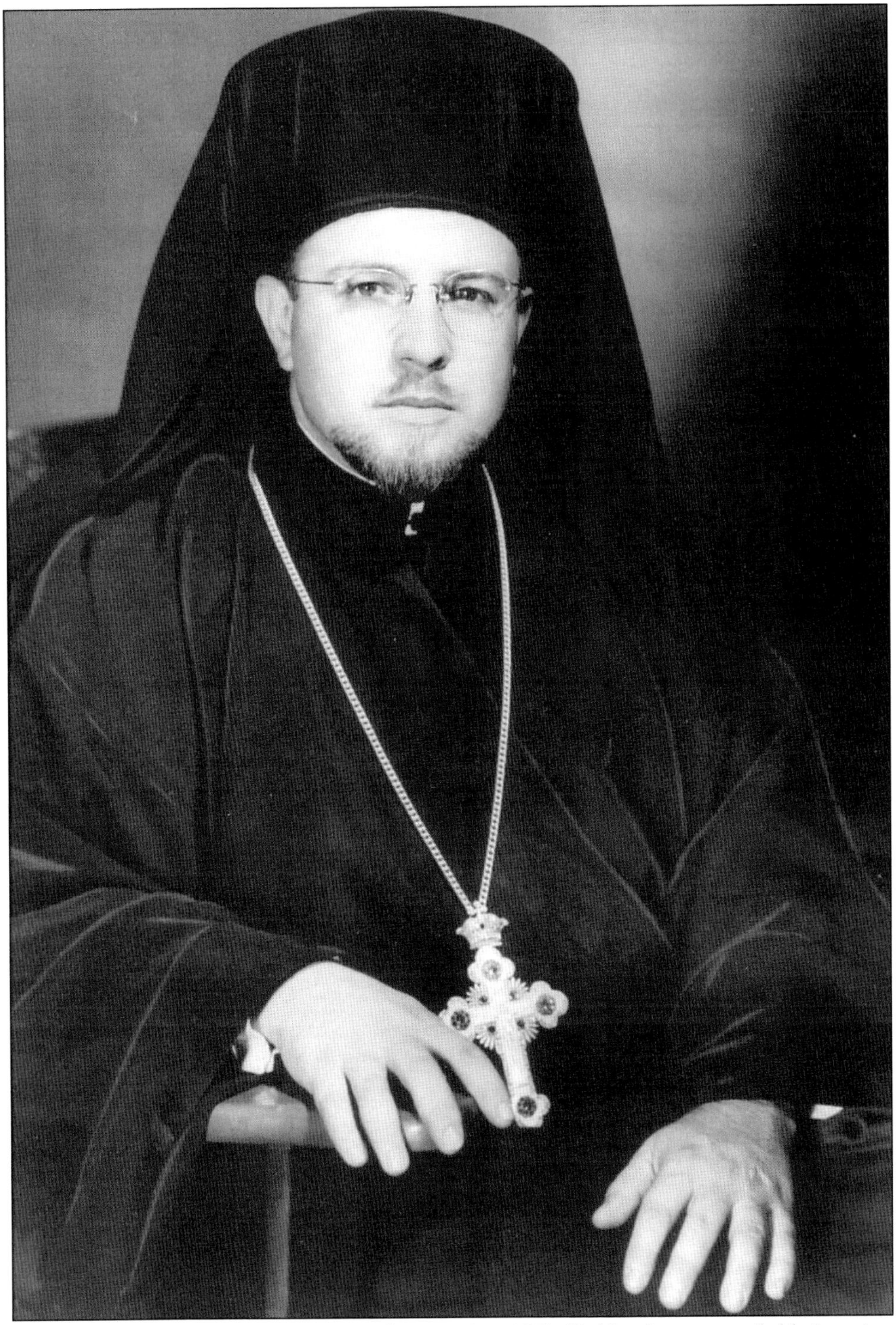

Rev. George Samaras served in Phoenix from 1949 to 1951. Unlike the priests of old, American-born Father Samaras had a gregarious and jovial nature. The younger generations loved Father Samaras. He was an extraordinary scholar and thinker, and he would go on to become a bishop of the church, taking the name Kallistos.

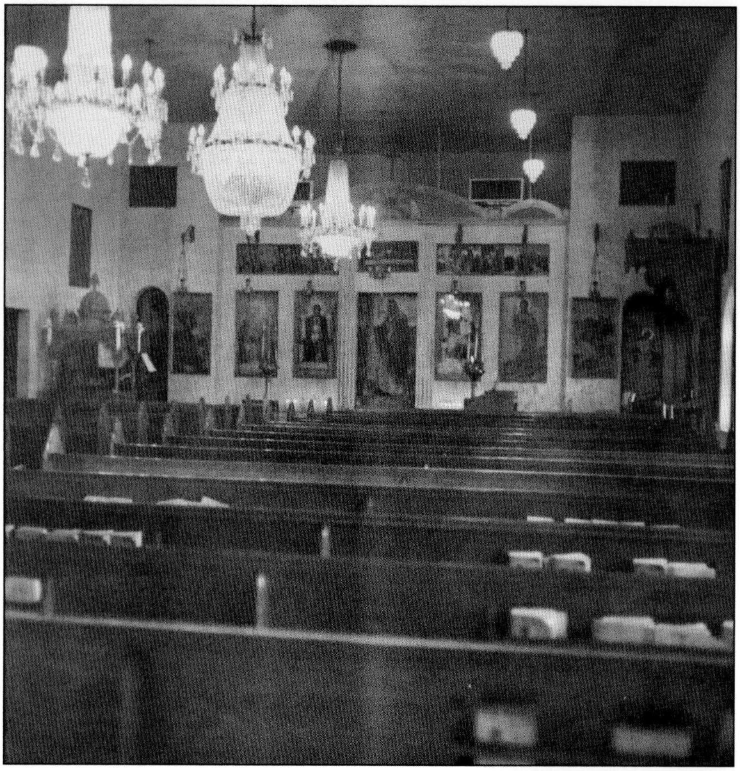

Shown is the inside of the new church at 333 East Virginia Avenue around 1947.

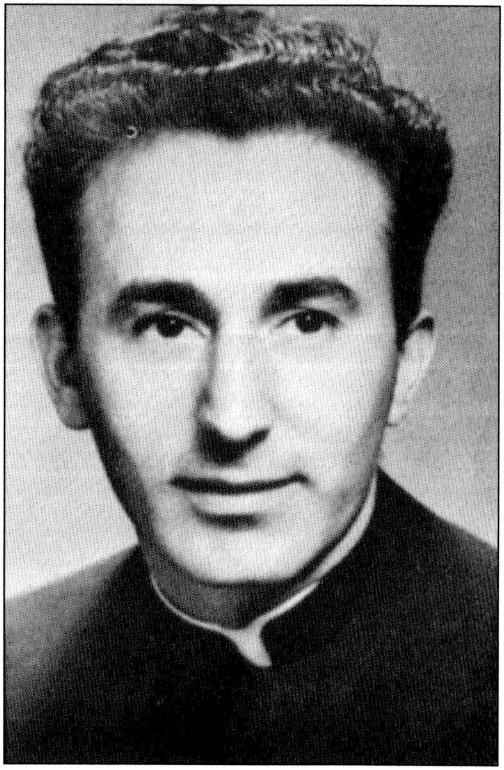

In 1951, Rev. Anthony Pentikis was the second of the new priests to arrive in Phoenix. He too was well liked by the youth and was very supportive of their activities. A year and a half later, this second of the new priests was transferred to another community.

In 1953, Ambrose Giannoukos became Holy Trinity's priest. No sooner had Father Giannoukos arrived and deposited his luggage in the priest's wood-frame house at the rear of the church property than the house somehow caught fire and rapidly burned to the ground, along with all of his belongings. His term as parish priest was brief.

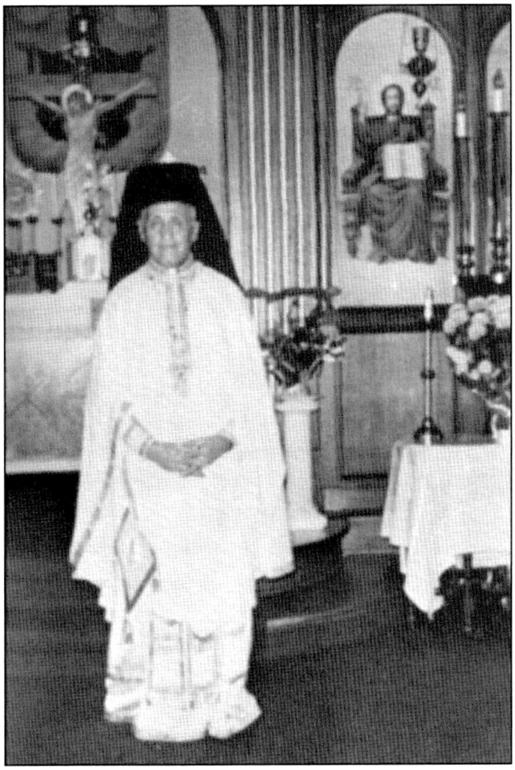

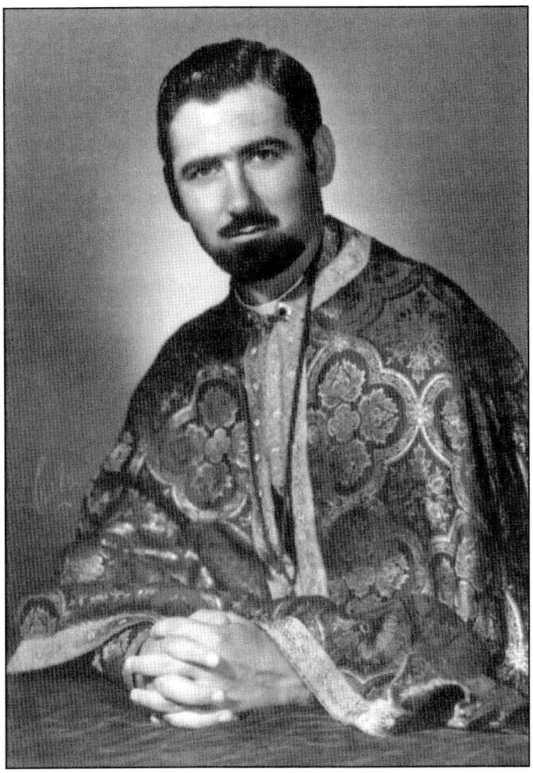

Rev. Chrysostom Selimos arrived in 1953 to assume the duties of parish priest. During his stay, he organized the first youth church summer camp in Prescott, Arizona, and the Junior GOYA (Greek Orthodox Youth of America). He also assisted the ladies of the community with the fund-raising church bazaar.

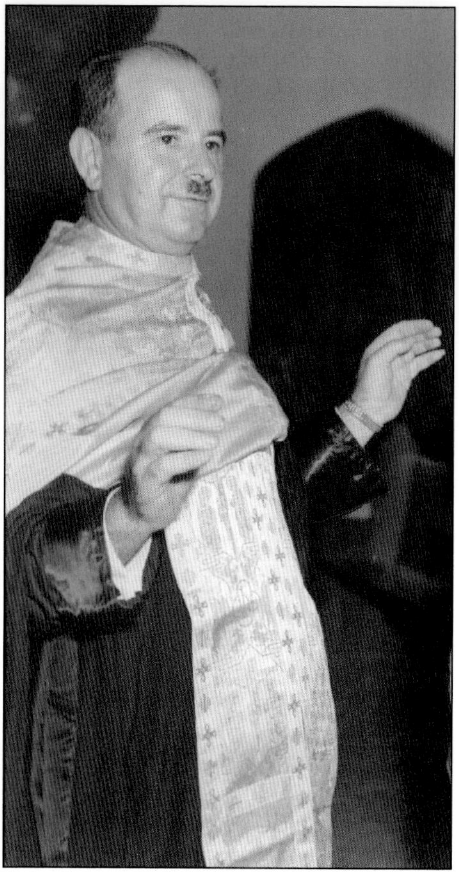

In 1957, the Holy Trinity community welcomed Rev. Kostas Poulakidas as its priest. Among his many accomplishments, he held several successful youth summer camps in Prescott. He was a strong spiritual leader and Greek language educator. He was the last priest to conduct Greek school classes.

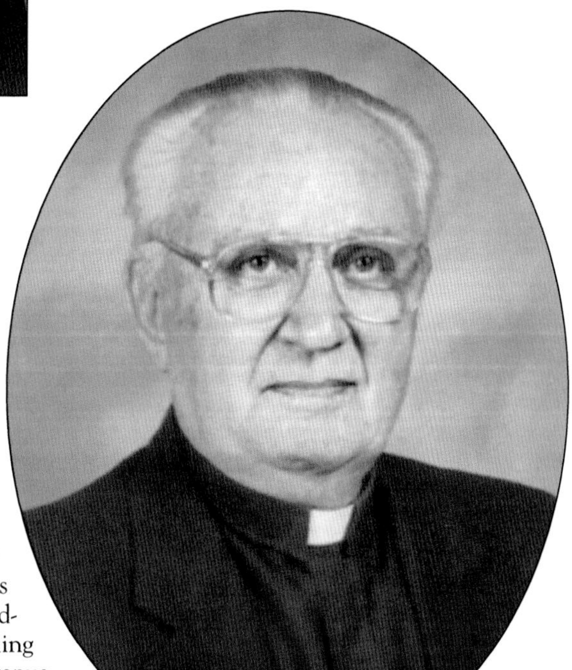

In 1965, Rev. James Tavlarides replaced Reverend Poulakidas. Father James served the community for 25 years. During this period, the Phoenix Greek community was growing so rapidly that a decision was made to move to a larger site; therefore, fund-raising was the primary focus. Besides working tirelessly during the move from Virginia Avenue to the new church location, he was instrumental in starting adult Bible classes and summer Bible classes for the youths.

Here is Rev. Chrysostom Selimos with altar boys Gus Theodoropoulos (left) and Chris Couretas (right) during Easter rites at the 333 East Virginia Avenue building in the early 1950s.

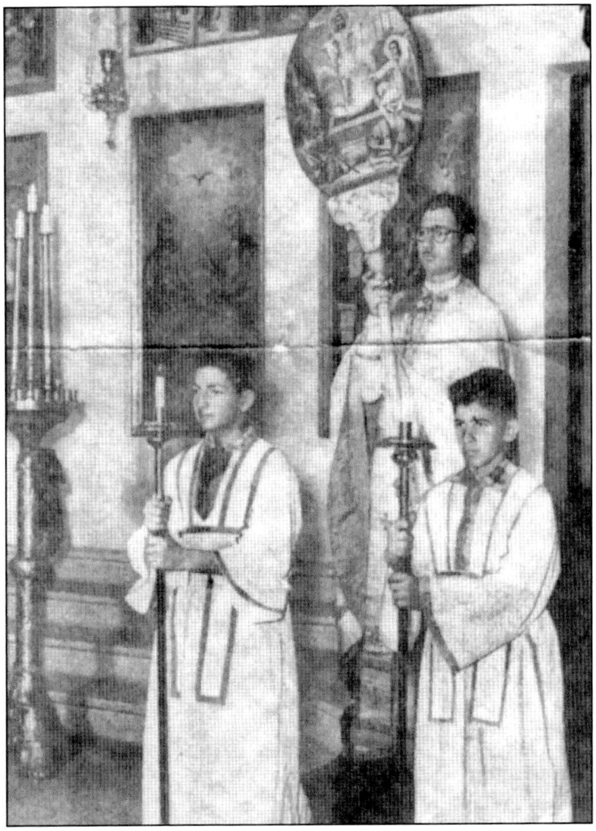

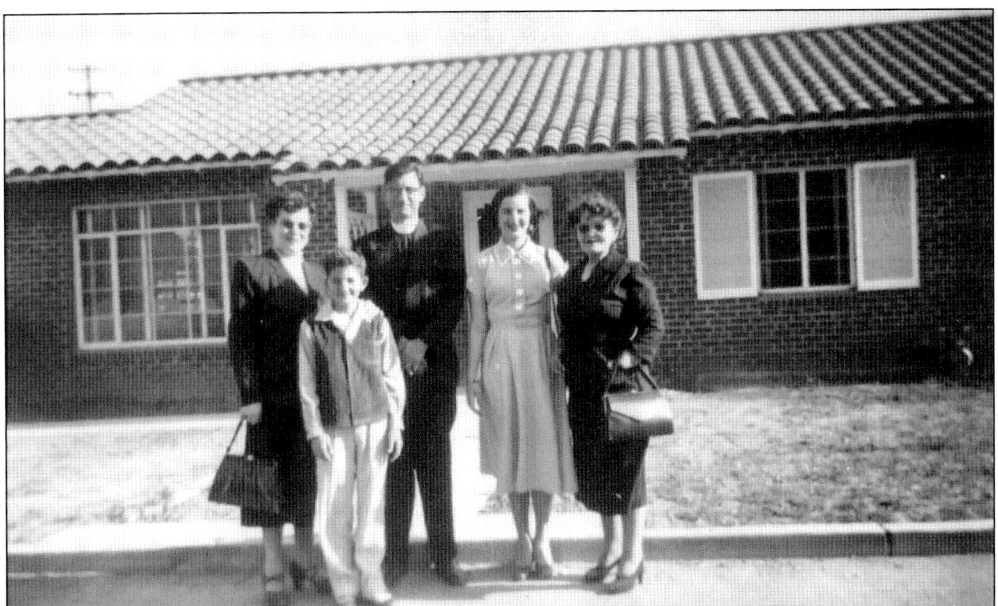

The newly built parish house was completed in 1953. The first occupants were Rev. Chrysostom Selimos and his *presbytera* (wife), Penny, to his left. Pictured from left to right are unidentified, Gus Theodoropoulos, Reverend Selimos, Penny Selimos, and Alexandra Theodoropoulos.

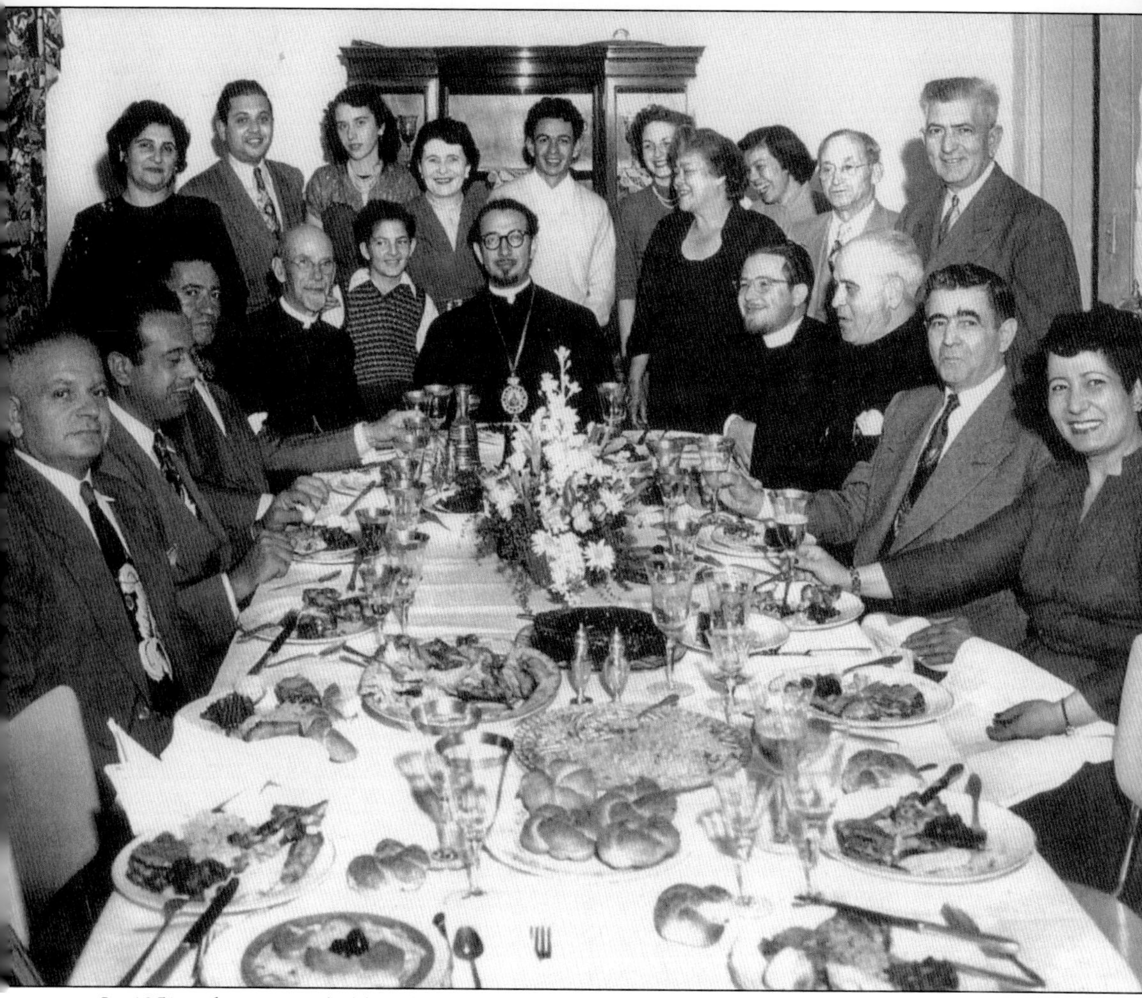

In 1951, a dinner was held at the home of the parish president Gus Metsopoulos (seated second from right) to welcome the diocese bishop. Seated to his right is retired reverend Ieronimos Koutroulis and to Koutroulis's left is the parish priest, Rev. George Samaras.

Thomas Katsenes was a chantor from the early 1930s. He assisted periodically through the early 1970s. Oftentimes, the chantors would travel with priests to assist with various services in small towns.

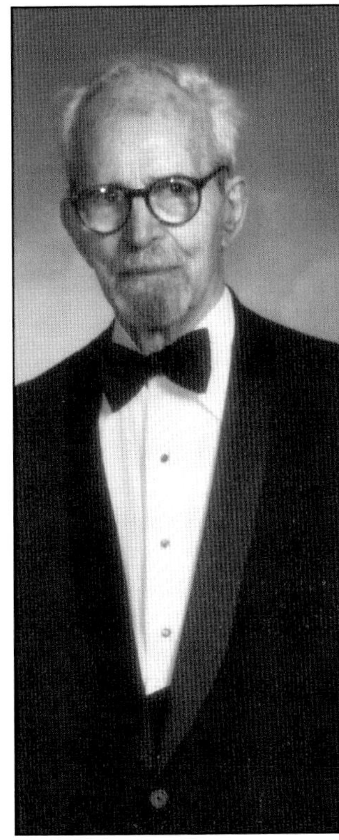

Trifon Petrouleas was the chantor at the new church, located at 1973 East Maryland. He retired at the ripe age of 84. He was assisted periodically by Andrew Poulakidas.

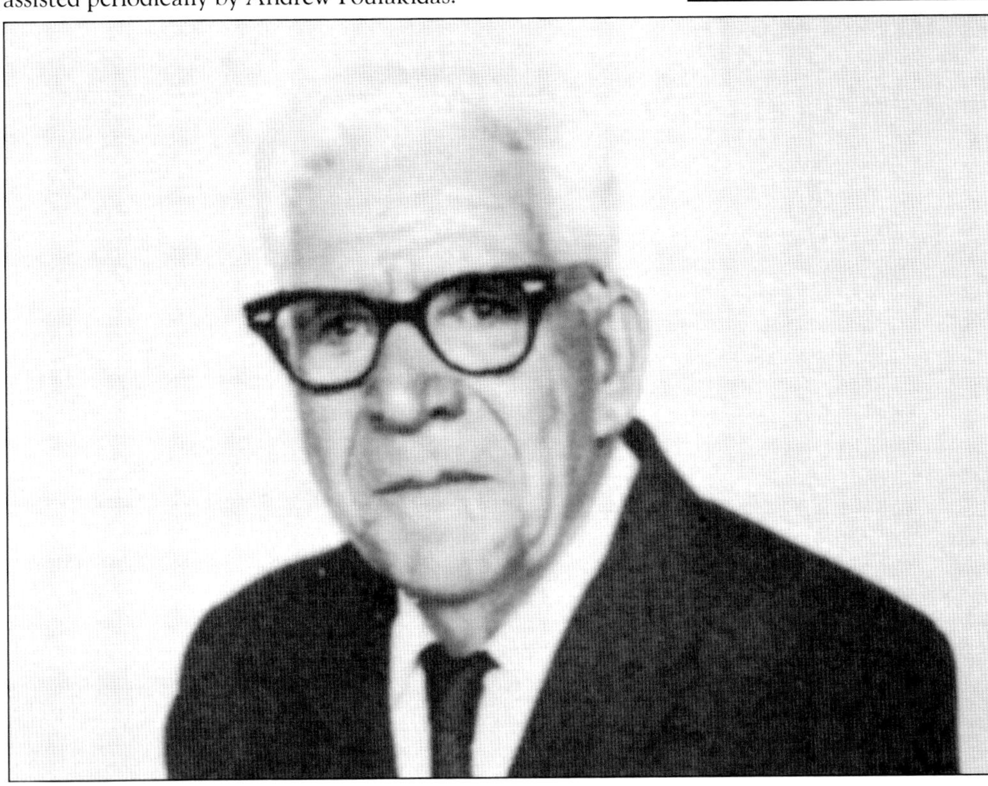

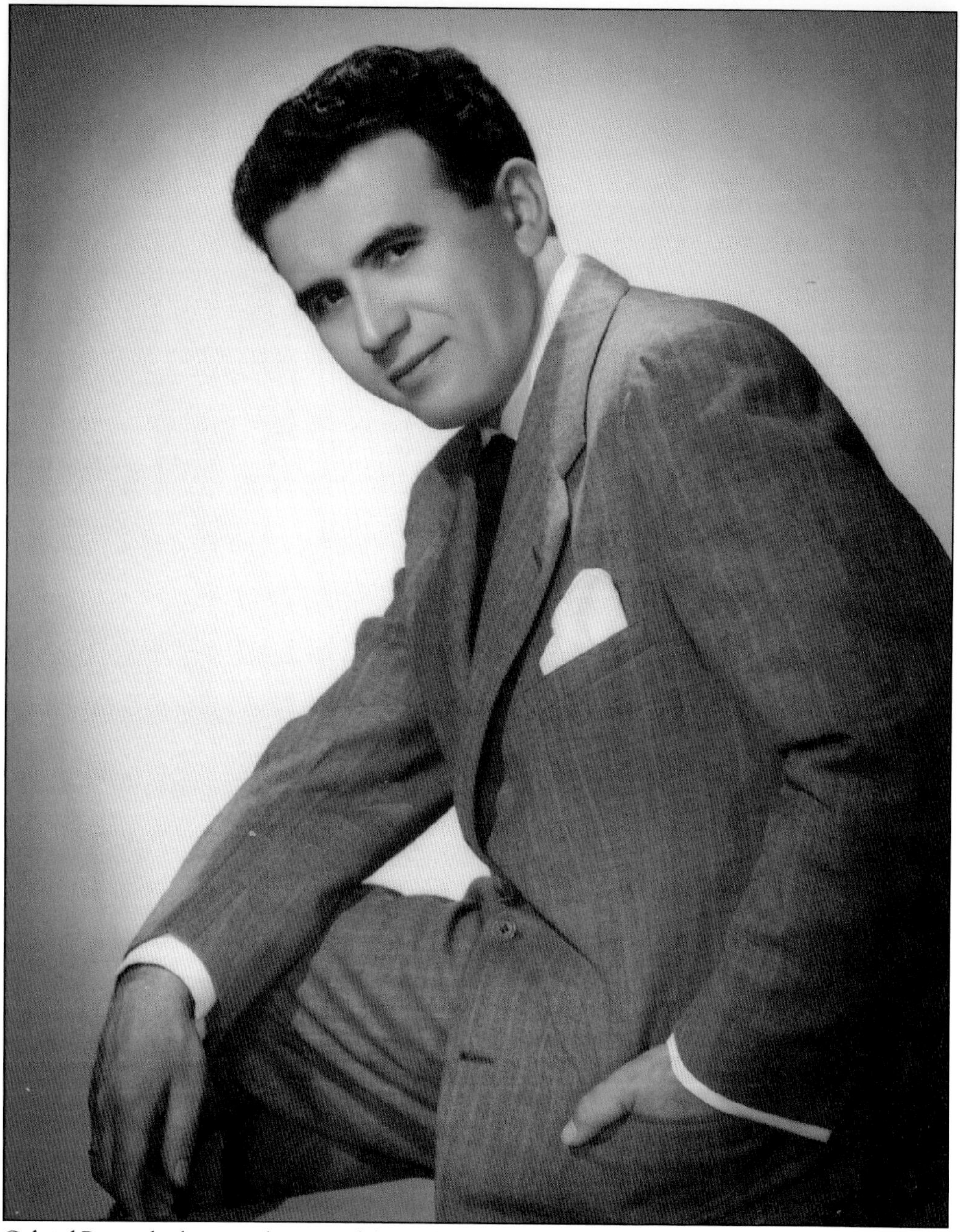

Gabriel Papagolas became director of the Holy Trinity choir in 1951. Under his capable leadership as director, monies were raised to replace the old choir robes. The choir also replaced the old church music with Frank Desby's Bysantine Liturgical music.

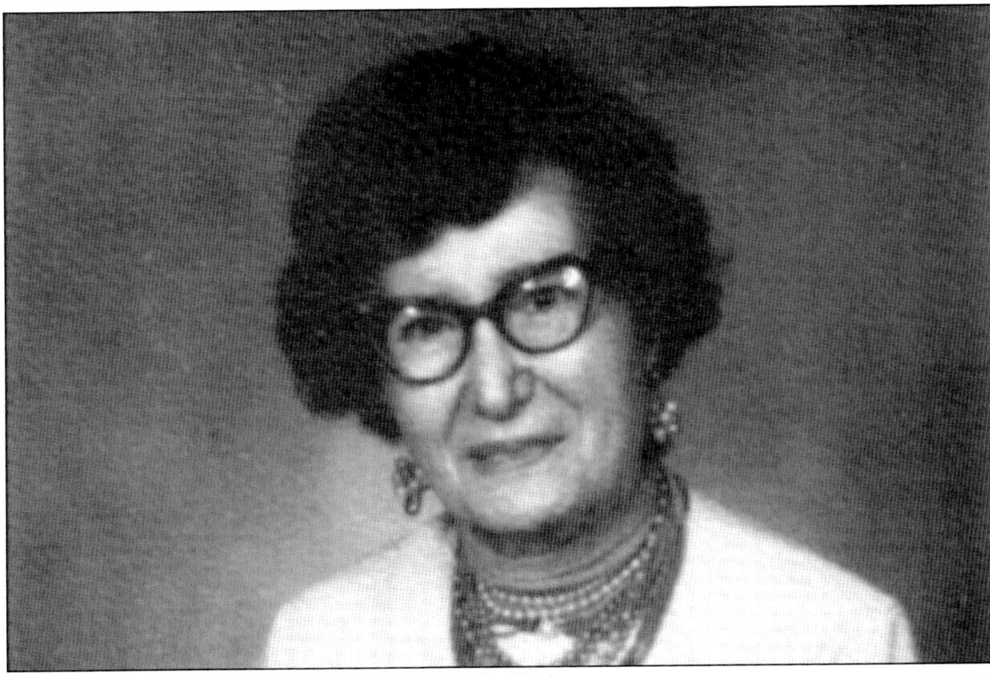

Shown here is Maria Mitchell, who directed the Holy Trinity choir in the later 1940s and early 1950s. She sang professionally and gave many performances. Her daughter, Helen Goodfriend, followed in her footsteps and also became an accomplished musician.

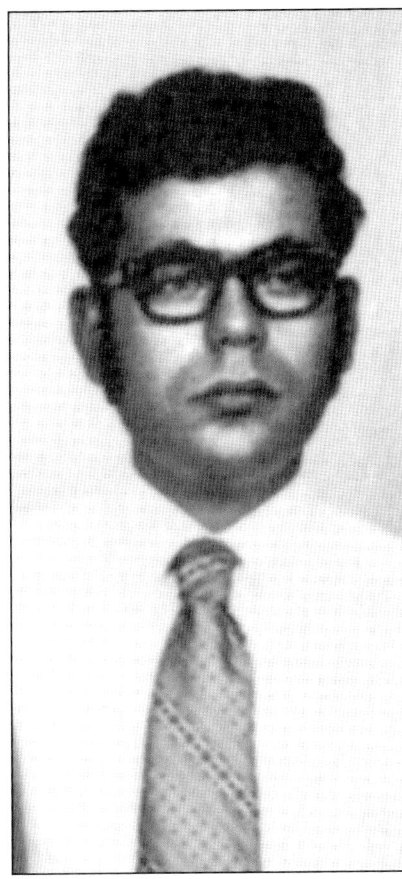

Jim G. Thomas was born and raised in Phoenix, the son of Gus and Antigone Thomas. Jim is a music teacher. He directed the Holy Trinity choir for a short period following Gabriel Papagalos, who left the post in 1966.

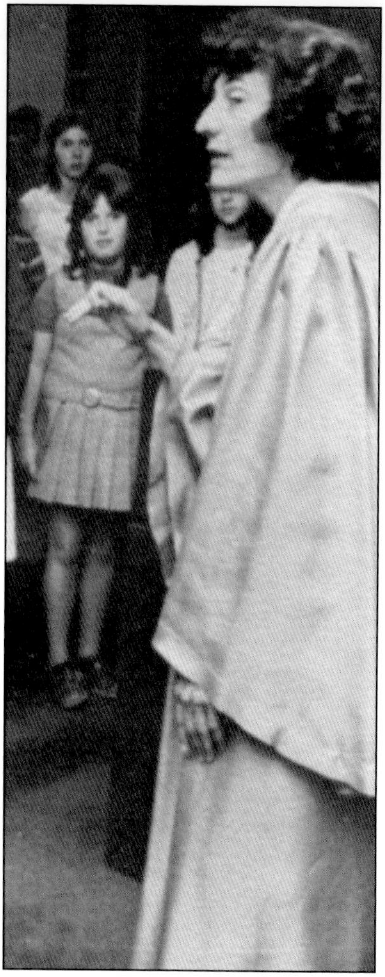

Helen Goodfriend was the daughter of Maria and Chris Mitchell. She was the organist at Holy Trinity. She accepted the duty of choir director and organist in the 1960s. She served for approximately 25 years.

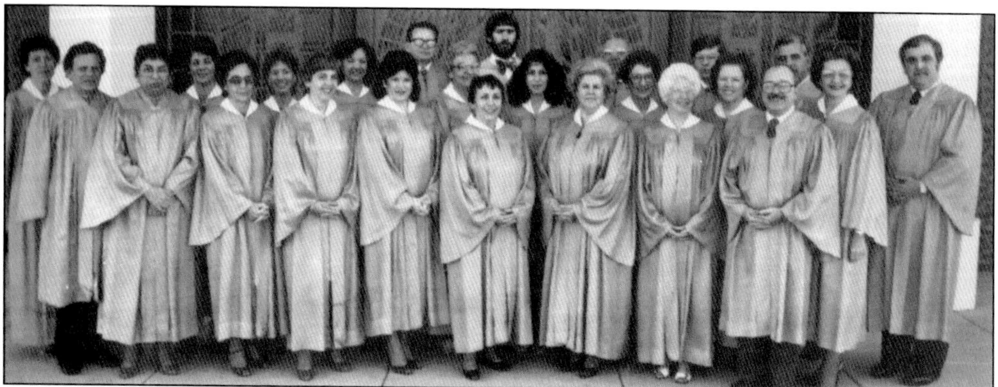

Shown here are choir members at the Holy Trinity Cathedral. These very dedicated members served many years at both the old and the new church.

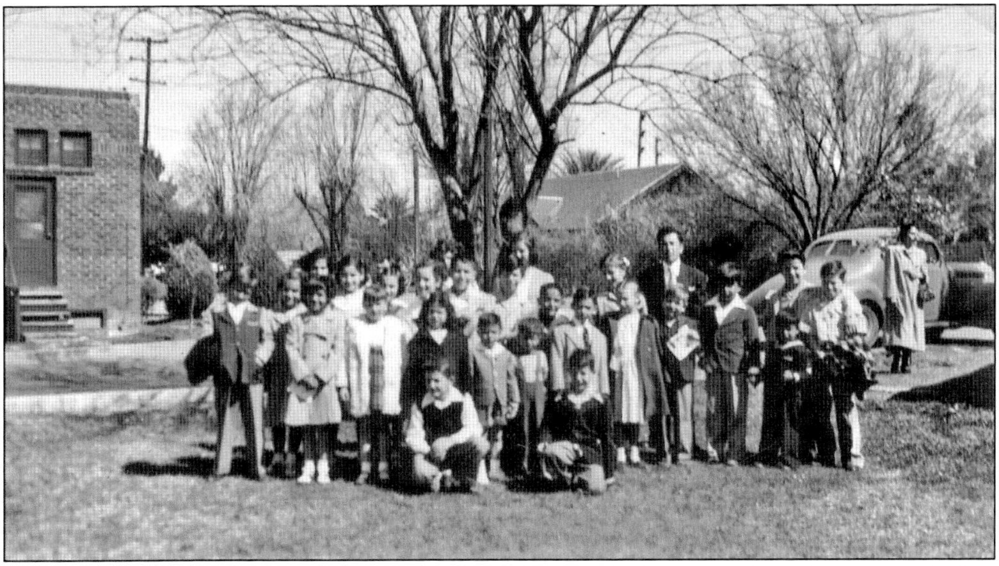

Shown here is the first organized Sunday school class taught by George Papadopoulos in 1950.

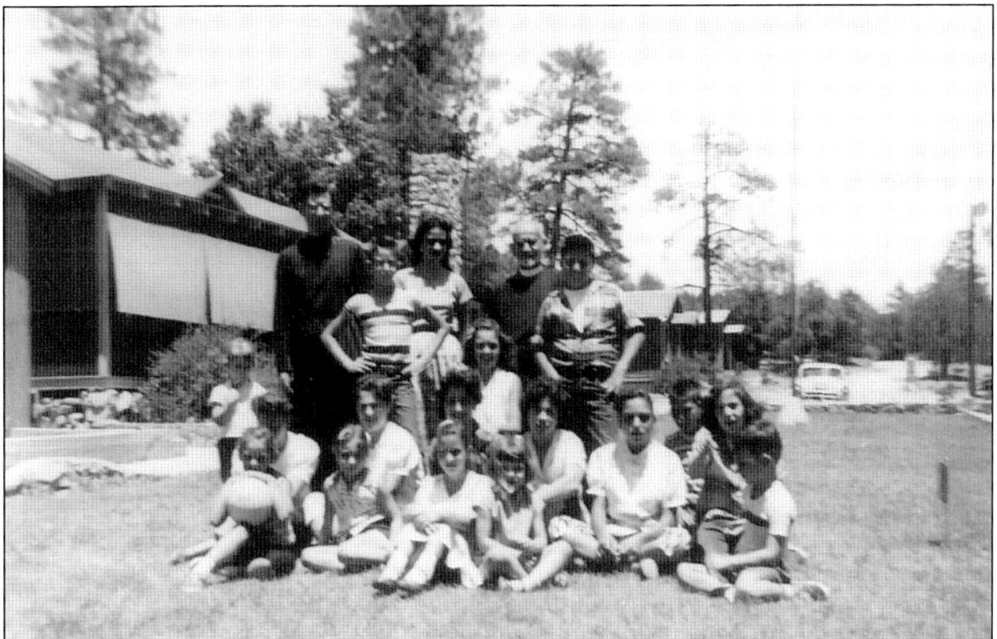

This is the first summer camp organized by Rev. Chrysostom Selimos (left) in Prescott, Arizona, held in 1955. Reverend Selimos was assisted by Rev. George Habib from St. George Serian Church.

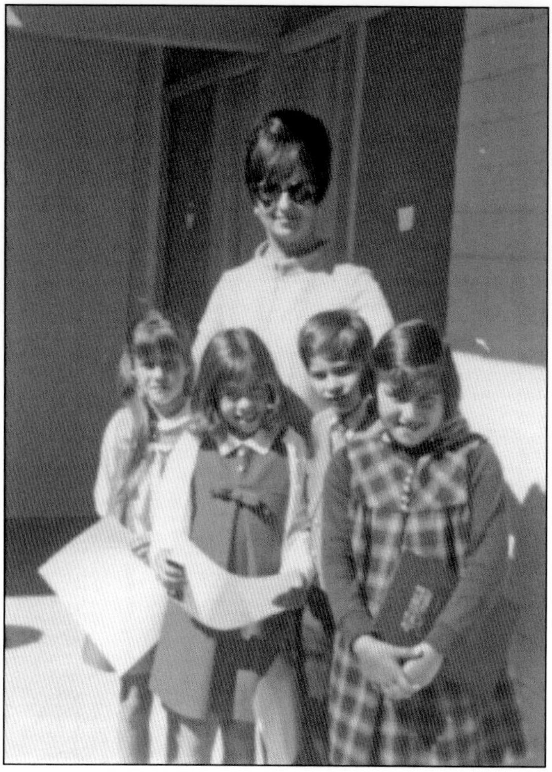

Bebe Speros is pictured with her Sunday school class in the 1960s. With the completion of an education building, the Sunday school continued to grow.

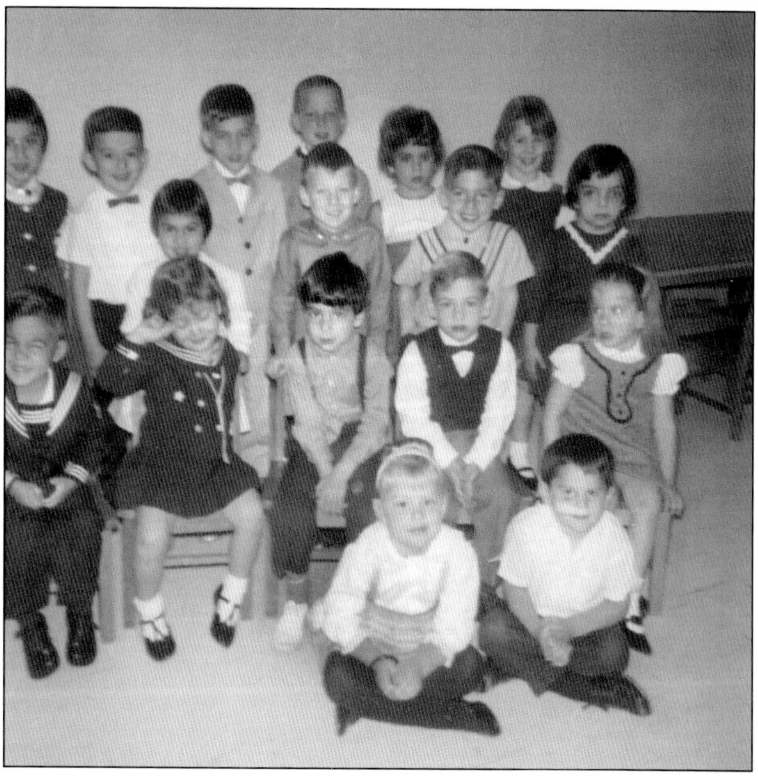

This 1965–1966 Sunday school class for pre-kindergarten children was taught by Georgia Poulo. As the years passed and more families moved to the valley, the community and the Sunday school grew rapidly.

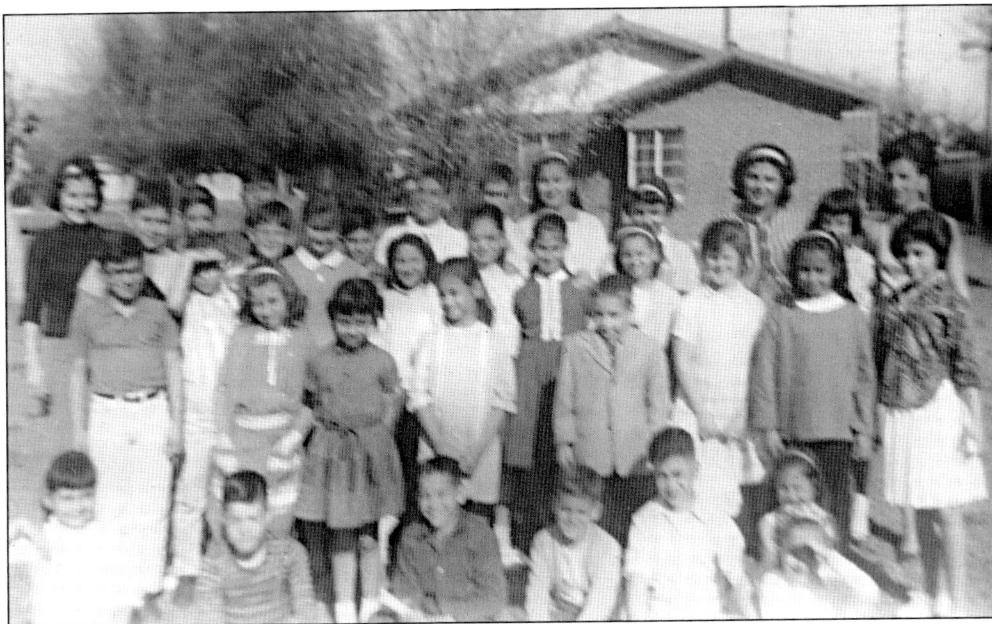

Rev. Kostas Poulakidas taught Greek school to this class in 1964. Reverend Poulakidas was the last priest to teach Greek school. The community then hired Greek school teachers to alleviate the additional duties of the priests.

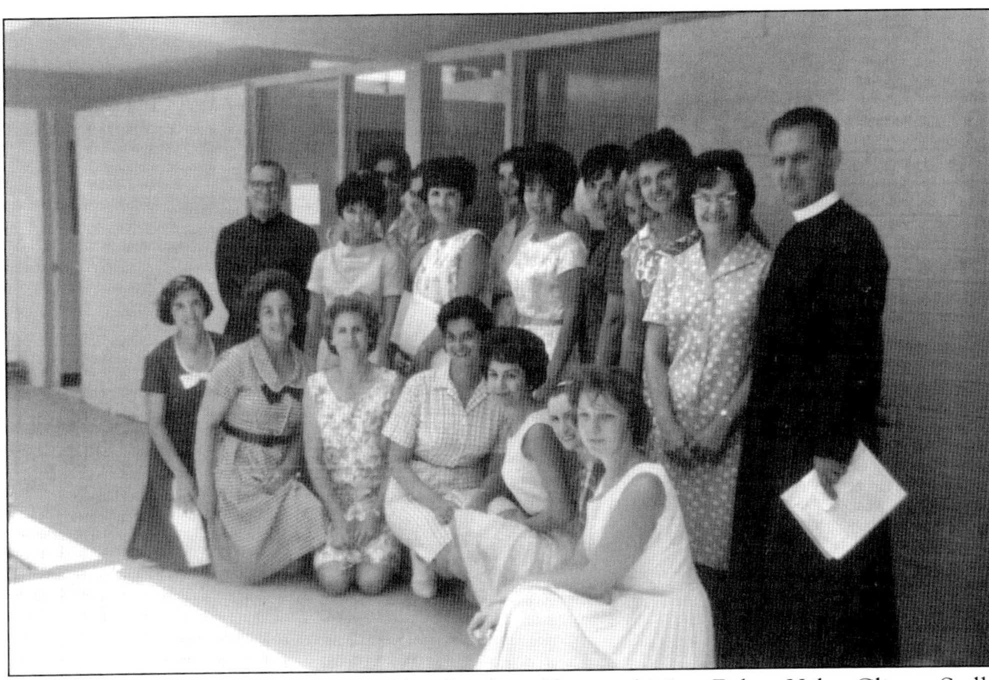

Participating in this 1966 summer Bible school are (first row) Mary Fisher, Helen Glitsos, Stella Glitsos, Mae Ducas, Georgia Poulos, Betty Georgouses, and Lois Sakkas; (second row) Fr. David Buss, Dorothy Kish, Bebe Speros, Betty Hraybar, Bessie Demos, Gloria Freije, Helen Moschovitis, Mena Bafaloukos, Millie Johnson, Agnes Andropoulos, Katherine Tavlarides, and Fr. James Tavlarides.

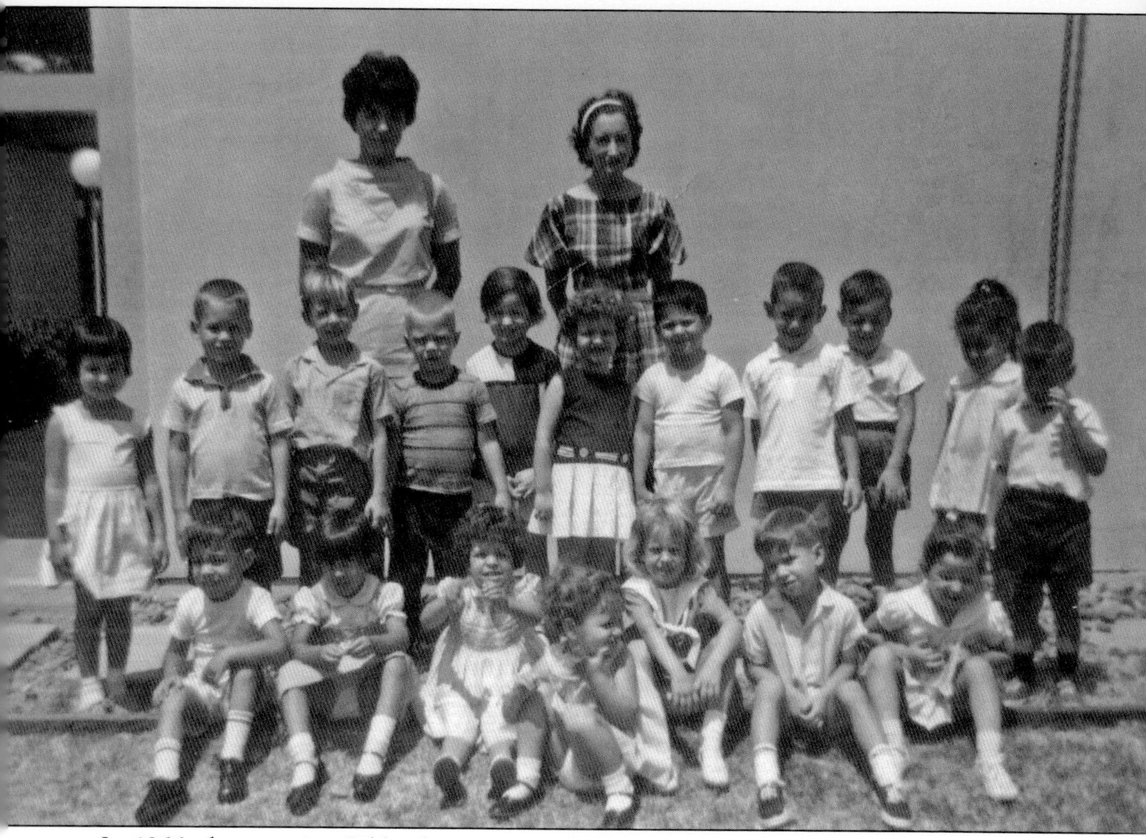

In 1966, the vacation Bible class poses with their teachers, Dorothy Kish (left) and Betty Georgouses (right).

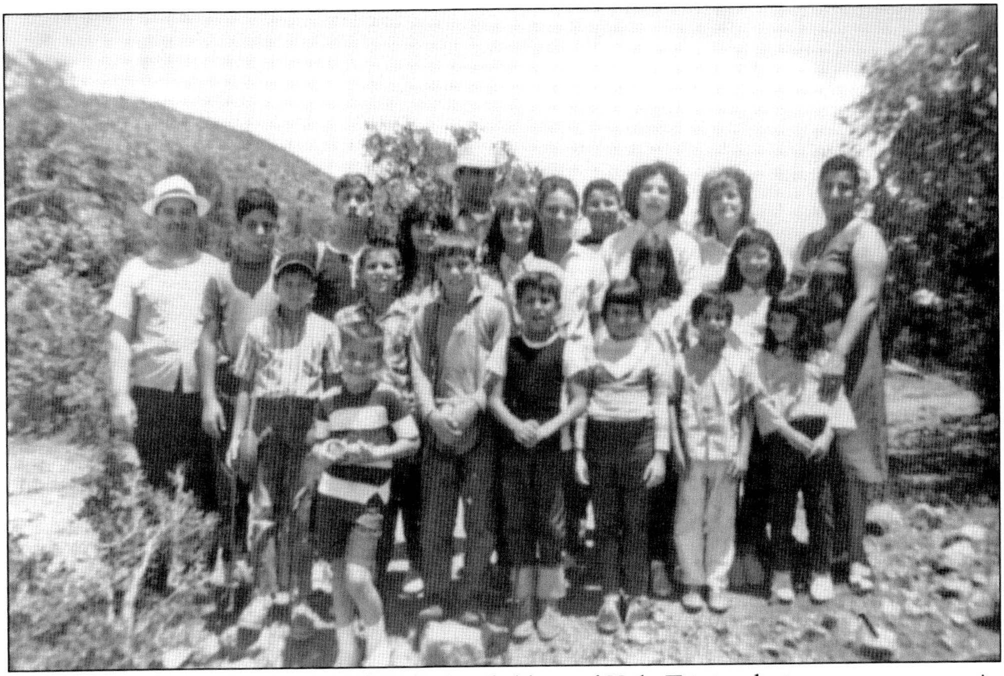

Rev. Kostas Poulakidas is pictured with the children of Holy Trinity during summer camp in Prescott in 1960.

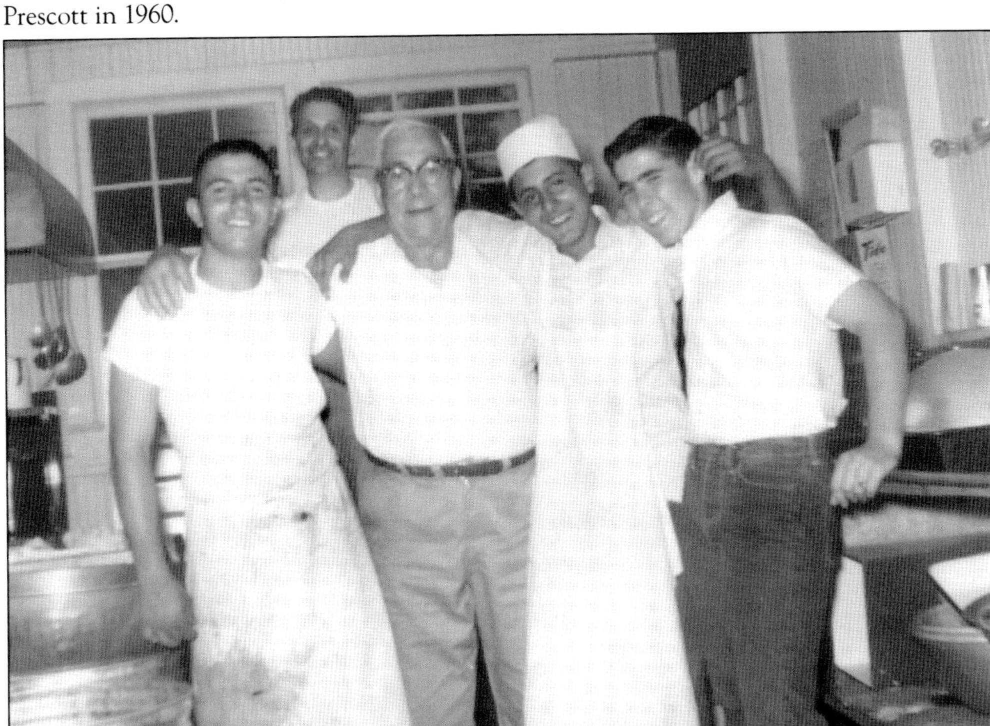

In 1960, summer camp was held in Prescott, Arizona. The fine cooks who attended camp were, from left to right, (first row) unidentified, Paul Christie, Chris Katsenes, and Leo Speliopoulos; (second row) Jim Anton.

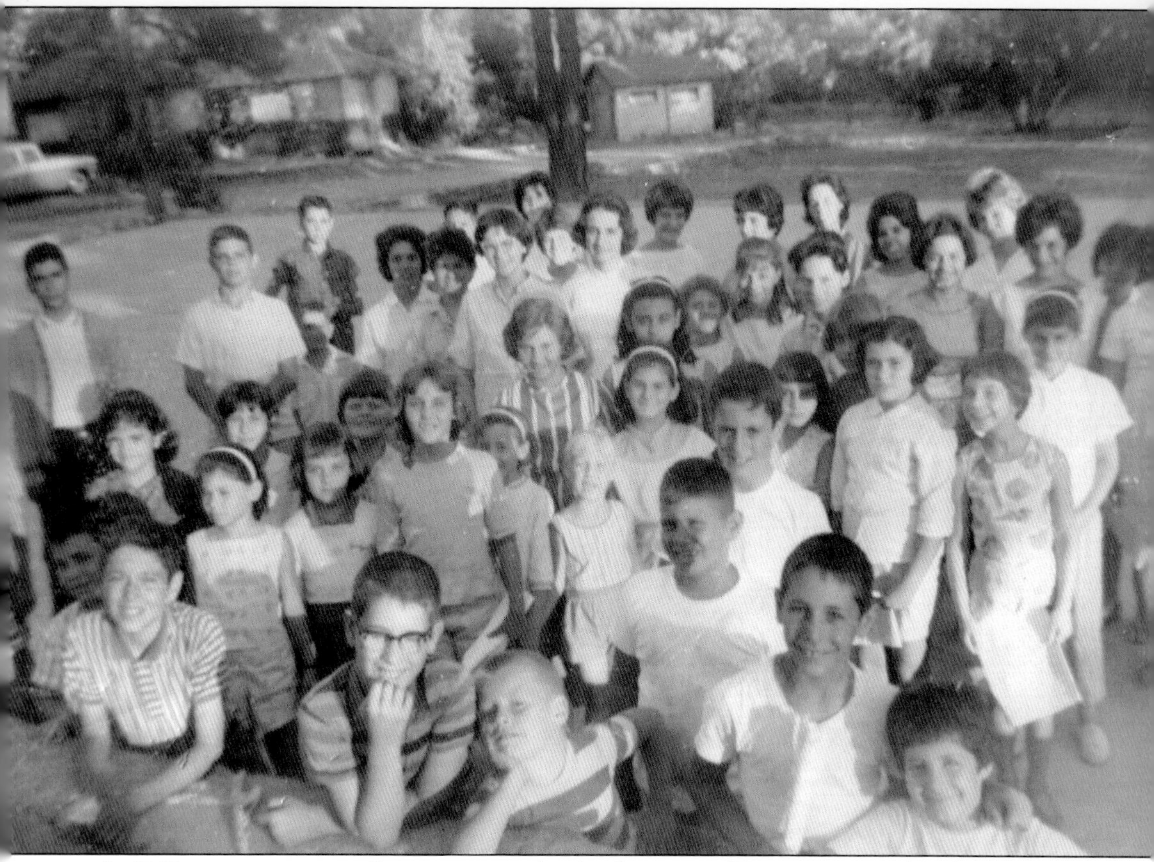

In 1963, summer camp in Prescott was under the direction of Rev. Kostas Poulakidas. The camp program consisted of sports, arts and crafts, and religious classes.

# *Five*

# BUSINESS

Eager to explore and benefit from the American dream, Greek immigrants became involved in numerous occupations. This included confectionery manufacturing and sales, shoe repair, fruit and vegetable vending, hat blocking and dry cleaning, bars and packaged liquor stores, and restaurants.

Ambitious and hard working, most of these men and women made successes out of their commercial endeavors, providing well for their families and becoming generous donors to their church and other community institutions.

The following is a list of the businesses owned and operated by Greek American families in Phoenix for which photographs were not available: the Blue Inn (Nick Gigicon and Gus Fotopoulos); Central Shoe Repair (James L. Speliopoulos); the Chicago Café (Jerry Theotokatos); Chiefs Café (Theodore Dadas); Colonial Coffee Shop (Joe and George Phacas, purchased by John Contos in 1940); Court House Café (Chris Petoumenos and Sam Condas, purchased by G. L. Golfinos in 1940); the Delicious Sandwich Shop (Jim Pritchard); Famous Sandwich Shop (Sam Pritchard); Giller-Konopisos Insurance Agency (James Konopisos); Gold Spot Lunch (Pete Tomaras); Gold Spot Café (Sam Krekos); Granada Café (Mr. Averkiou); Gus's Cigar Store and Tony's Shoe Stand (Gus Georgouses and Tony Thomas); H and J Construction (Harry and John Riskas); Leonard Custom Tailors (James G. Ganos); Mike Londos Union Café (Mike Londos); John S. Marakas Produce (John S. Marakas); Mohave Auction (Paul Souris and George Mates); Pete's News Stand (Pete Kargas); Rainbow Café (Sam Checuras, previously owned by Louis Zeotopoulos); Tom J. Riskas Construction Company (Tom Riskas); Seven Seas Club (Gus and Margaret Curtis); Michael P. Theodore, Insurance Broker; Tony's Shoe Repair (Tony Thomas); the Troc Tavern (Gus P. Contos); and Hammond Café, Ideal Café, Fox Cavern, and Z-Bar (Vasili G. Zorbas).

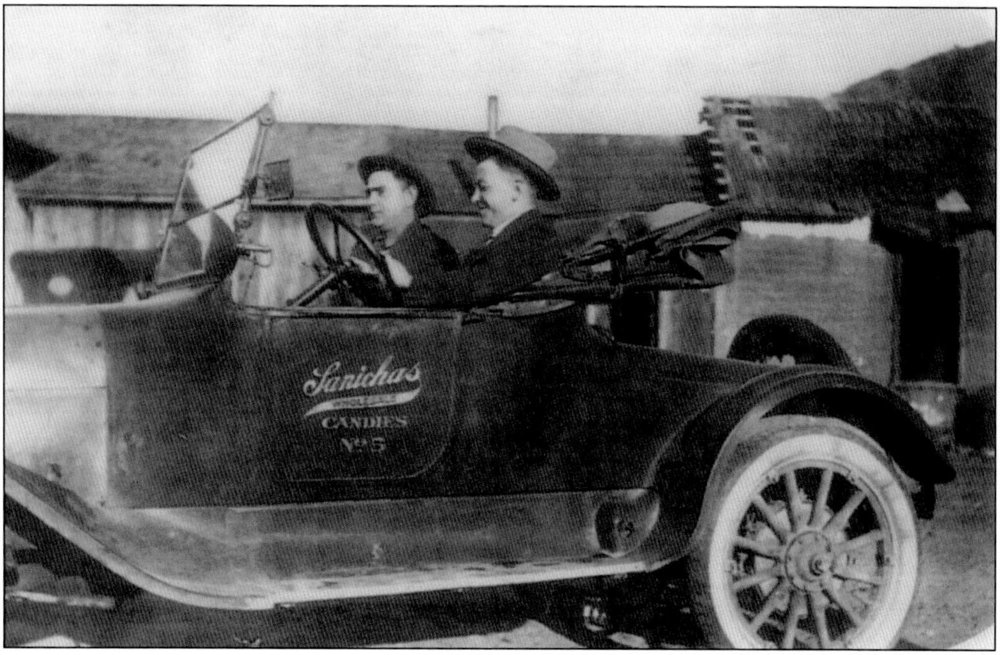


The Sanichas Candy Company was established in 1908 and was owned and operated by Chris Sanichas. The candy and ice cream factory was located at 305 West Madison Street. In the 1930s, the company changed ownership to Nick Gannis, who changed the name to Southwest Candy Company.

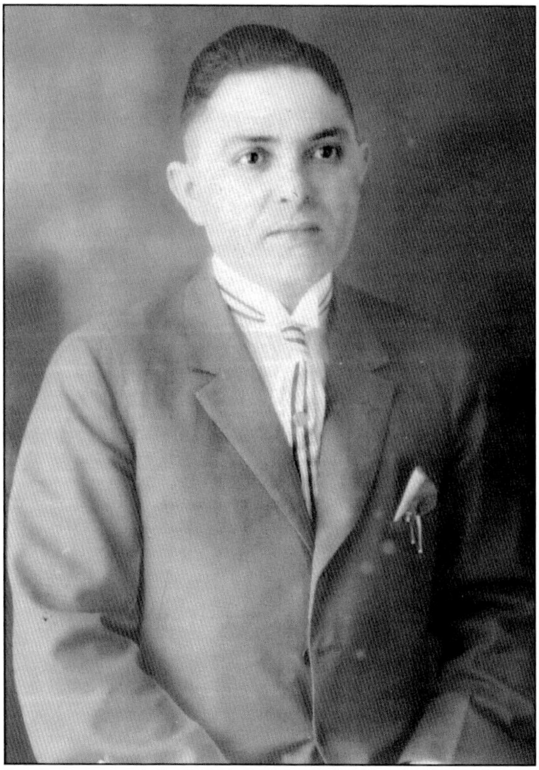

Gus Thomas first came to Arizona in 1917. He worked in Douglas, Arizona, until 1920. He returned to Arizona in 1927 and opened a sandwich shop in Gila Bend (he was one of two Greek men in Gila Bend.) In 1946, he became partners with Chris Panagos in the El Paso Buffet on Third Street and Washington Street in Phoenix, which he later sold to his nephew, Tony Hotis. Gus and his wife, Antigone, had a son, Jim.

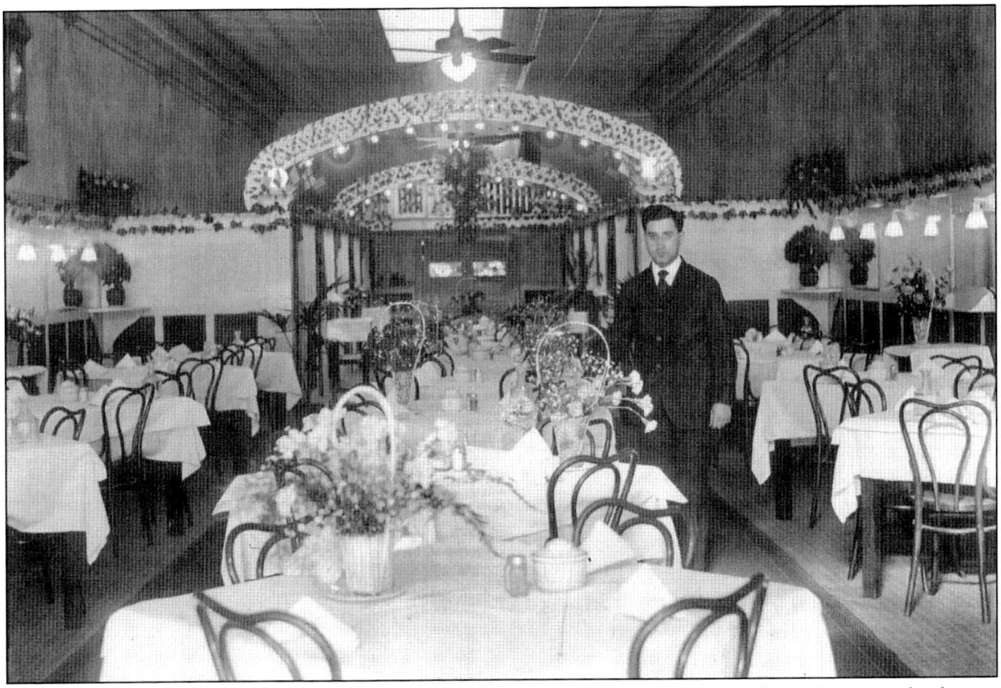

Milton Stamatis, shown here, opened the St. Francis Café at 34 West Adams Street, which was destroyed by fire in 1922. He later opened the Grand Café at the same location. In addition, he owned the Country Club on North Central Avenue, north of the Grand Canal, during the late 1930s.

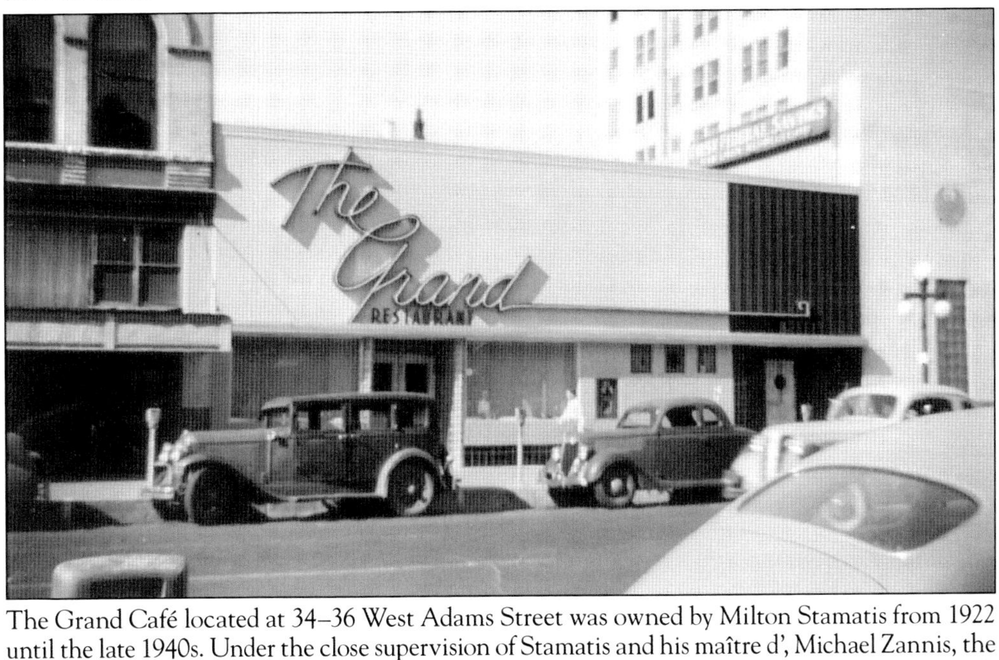


The Grand Café located at 34–36 West Adams Street was owned by Milton Stamatis from 1922 until the late 1940s. Under the close supervision of Stamatis and his maître d', Michael Zannis, the Grand quickly established itself as the only fancy eating and drinking place in town with nightly dancing. At lunch, the restaurant was a meeting place for professional people from the new Phoenix Title and Trust building. In the late 1940s, the Grand was sold and renamed the Flame.

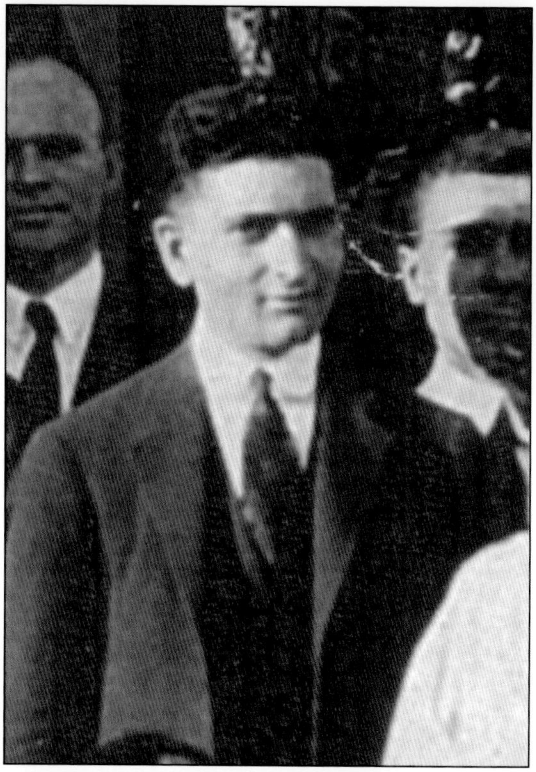

In the 1920s, Chris Mitchell owned and operated Mitchell's Sweet Shop. He was the originator of Cactus Candy. Chris and his wife, Maria, had two daughters: Alice and Helen.

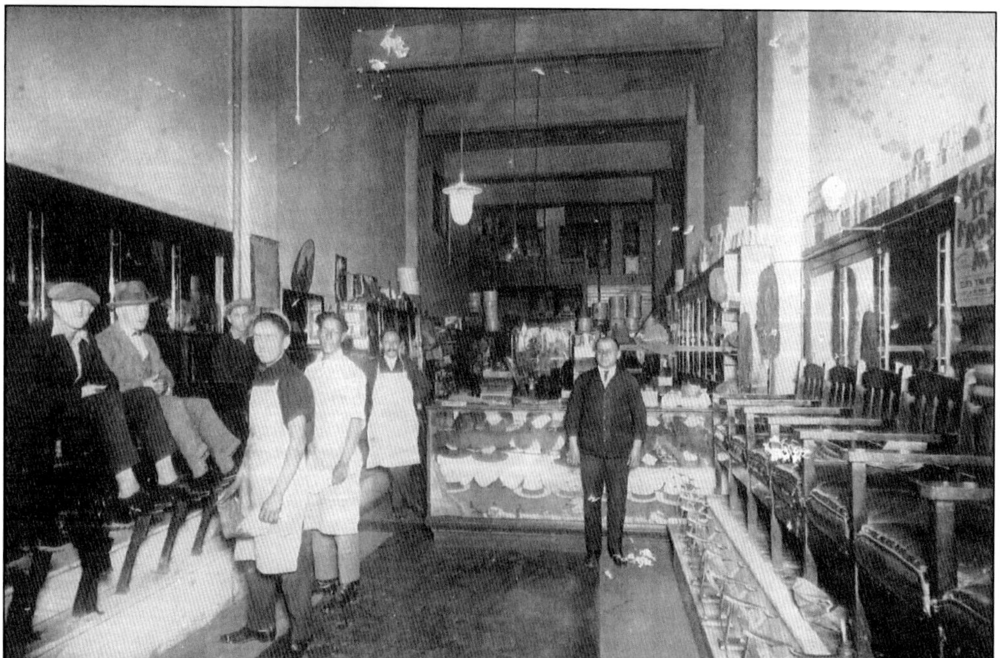

John Thomas owned and operated the Shoe Shine Parlor, where he also cleaned and blocked hats, in the 1920s. Thomas is standing next to the counter in the background, wearing an apron. One of his sons, Tony, opened several shoe repair shops in the 1940s.

Athens Hat Shop was owned and operated by George Falkedes. He was known as "George the Greek" to his customers. His shop was located in the Jefferson Hotel at 121 South Central Avenue, where he cleaned, blocked, and sold in excess of six million hats. He owned the shop from 1921 to 1969. Even after retiring, he still did business with a few customers, working from a building in his backyard.

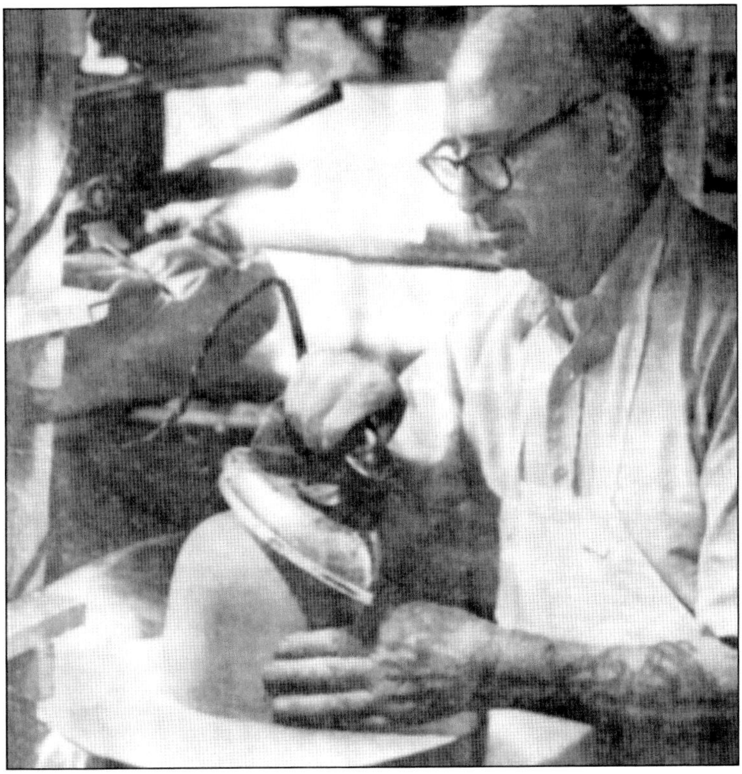

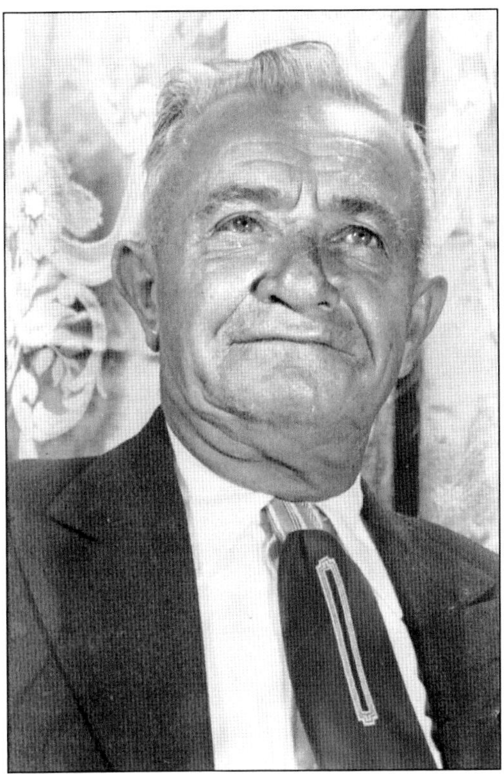

Chris Pallas came to Phoenix in the early 1920s and opened a restaurant at 37 West Washington Street. He then opened the Palace Café at 315 South Fourth Avenue, across from the Phoenix Union Station (railroad). The Palace Café had the largest packaged liquor department in the city at that time.

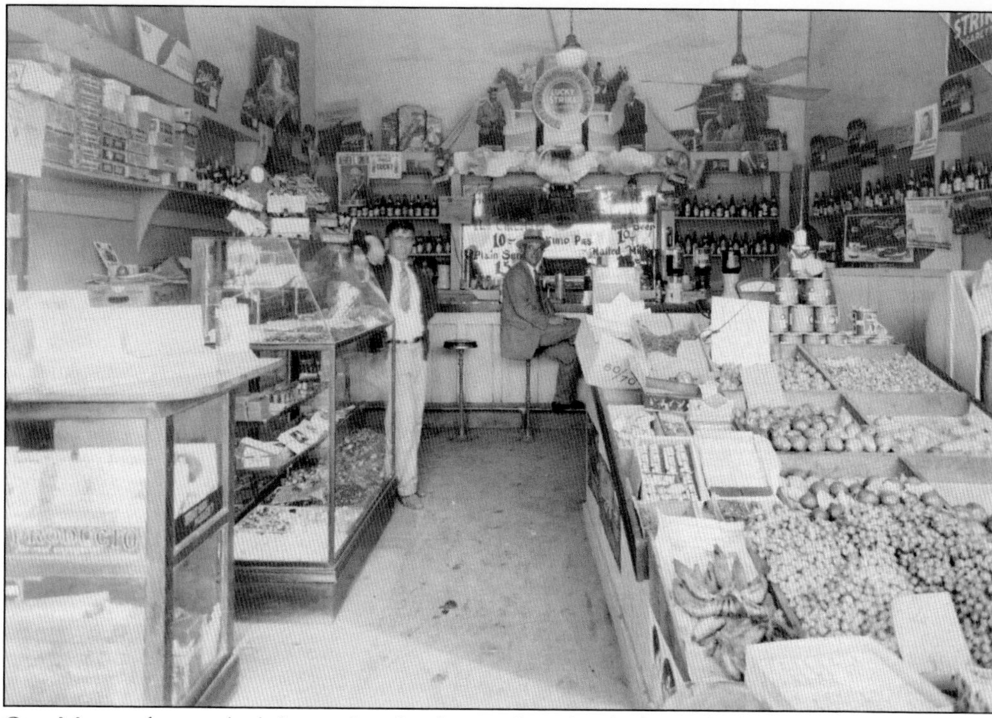

Gust Metsopolos, on the left, stands in his fruit and sandwich shop, which was established in 1923 and located at 311 East Washington Street. In the 1940s, he changed the name to Gust's Chili Parlor. After extensive remodeling in the 1950s, it became Metsos Cocktail Lounge.

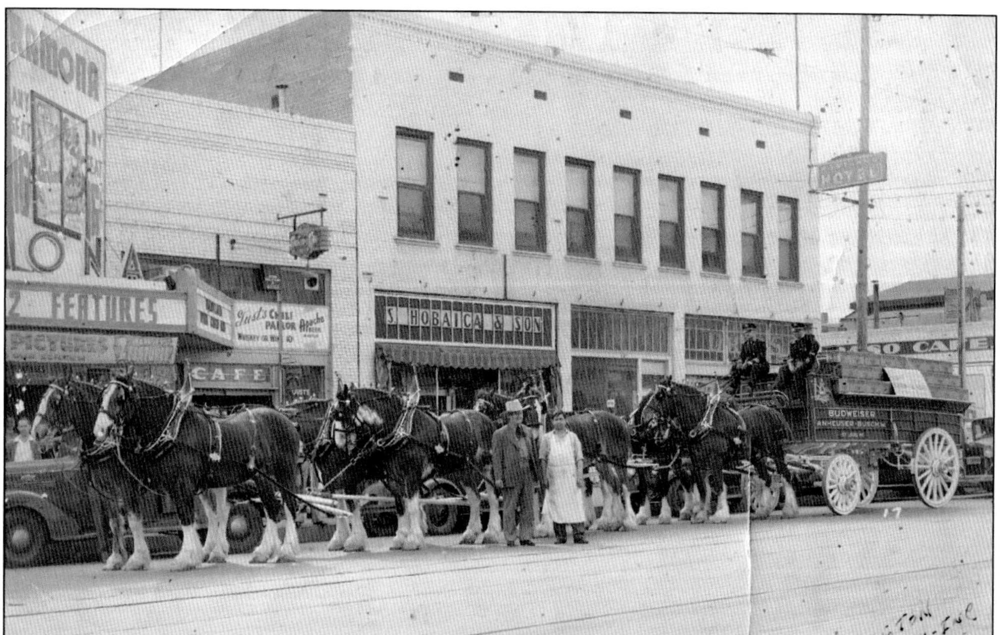


Shown here is Gust Metsopolos standing outside his establishment, Gust's Chili Parlor at 311 East Washington Street, with the famous Anheuser-Busch Budweiser Clydesdale Horse Team.

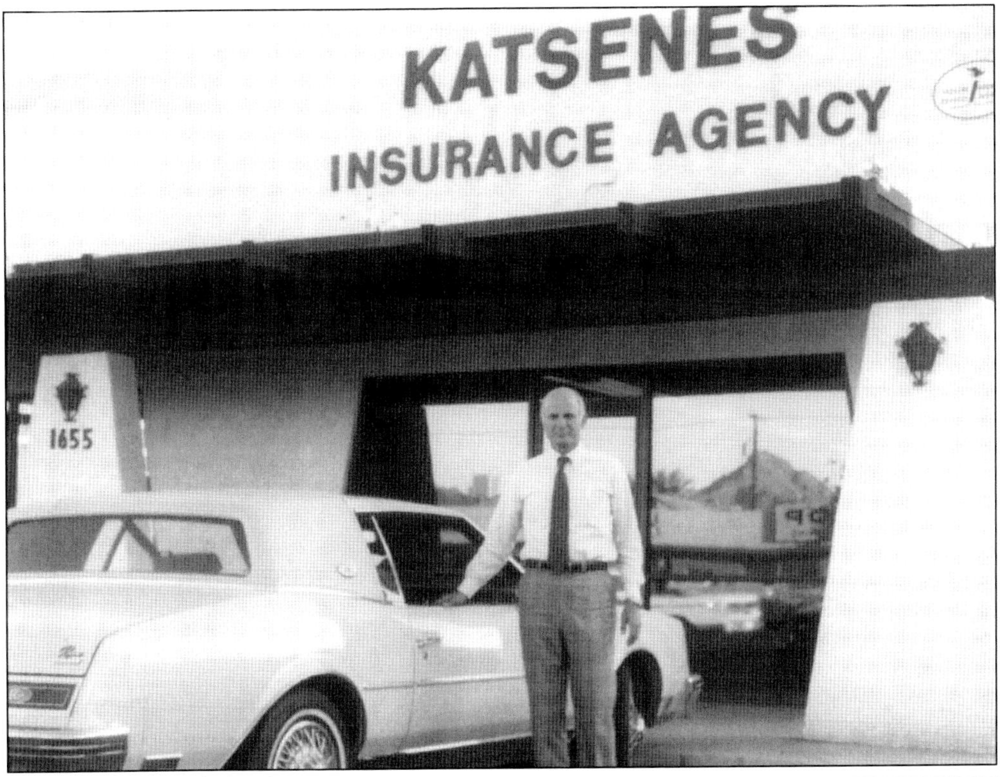


The Katsenes family has been in the insurance business since 1925. Tom Katsenes was a New York Life salesman with an office downtown. He later worked out of his home office. Pictured above, his son John went into the general insurance business in 1940. He built the office at 2325 North Sixteenth Street. In 1972, they moved to a new location, 1655 East Indian School Road. John's son, Tom Katsenes, took over the business in 2006. John and his wife, Mary, have three children, Athanasia "Sia," Tom, and Karen.

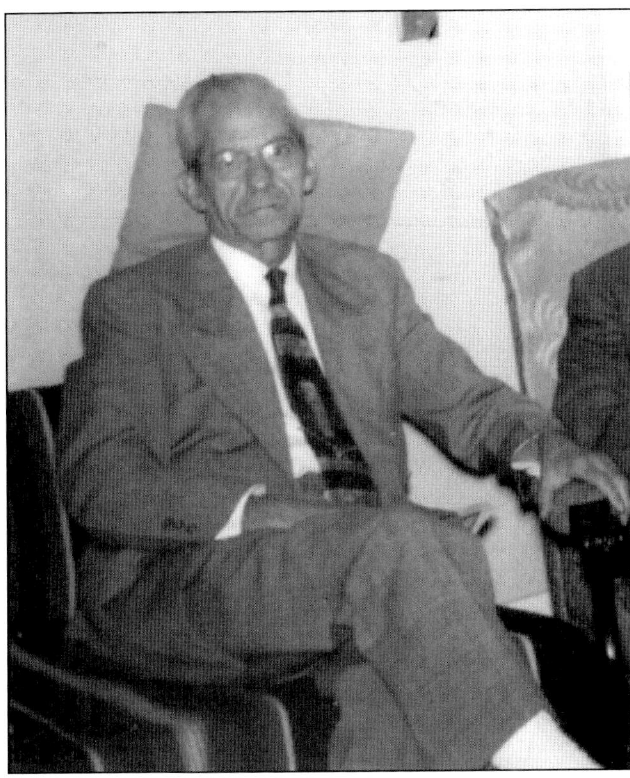

In the 1940s, Spyro Diamond owned a pet supply store, Canine Caterers, on Seventh and Roosevelt Streets. Diamond and his wife, Rita, had two sons: Gus and Tally.

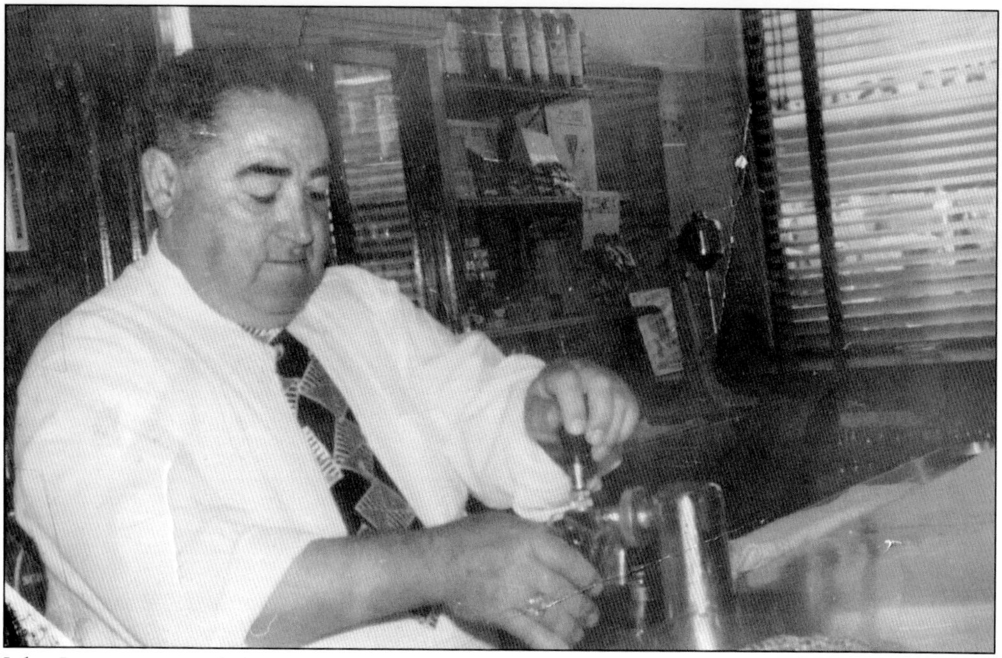

John Pappas, pictured above, was a partner in the Busy Bee Café, located at 45 West Washington Street, from 1928. Pictured below are Theodore Theodoropoulos, in front of the counter, and Pete Chotras, third from the right. They became partners with John Pappas in 1938. The Maricopa County Courthouse/Phoenix City Hall was located across the street, leading lawyers and reporters to eat lunch at the café. During World War II, thousands of soldiers on weekend passes swarmed downtown Phoenix. Diners were so packed they stood over the sinks in the kitchen to eat their steaks and seafood.

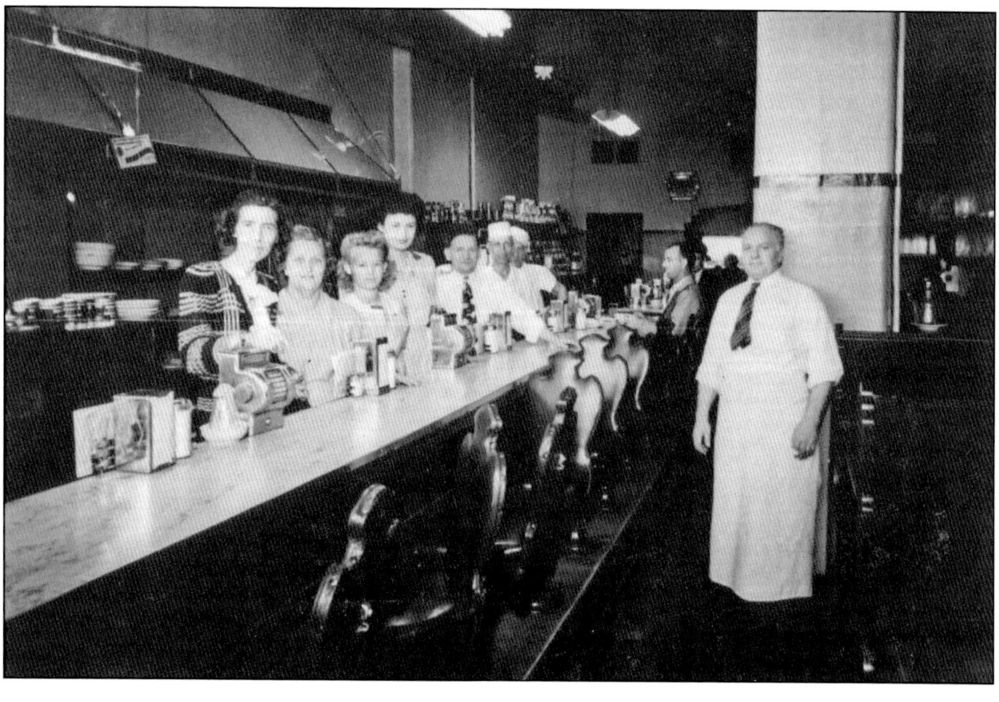

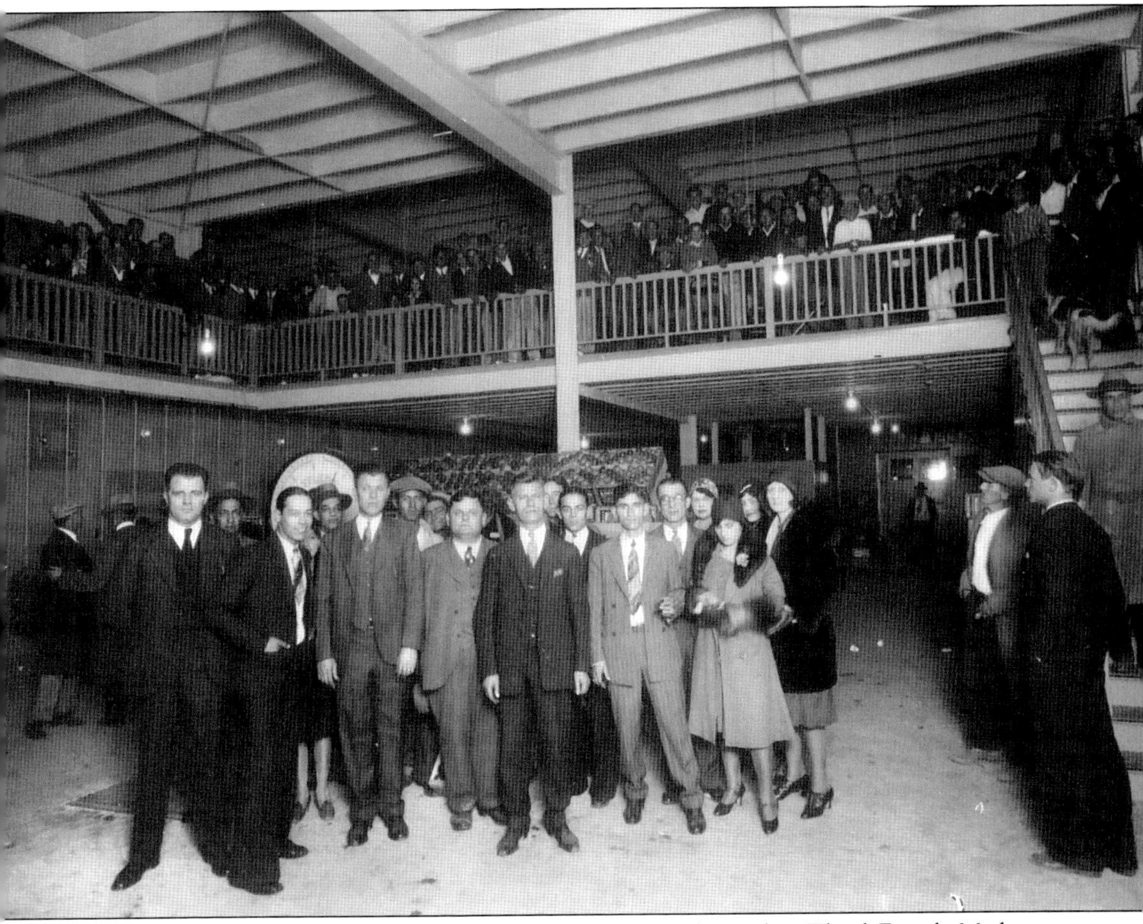

This is the 1929 grand opening of Farmers Produce Company, located on Third, Fourth, Madison, and Jackson Streets. Chris Johnson (third from right in the front row) and James Poulos (to his right) were partners. Poulos managed the store in Miami. When Chris Johnson passed away, Poulos moved to Phoenix, and Harry Johnson took his brother's place as a partner. He is pictured in the front row second from the right with his wife, Paraskevi, next to him.

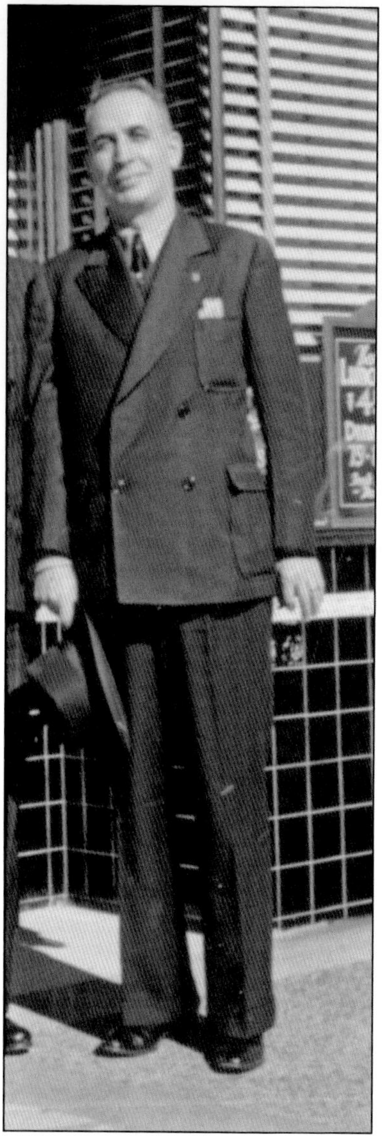

Jim Konomos had an auto repair shop on Third Avenue and Madison Street in the 1930s. He opened General Auto Repair at 722 East Culver Street in the 1940s. He later married Georgia, and they had five children: George, Peter, Becky, Philip, and Tessie.

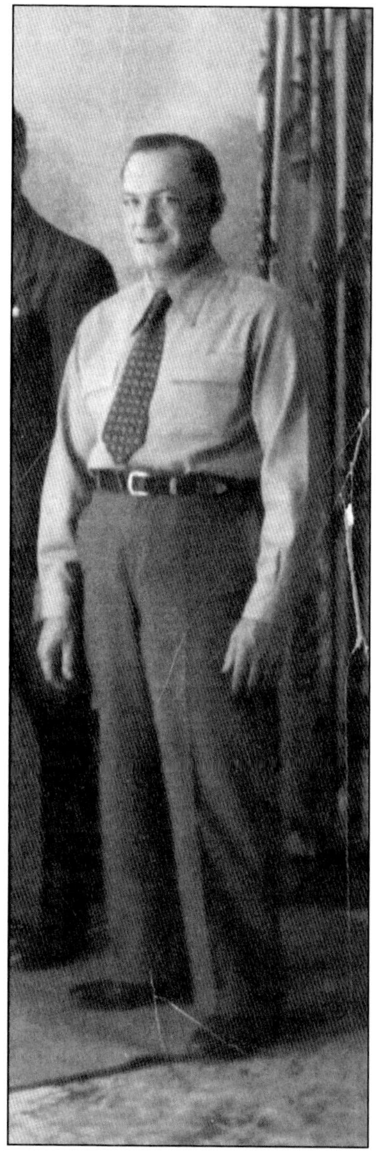

Nick Cuimanes was a chef at the Saratoga Café in 1931 and later became a partner. He married Irene Montague and raised two daughters, Demitra and Evelyn.

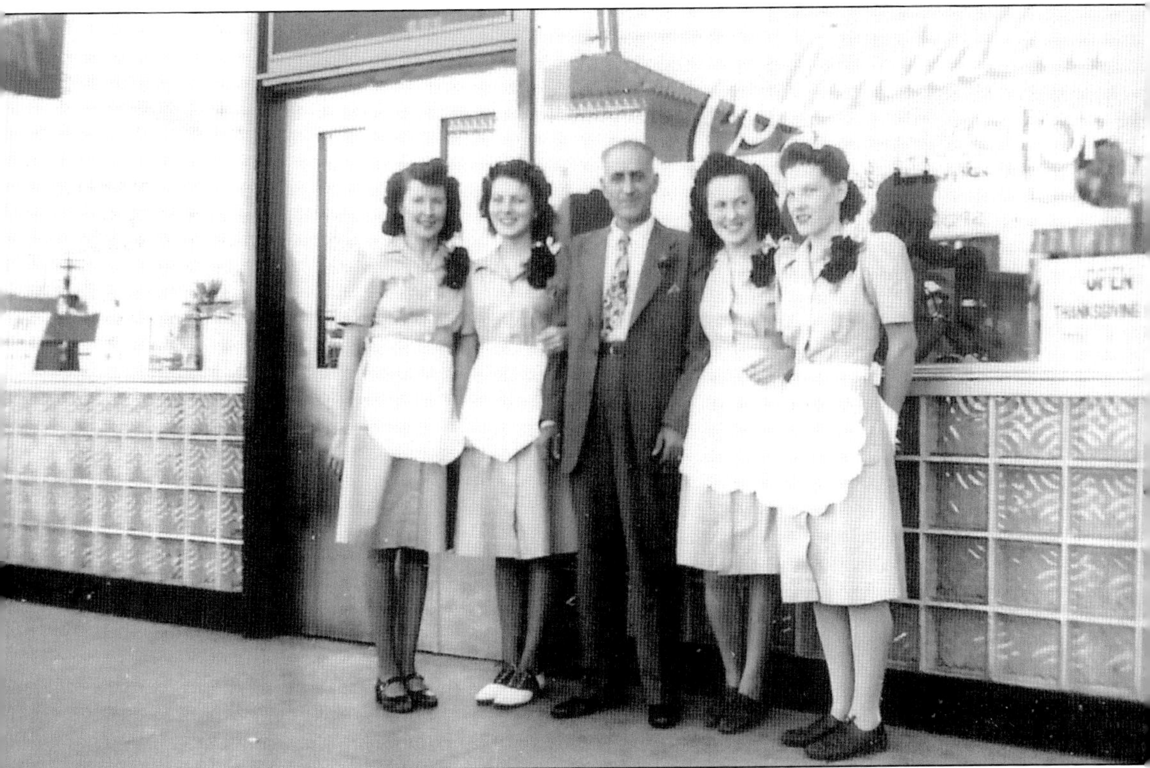

John Contos and his staff are pictured in the 1940s in front of the Colonial Coffee Shop, located at 37 East Monroe Street. He also owned the White Hotel in downtown Phoenix. John and his wife, Zoe, had two children: Dora and Gus.

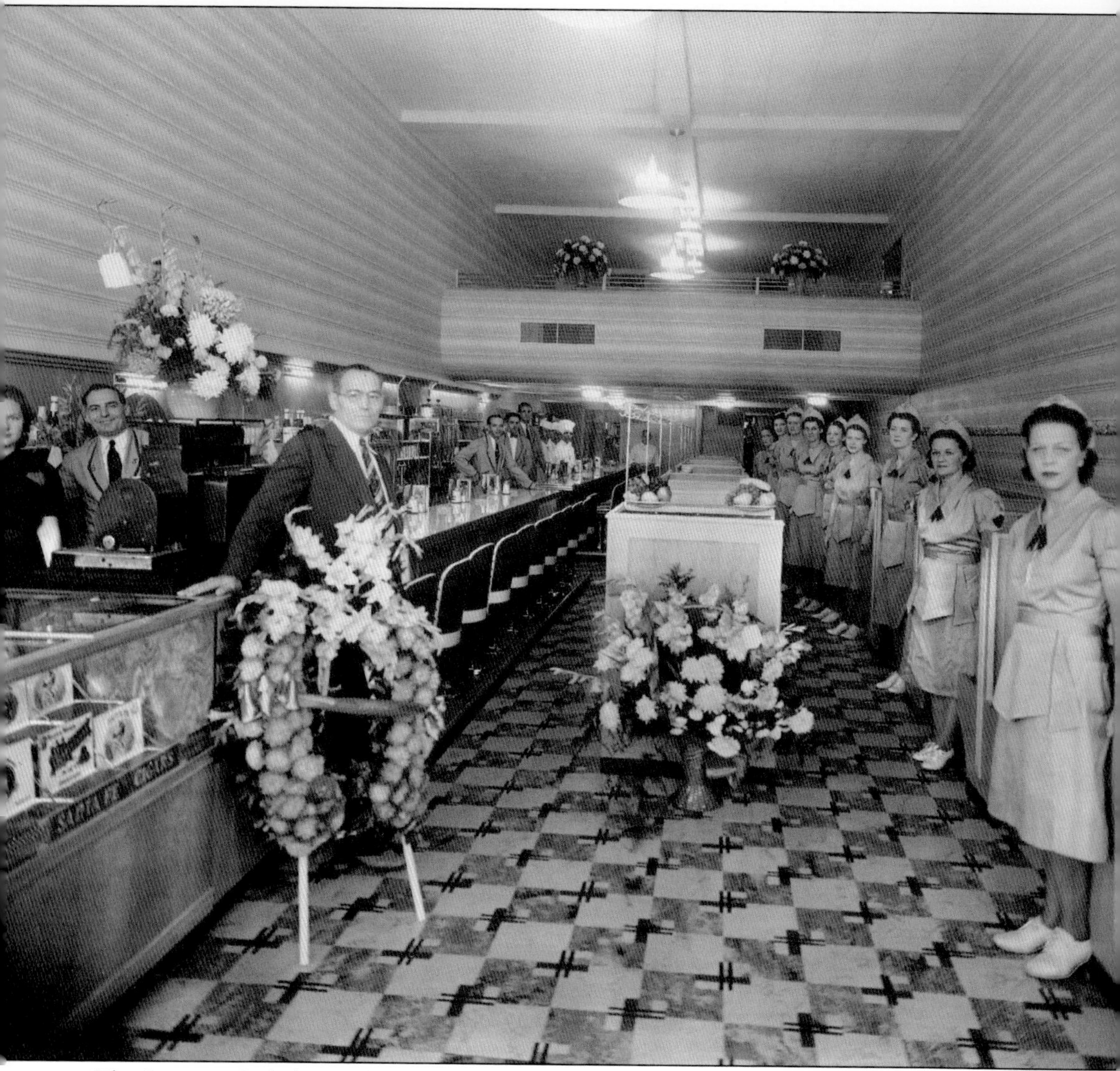

The Saratoga Café, located at 11 West Washington Street, was opened in 1920 by Sam Colachis (pictured in front of the counter). In 1925, Michael Zannis joined him and was a partner until 1928. In 1926, Harris Kalogeras joined the business. In the late 1920s, Nick Cuimanes and Chris Fotinos became partners. It was a place where new recruits ate their last meal before shipping out during World War II. Visiting sports teams, along with judges and lawyers, frequented the restaurant.

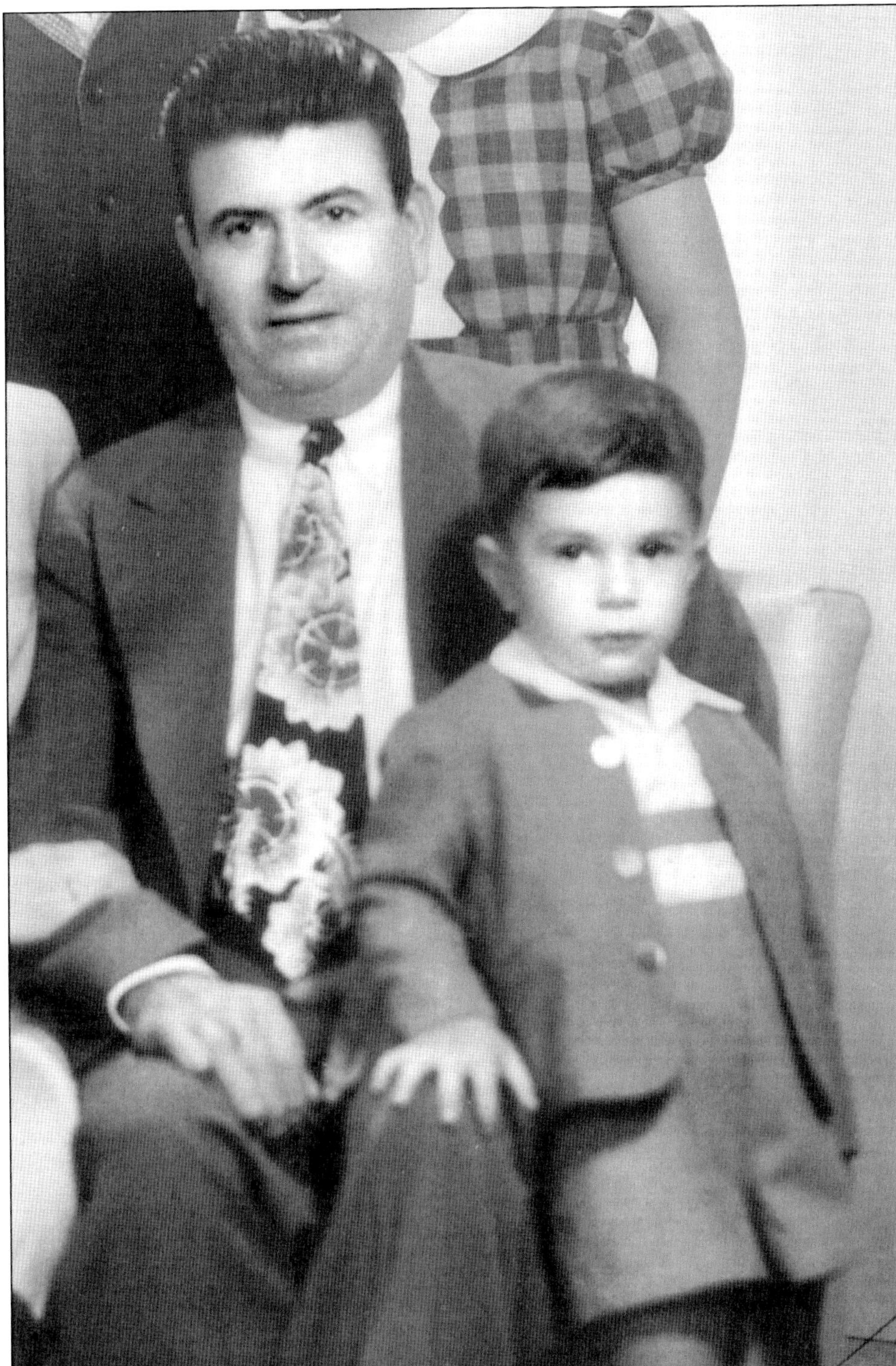

Chris Fotinos came to Phoenix in 1928. He married Dimetra Tseguris in 1936. They had four children: Steve, Irene, Tony, and Nick. Chris Fotinos worked as a chef at the Saratoga Café and in the late 1920s became a partner. He later opened the Skylark on Central Avenue.

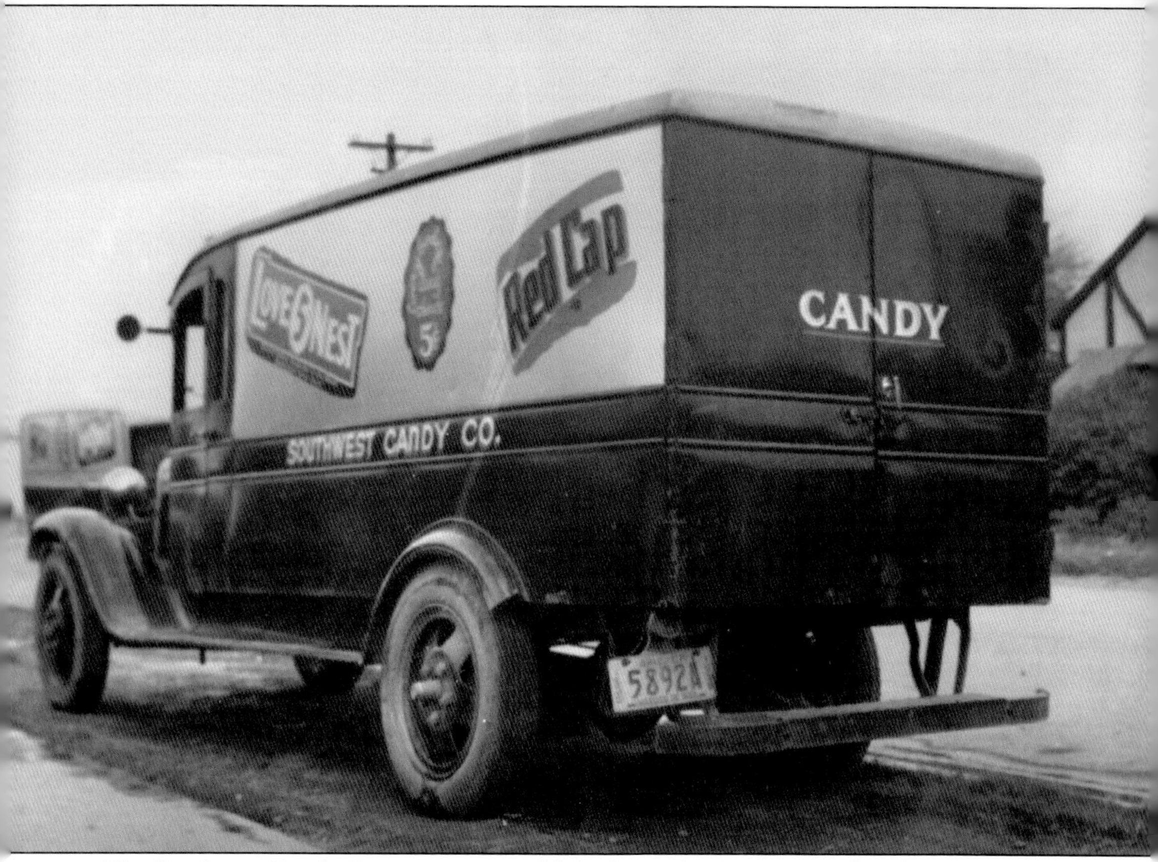


The Southwest Candy Company was established in 1938. It was owned and operated by Nick Gannis. The company distributed candies, gum, and cigarettes to various surrounding retail stores, including cities in northern Arizona. Nick's wife, Meropy, and children, John, Emily, Fannie, and Mary Louise, assisted him with his business, including stocking (and sometimes eating) the various candies. Nick retired in 1945 and closed his business.

In the 1940s, Gus Georgouses and Tony Thomas operated shops at 47 West Washington Street, including Gus's Cigar Store and Tony's Shoe Stand. Later Tony Thomas opened several other locations.

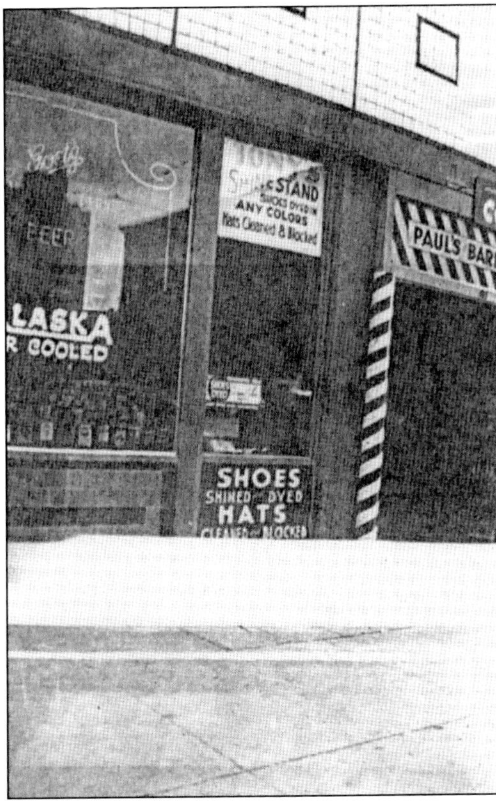


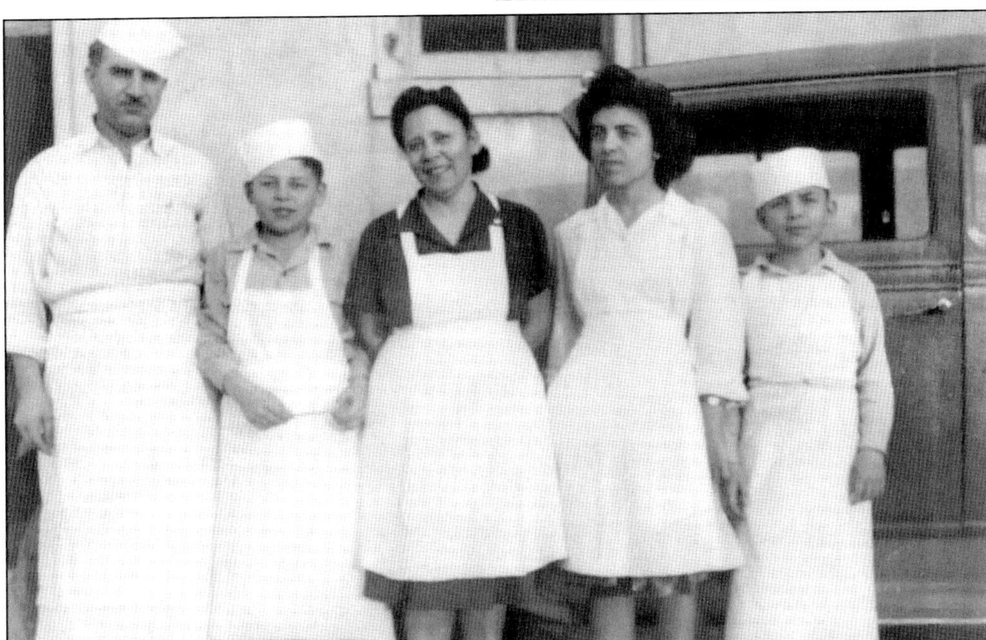

In 1941, Tom Annos opened the Nogales Café at 27 South Second Street. In 1983, the City of Phoenix purchased the property for the development of a fourth hotel. Pictured are, from left to right, Tom, Pete, Mercedes, Katherine, and William Annos.

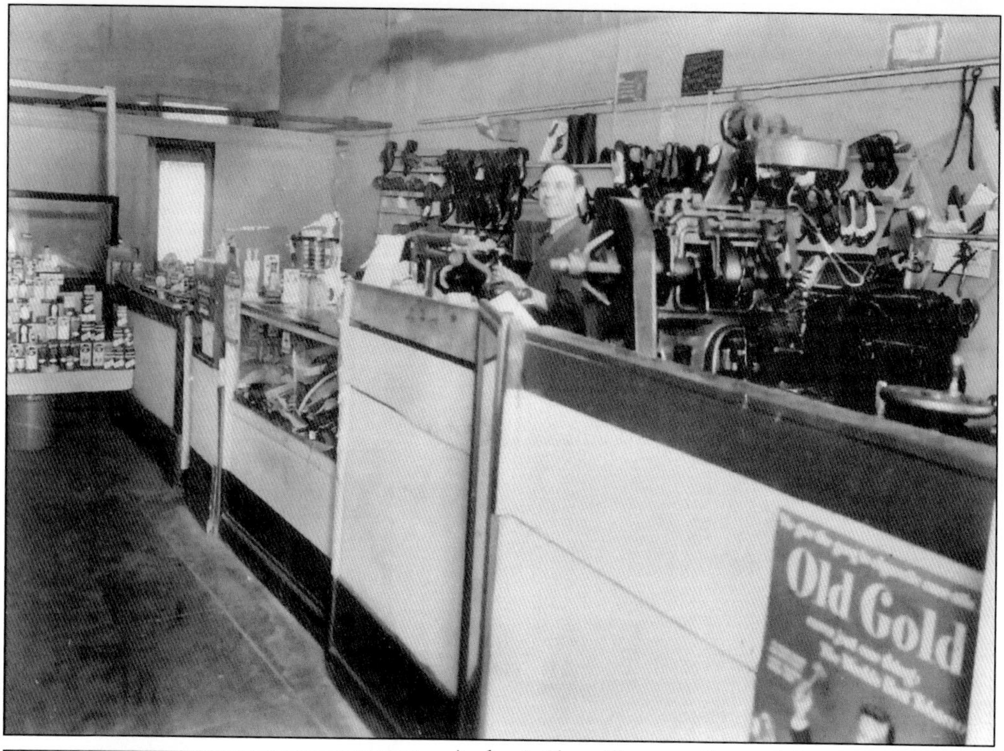


Arthur's Shoe Shop, on Second Avenue and Adams Street, was owned by Arthur Kostopoulos from 1942 to 1960. Arthur and his wife, Julie, had three children: Doris, Alexandra, and Helen.

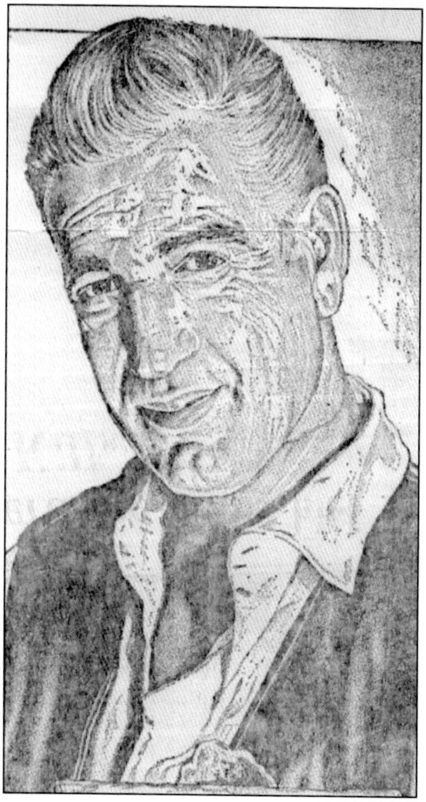

Ed Scarla moved to Phoenix in 1942. He ran the Home Produce Company for the A. J. Bayless stores. The Home Produce Company was located at the Farmers Produce Company warehouse on Third, Fourth, Madison, and Jackson Streets.

George and Viola (Paraskevi) Handgis moved to Phoenix in the mid-1940s. They opened George's Shoe Repair south of Roosevelt Street on Sixteenth Street. This photograph appeared with an article in the *Phoenix Gazette* on Labor Day, Monday, September 1, 1969, with the caption that read "Hands of working man keep nation strong. The shoemaker uses his hands and we walk comfortably." They had six children: Helen, Nicholas, Demosthenes (Moss), John, Socrates (Sox), and Alexander.

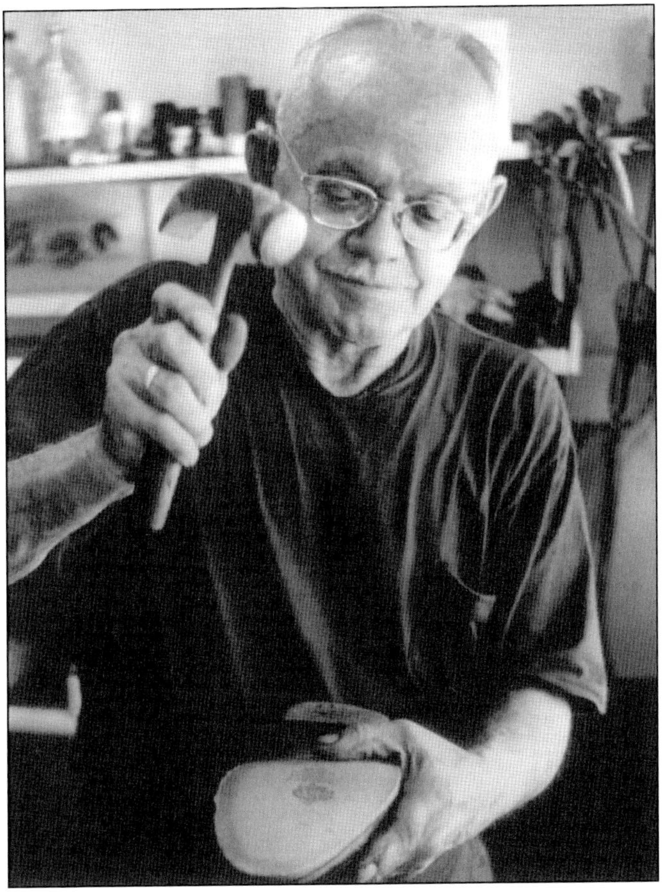

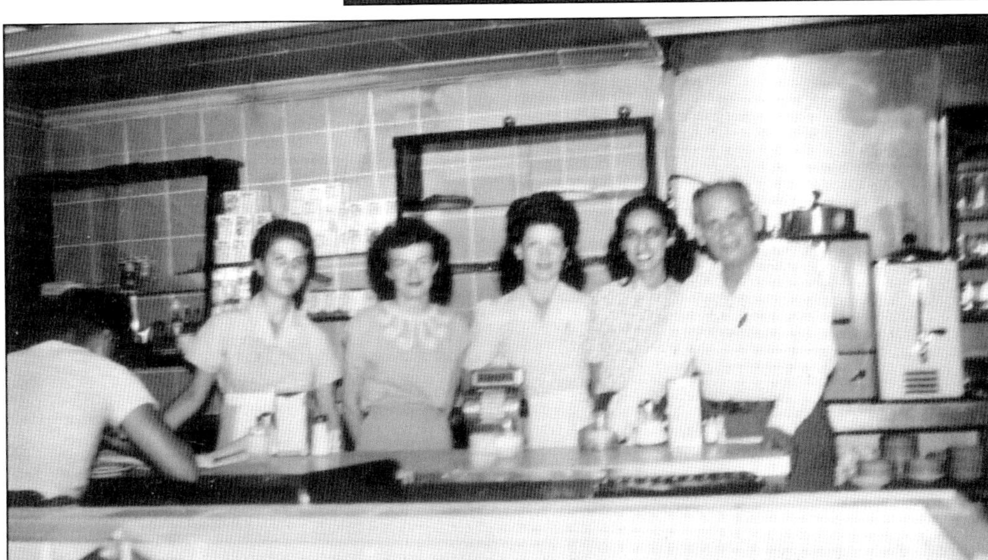

The Majestic Café, located at 200 West Washington Street, was purchased by Alexander Limberopoulos in 1945. Next to Alexander (at far right) is Ethel Gianoulis, who was a cashier and who returned to her native Chicago in 1947. Limberopoulos and his wife, Toula, had a son, Andrew.

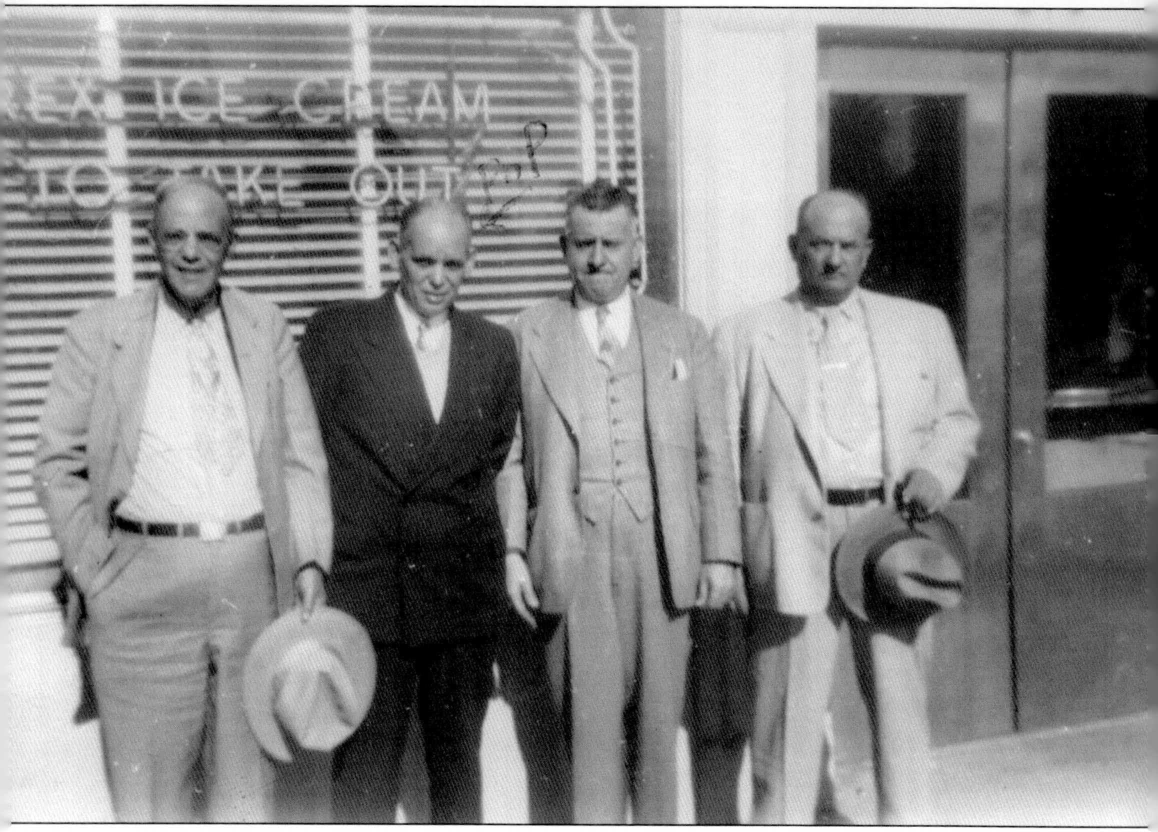


In 1946, Alexander Limberopoulos (second from left) bought and remodeled the Rex Ice Cream Store at 210 West Washington Street, next to the Majestic Café. (The site of the Majestic and the Rex is where the new Phoenix City Hall now stands.) When Alexander died in June 1948, his 12-year-old son Andrew took over, taught his mother the business, and became what was probably the youngest retail store operator in Phoenix. The first *kafenion* (a Greek coffee house) in Phoenix, the Arcadia Club, was opened by Alex Limber in early 1945. He opened it not as a business venture, but so that he and other Greek men could have a place to play poker and *tavli* (backgammon). He took in a partner, longtime Phoenix resident Ted Speropoulos, to cook and run the place. The Arcadia Club was on the west side of Central Avenue, mid-block between Washington and Jefferson Streets, on the second floor of a commercial building.

Dick's Flamingo Club, located at 2842 West Van Buren Street, was owned by Richard Doukakis from 1947 to 1969. Richard and his wife, Pauline, had three children: Rick, Gail, and Debbie.

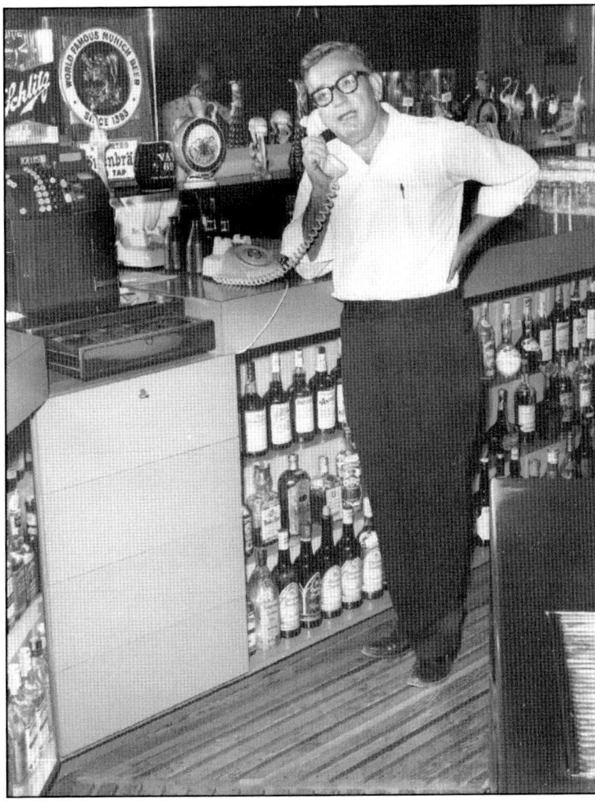


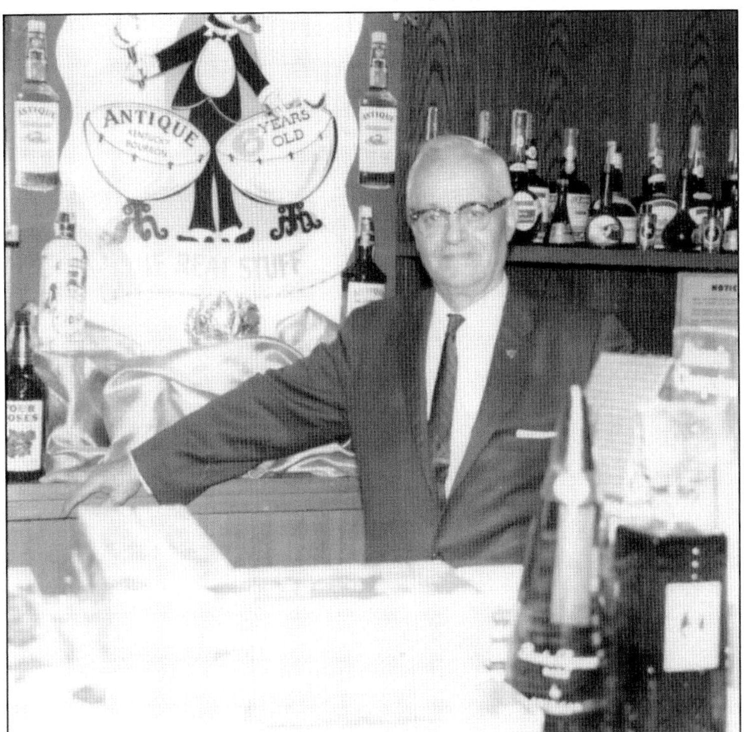


Michael J. Zannis operated the Buttery at the Westward Ho Hotel from 1947 to 1968, when he retired at age 81. He moved to Phoenix in 1925 and became a partner in the Saratoga Café until 1928. He opened his own Saratoga Café in Los Angeles, California, which he sold in 1934 and moved back to Phoenix, where he worked at the Grand Café until 1946.

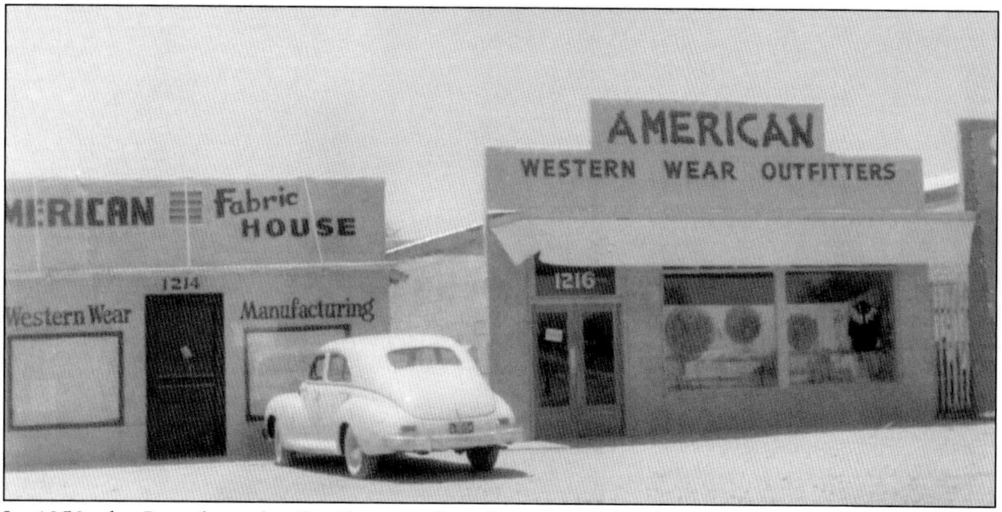


In 1950, the Papadopoulos family owned and operated the American Fabric House at 1214 North Thirty-fifth Avenue. They specialized in custom Western wear and supplied businesses like Goldwaters, Porters, Sabas, and J. C. Penney. They also supplied some shops in Las Vegas. The parents, Vasilios and Magdalene, and their children, George, Lazaros, Penny, and Athena, designed and manufactured the Western clothes.

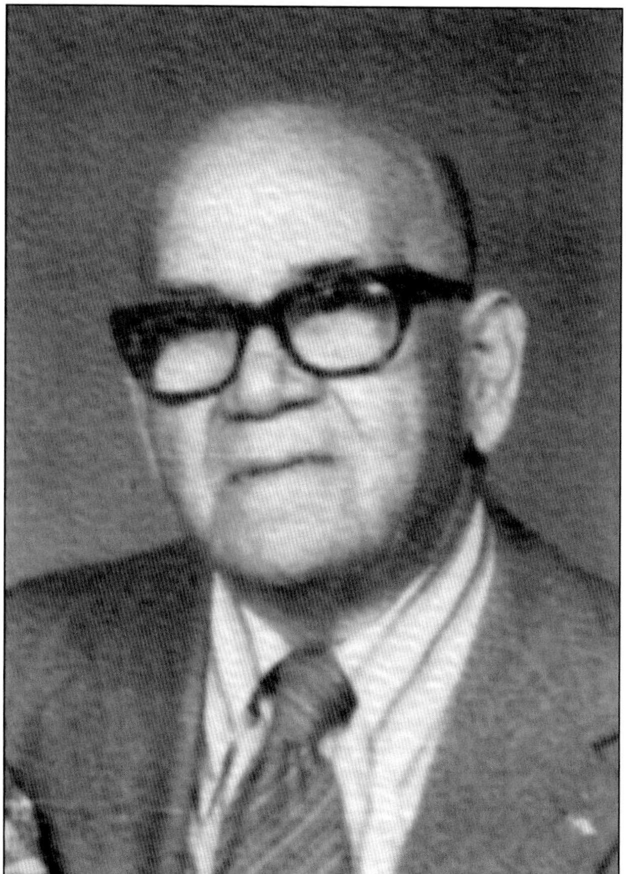

In 1951, William Mallas purchased the Rex Ice Cream Store at 210 West Washington Street. He was assisted by his wife, Alexandra, and son, George.

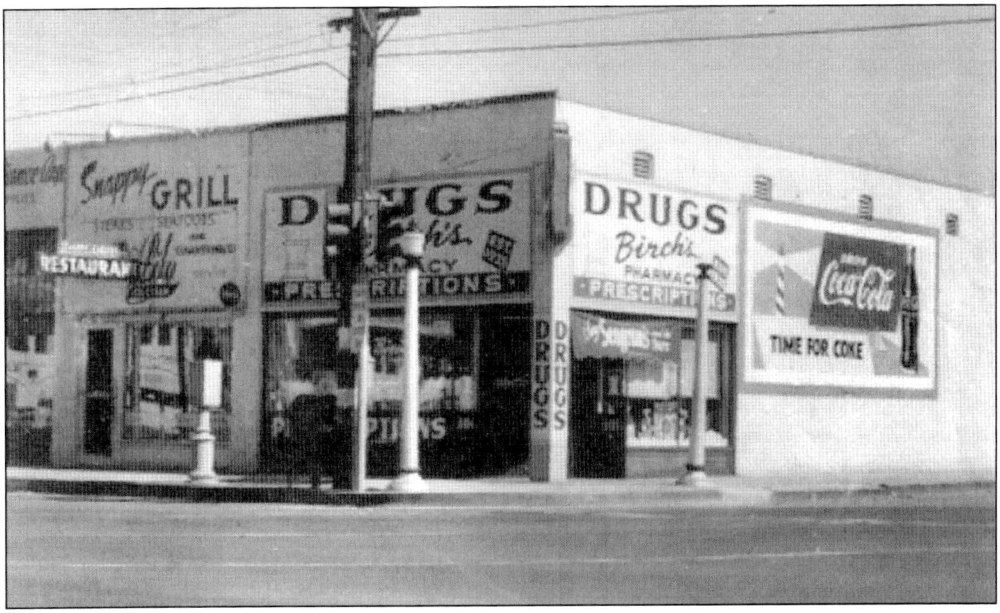


The block between Third and Fourth Streets facing Roosevelt Street had a number of stores and services utilized by Greek families living in the area. The Snappy Grill, next to Birch's Pharmacy, was owned by the Petenakis family, who moved to Phoenix from Mason City, Iowa, in 1950. Athena Petenakis is pictured at right. Her daughter, Claire, also worked in the Snappy Grill.

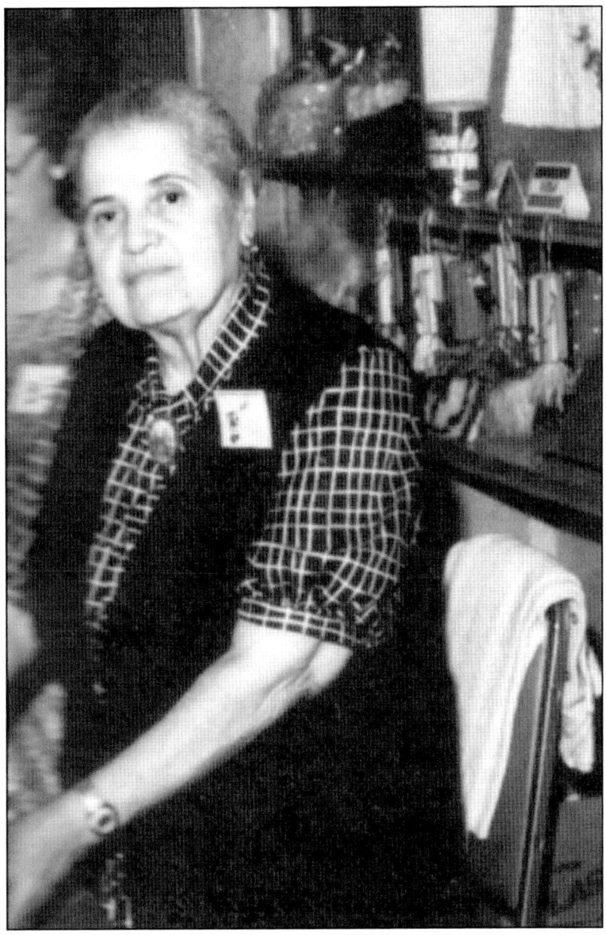

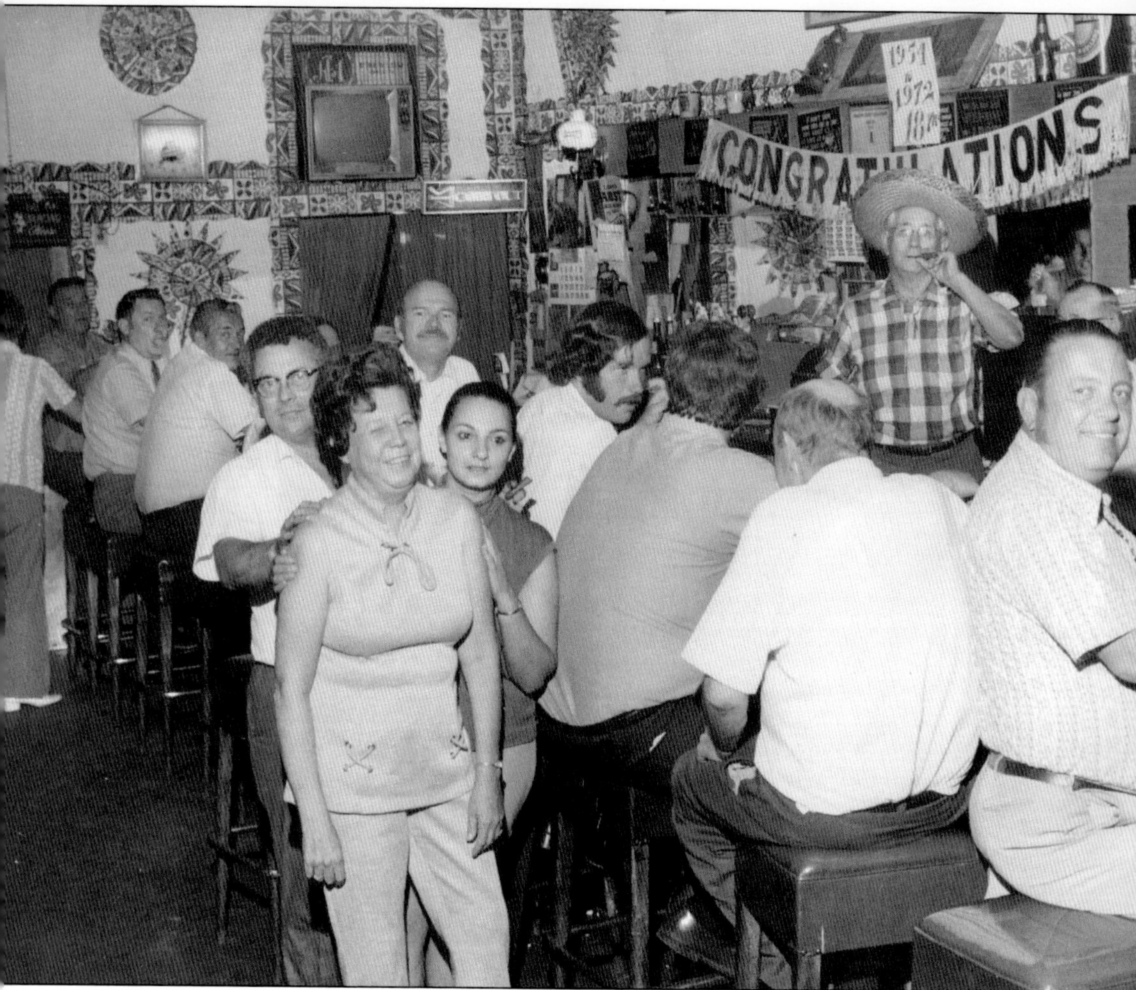


Located at 1413 West Indian School Road, YoYo Tavern was owned by Stefanos Stefanopoulos (Steve Stephens) from 1957 to 1980. Stephens and his wife, Helen, had two children: Pano and Aspacia.

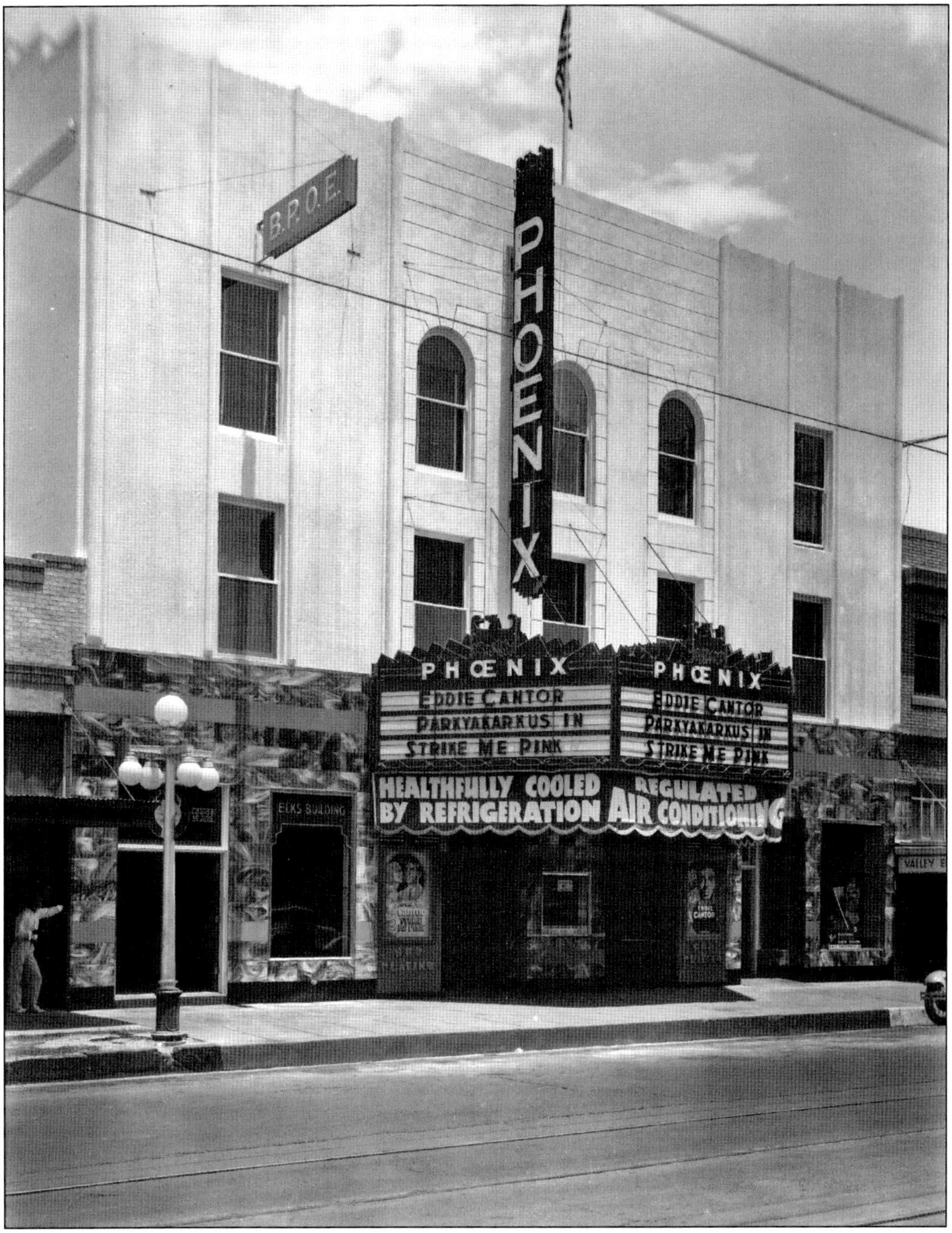


The Phoenix Theater, shown here in 1936, was the oldest theater in Phoenix at the time. Located at 328 West Washington Street, it opened in 1898. It had several owners and names: Patton's Grand Theater, Dorris Opera House, and Elks Theater. In 1957, John Diamos and his brothers purchased the theater and renamed it the Phoenix. They also owned theaters in Tucson, Nogales, Douglas, Bisbee, and Tombstone, while John operated the Phoenix Theater. Paul Ladas, the projectionist, and Sophie Ladas, cashier, were employed at the Phoenix Theater for many years. (Courtesy Arizona Collection, Arizona State University.)

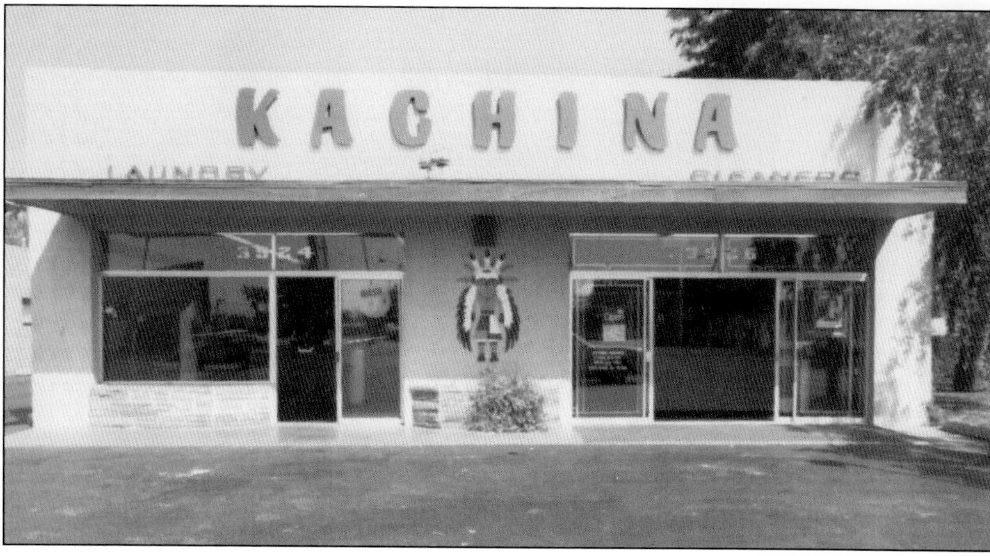


On September 17, 1959, Jim and Bessie "KiKi" Tsantilas (pictured below) opened and operated the Kachina Cleaners at 3926 East Indian School Road. They had two sons: Dean and Perry. Dean and his wife, Stella, took over the business for many years. Their son, Stacy, now owns and operates the business.

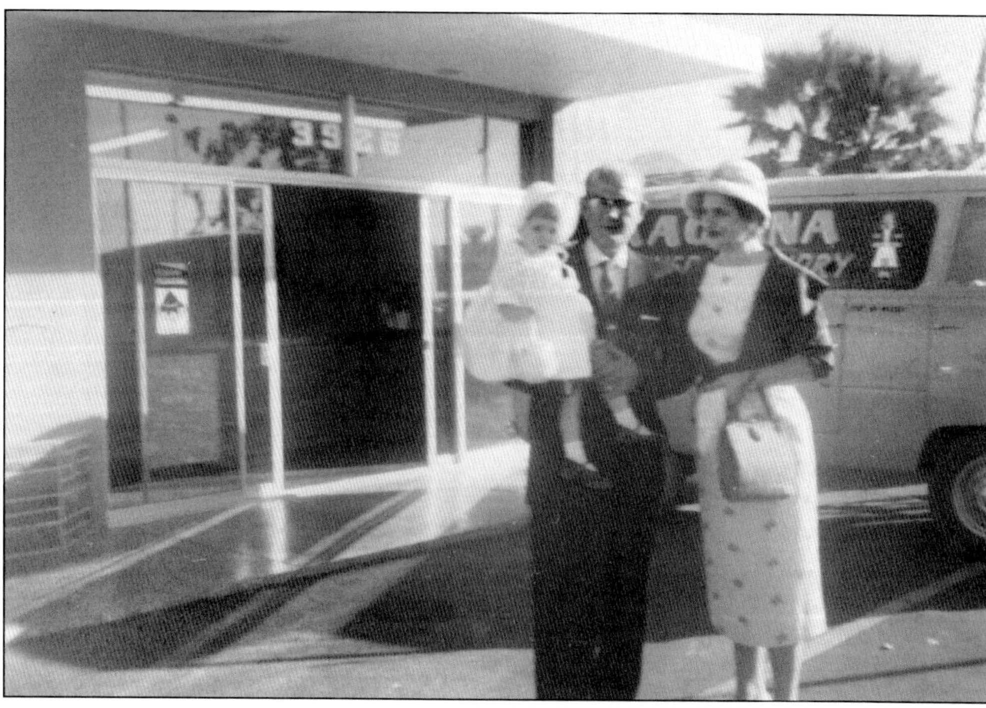

# *Six*

# ORGANIZATIONS

Philoptochos, "the Ladies Society," is a local Phoenix organization founded in the 1920s with Chrysanthe Stamatis as president. This organization felt the need to help their compatriots who were ill, so they solicited funds from local businessmen (some were their husbands) and began to offer financial aid. Frequently the women provided funds for burial expenses. In 1933, the ladies organized the group as the Women's Auxiliary of Holy Trinity Church and elected Fannie Katsenes president. In 1944, the auxiliary officially joined the National Philoptochos Society and received their charter. The name St. Katherine Philoptochos Society was selected.

The presidents were Fannie Katsenes (1933–1935, 1967–1969); Eftihia Mitchell (1936–1937); Chrysanthe Stamatis (1937–1940); Christina Pallas (1940–1942); Joan Zannis (1942–1945, 1950–1952, 1960–1965); Rosalia Manos (1945–1948); Alexandra Theodoropoulos (1948–1950, 1952–1953, 1958–1960, 1965–1967); Georgia Williams (1953–1955); Cleo Mates (1955–1957); Harriett Pappas (1957–1958); Agnes Andropoulos (1969–1971); Helen Kuzmanoff (1971–1973); Stella Michalakes (1973–1975); and Mary Johnson (1975–1985).

GOYA (Greek Orthodox Youth of America) was a national Orthodox youth movement taking place in the post–World War II years, and the newly arrived priest, Rev. George Samaras, helped set the stage for the Phoenix youth in 1949. Young people of the Greek community elected Louis J. Poulos president. The "Youth Club," as it was known, was organized from the onset with social and athletic activities to acquaint the young people with the Orthodox faith and to bring them closer to the church. By 1957, the Youth Club had become part of the National Greek Orthodox Youth of America.

A Junior GOYA was formed in 1954 by Rev. Chrysostom Selimos. This group was very active in parish activities. Their activities within the parish continued, but their services extended to the greater community.

Other organizations of the Hellenic community included: AHEPA (American Hellenic Educational Progressive Association), Daughters of Penelope (the women's auxiliary of AHEPA), Maids of Athena (the junior auxiliary of the Daughters of Penelope), Sons of Pericles (the junior auxiliary of AHEPA), and Pan Messinians.

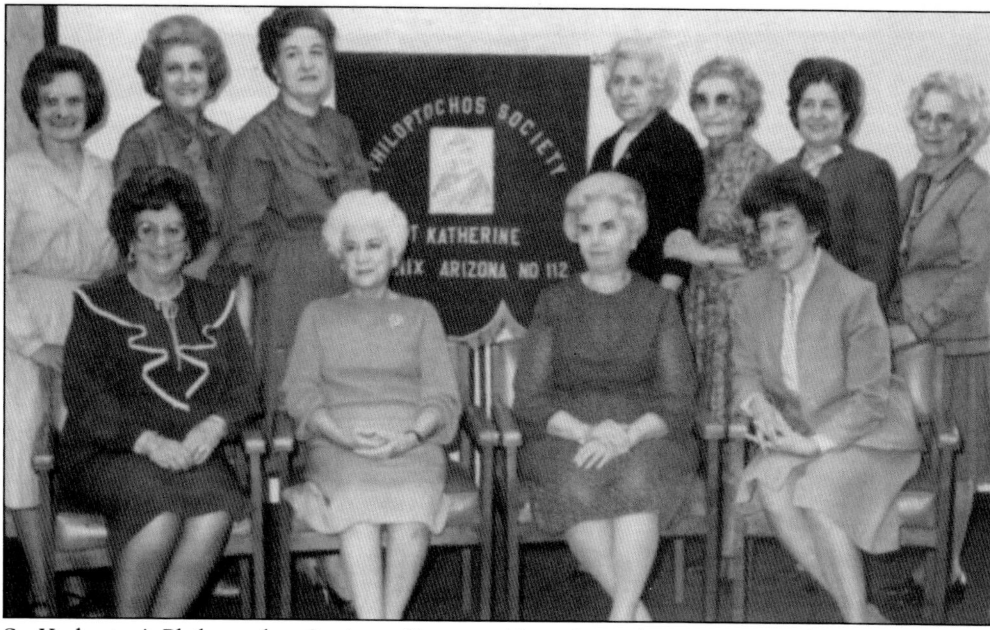


St. Katherine's Philoptochos Society officers and board members are pictured here. Seated are, from left to right, Helen Stamatis Glitsos, vice-president; Mary Ladas Johnson, president; Fannie Ganolis, secretary; and Mary Fraenkel, treasurer. The board members are, standing from left to right, Presbytera Catherine Tavlarides, Stephanie Kokalis, Helen Haritos, Fannie Ladas Katsenes, Joan Zannis, Irene Annos, and Diane Crist.

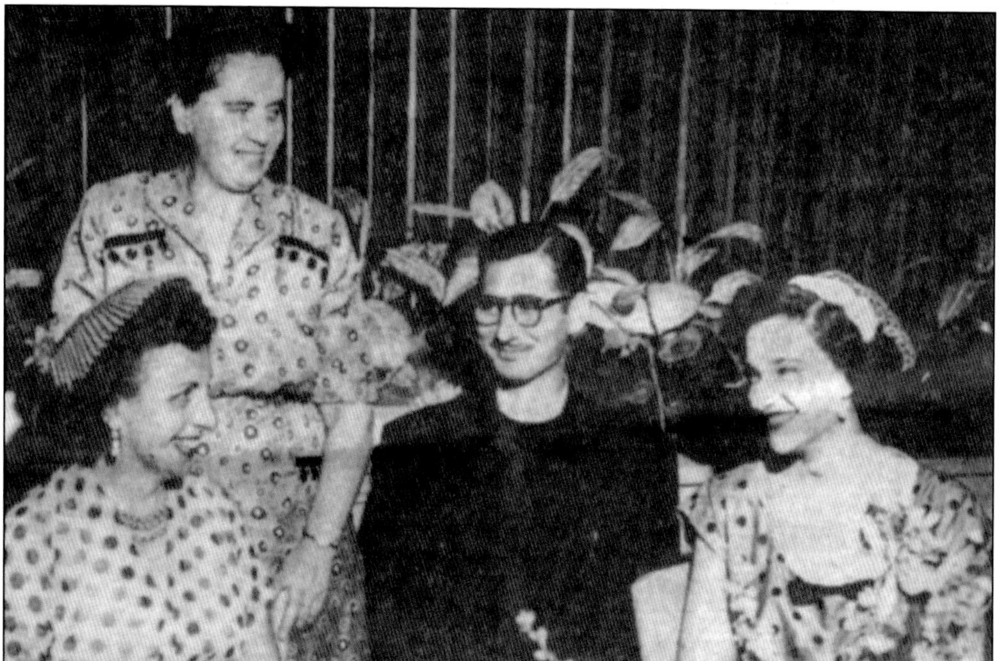

Members of the Philoptochos Society held a social in 1953 to welcome the new priest, Rev. Chrysostom Selimos, and his wife, Presbytera Penny. Pictured above from left to right are Maria Zorbas, Fannie Ganolis, Rev. Chrysostom Selimos, and Presbytera Penny.

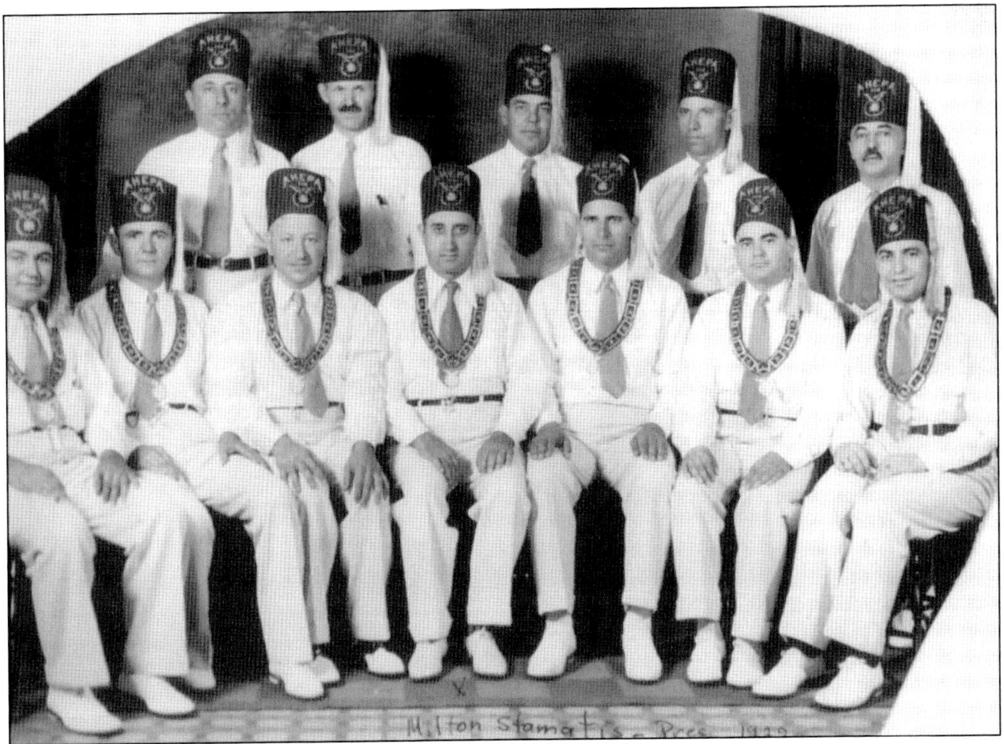


The officers and board of the order of AHEPA Chapter No. 219, established in 1929, are, from left to right, (first row) unidentified, Paul Plumis, Nick Gannis, Milton Stamatis, Tom Katsenes, Nick Annos, and unidentified; (second row) three unidentified, Paul Kouris, and unidentified.

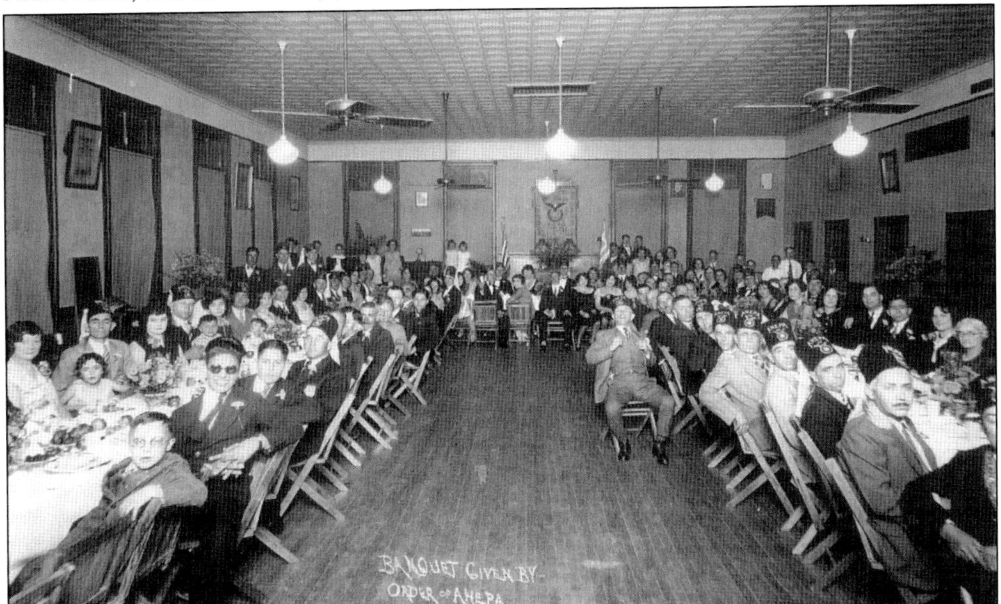


In 1929, AHEPA held a banquet at the WOW Hall to raise money for the building of the church community hall. The AHEPA chapters throughout the United States were known for helping the Greek communities establish themselves.

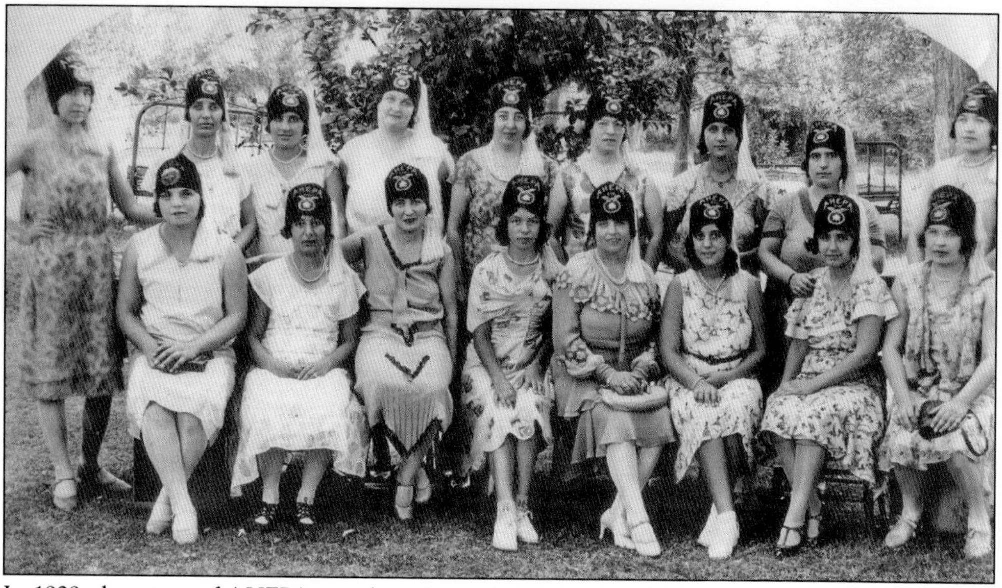

In 1929, the wives of AHEPA members donned their husbands' fezzes at the Tamaras farm (on Third Avenue and Osborn Road) at a picnic following a meeting. From left to right are (first row) unidentified, Meropy Gannis, Maria Mitchell, Mary Georgantos, Chrysanthe Stamatis, Helen Stamatis, Garifalia Annos, and unidentified; (second row) Lenora Colachis, Mrs. Zambaros, Paraskevi Johnson, unidentified, Eftihia Mitchell, Venetia Georgantos, Fannie Katsenes, Anna Fotinos, and unidentified.

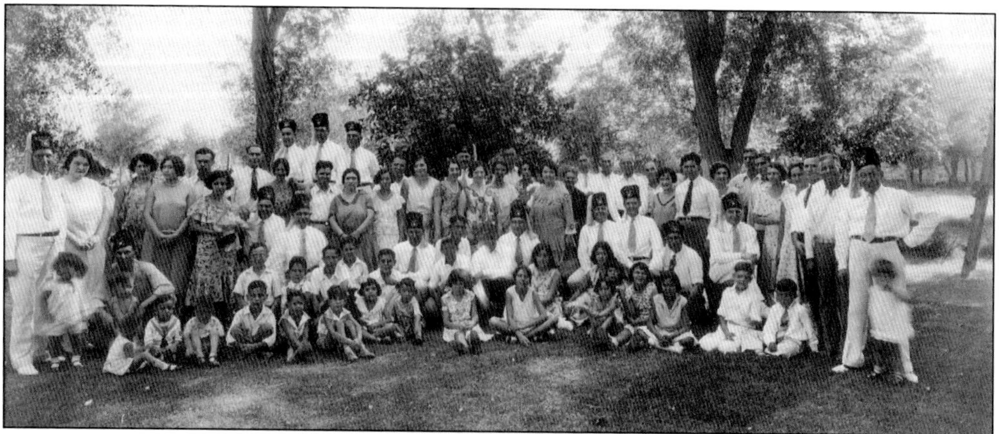

The gentlemen of AHEPA then recovered their fezzes and took a family picture with their wives at their Tamaras farm picnic. Many activities were held on this farm.

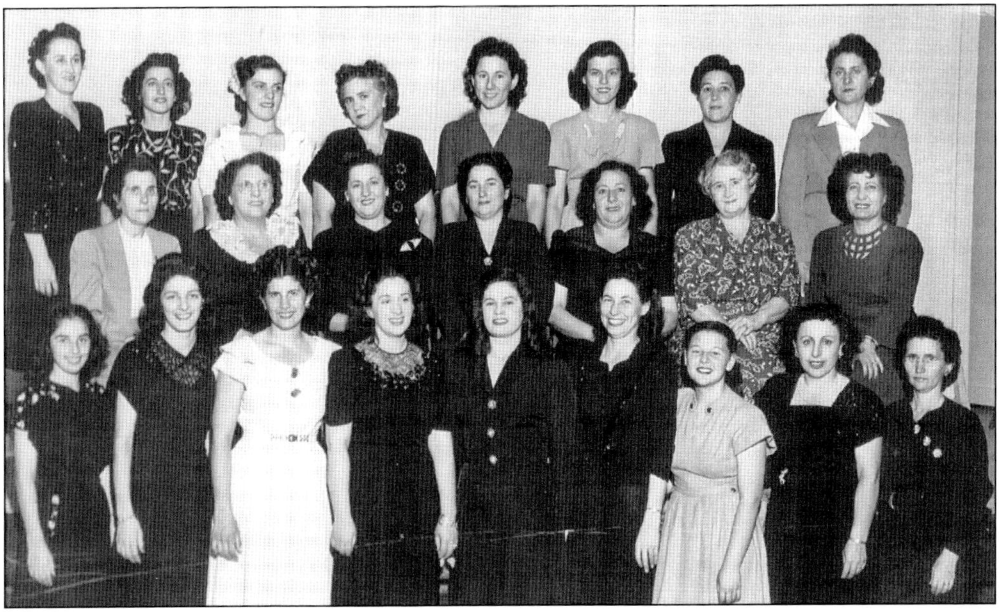

In 1947, the Hellespont chapter of the Daughters of Penelope was formed. The Daughters of Penelope was the women's' auxiliary of AHEPA. From left to right are (first row) Helen Chrison, Stella Malapanes (Scarla), Katherine Katsenes, Helen Stamatis Glitsos, Efftehia Poulos, Alexandra Theodore, Fannie Gannis Pappas, Marika Zorbas, and Julie Kostopoulos; (second row) Christina Pallas, Chrysanthe Stamatis, Zoë Contos, Tasia Pritchard, Meropy Gannis, Lena Trakas, and Maria Mitchell; (third row) Hazel Stamatis, Zella Zannis, Alexandra Diamos, unidentified, Martha Theodore Trakas, Doris Kostopoulos, Agnes Malapanes, and Fannie Katsenes.

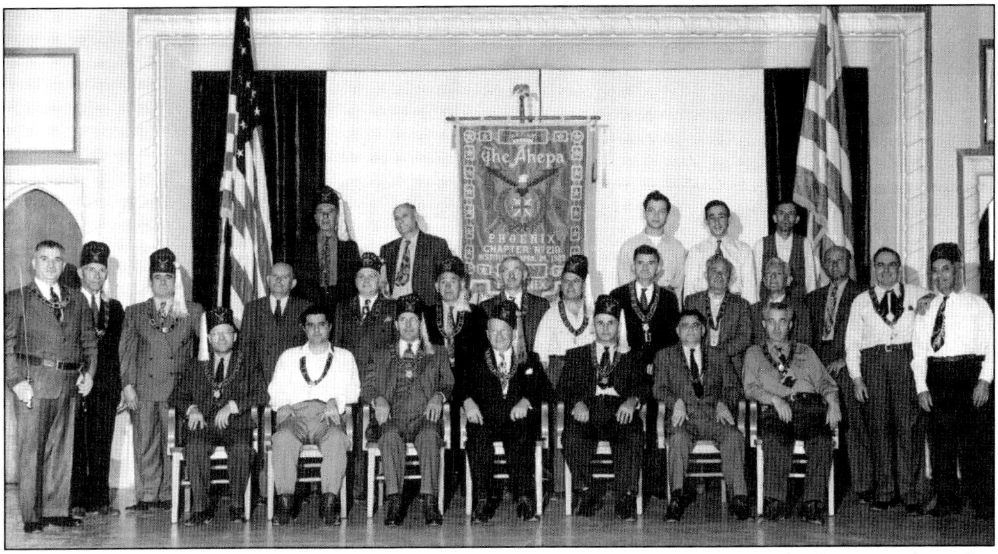


In 1947, AHEPA was thriving and continuing to do its philanthropic and educational works. From left to right are (first row) Sam Checuras, Gus Georgouses, Tom Katsenes, Nick Gannis, Jim Georgouses, Nick Annos, and Milton Stamatis; (second row) Tom Annos, Paul Kouris, Gust Metsopoulos, unidentified, Theodore Theodoropoulos, Louis Zeotopoulos, unidentified, Tony Fotinos, Chris Pikoulas, Chris Pallas, two unidentified, Peter Speropoulos, and Peter Manos; (third row) three unidentified, John Gannis, and unidentified.

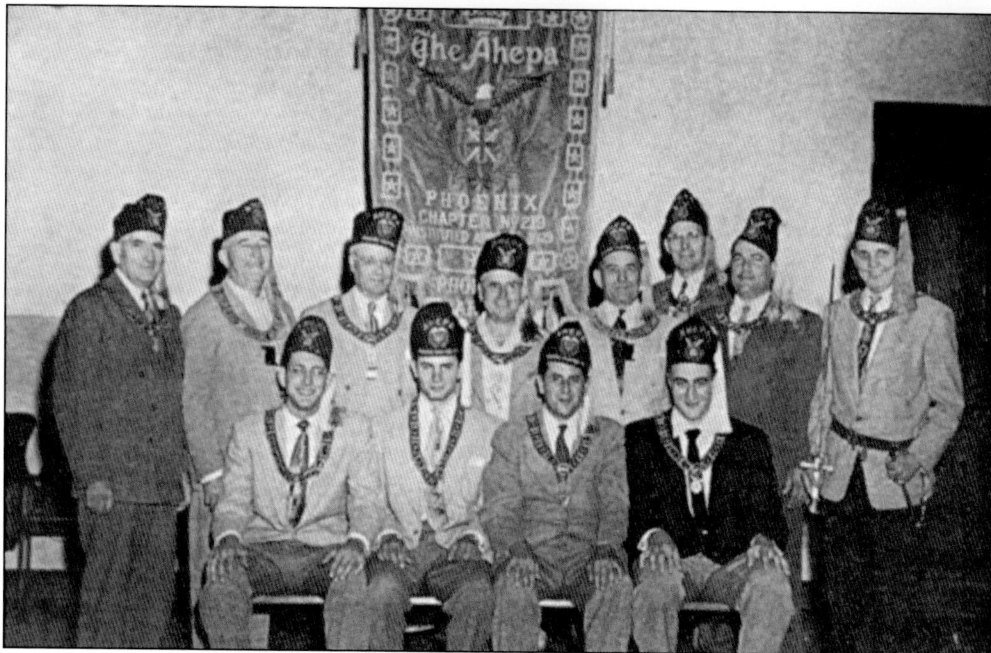


The 1952 AHEPA officers and board of directors are, from left to right, (first row) Stacy Hotis, vice president; John Katsenes, president; Paul Ladas, secretary; and George Christie, treasurer; (second row) Chris Mitchell, Michael Kantsi, Michael Zannis, Tony Fotinos, George Picoulas, Thomas Katsenes, Peter Speropoulos, and Louie Malamas.

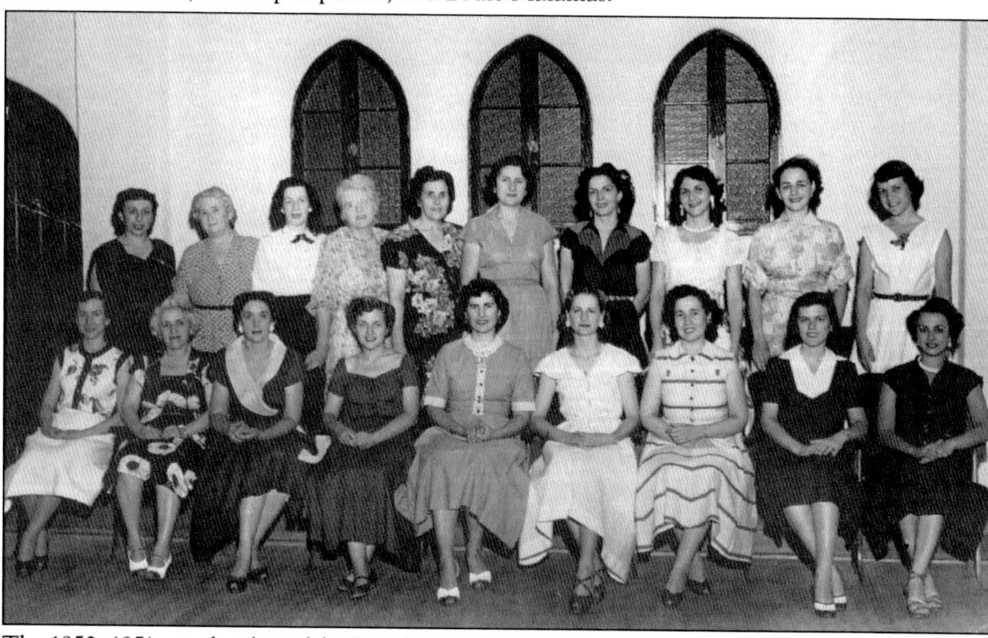

The 1950–1951 membership of the Daughters of Penelope included the following, from left to right: (first row) Tassie Ladas, Lucy Janas, Helen Stamatis Glitsos, Bessie Theodoropoulos, Katherine Katsenes, Stella Glitsos, Cleo Mates, Doris Kostopoulos, and Amelia Christakis; (second row) Marika Zorbas, Lena Trakas, Sandy Gigicon, Chrysanthe Stamatis, Christina Pallas, Fannie Katsenes, Jenny Prato, Mary Falkedes Scarla, Angie Scarla, and Sophie Kirk.

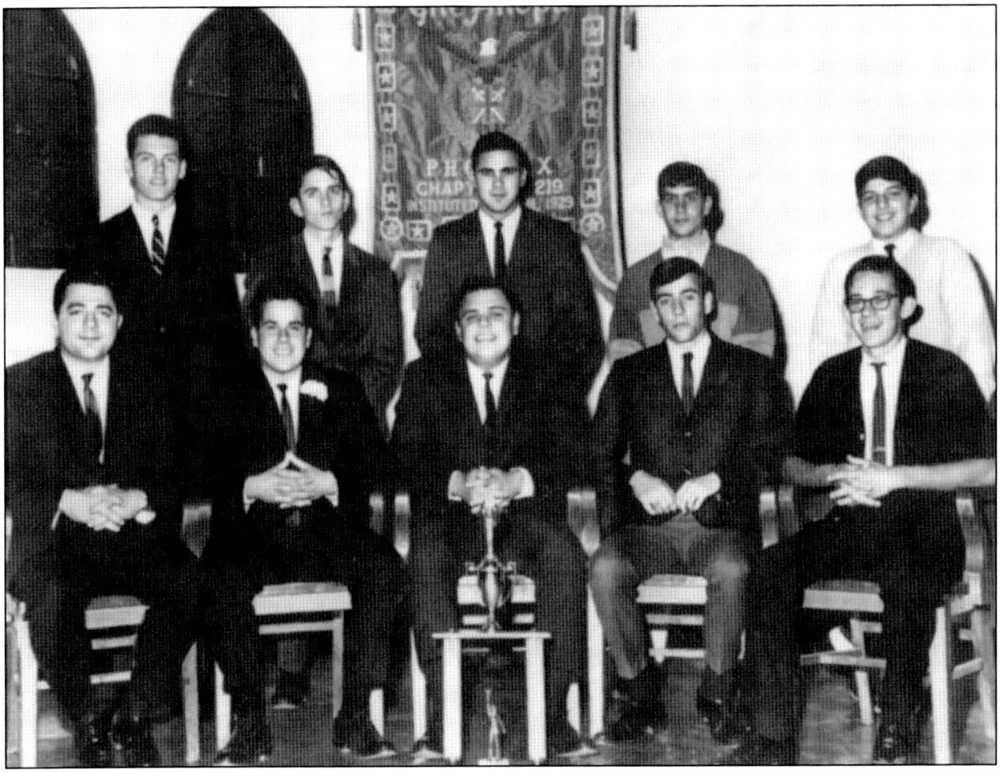

In the 1960s, the Sons of Pericles, the junior auxiliary of AHEPA, won the district basketball tournament. Leon Stavrou was the first president of this chapter when it was formed. From left to right in this picture are (first row) two unidentified, Perry Contos (current president), unidentified, and Danny Mortenson; (second row) Mike Sorich, unidentified, Leon Stavrou, Bill Tavlarides, and John Zacharoudis.

**GEORGI KIMMEL**
Grand Vice President

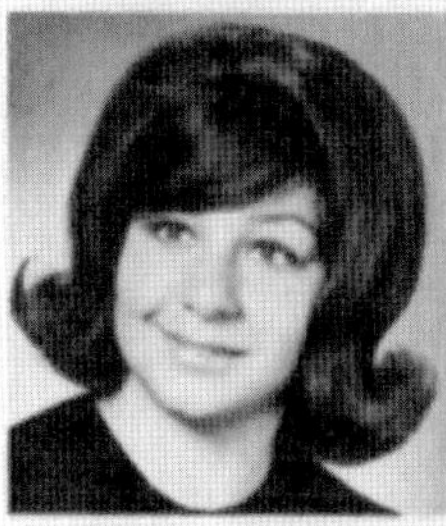

Georgi Kimmel, Grand Vice President of the Maids of Athena from Phoenix, Ariz., is no newcomer to the Maids. This 22-year-old member has been very active in both her chapter and district. Miss Kimmel served her chapter, Aphrodite No. 158, as president; she served the district in the capacities of District Treasurer No. 20, District Lieutenant Governor, and District Governor. During her term as District Governor she was presented the Outstanding District Governor's Trophy in the nation. In 1967 she was crowned Queen of the Sons and Maids Spring Ball, and in 1968 she was elected Governor.

Georgi is a graduate of Phoenix College, and is presently attending Arizona State University. She is majoring in sociology and is planning to do graduate work in social psychology.

She is the daughter of Mrs. Emily Kimmel, who is a member of the Hellespont Chapter of the Daughters of Penelope in Phoenix. Georgi has one sister, Karen, who is a member of the Maids of Athena Aphrodite Chapter in Phoenix.

In 1970, Georgi Kimmell served as the grand president of the Maids of Athena. She also served as president of the Phoenix chapter, district treasurer, district lieutenant governor, and grand vice-president.

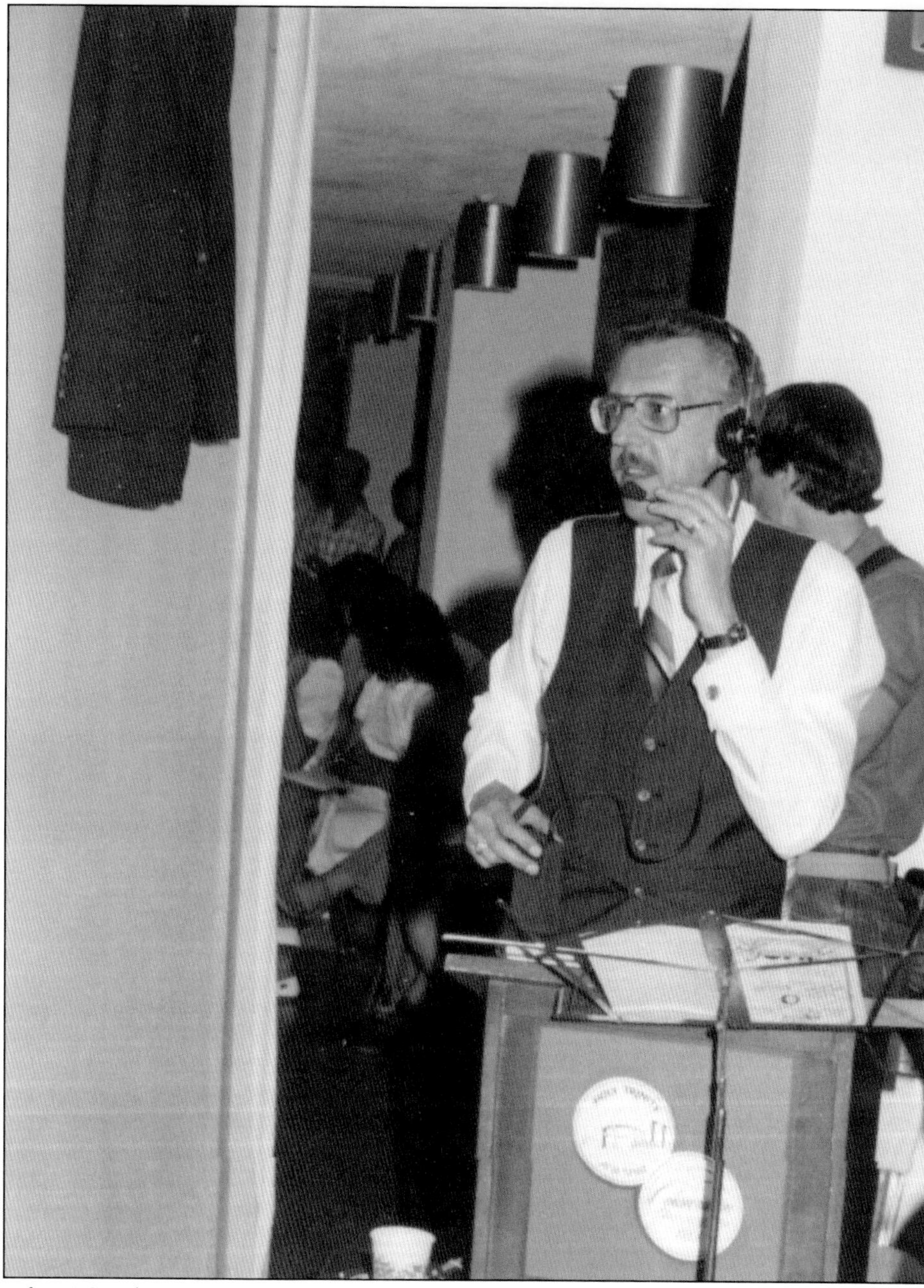

The first "Greek Hour" on the radio in Phoenix was started in 1953, when Andy Limber was president of the Phoenix Chapter of the Greek Orthodox Youth of America (GOYA). Heard at 3:00 p.m. every Sunday afternoon on KRUX Radio (1360 AM), broadcasting from Glendale, the program featured recorded Greek music and community news. These spoken segments were aired in Greek by Andy, followed with the same topics read in English by Jenny Pappas. The youth members at the time, all around 16 to 18, produced, wrote and aired the show, as well as selling advertising time and writing the commercials. Also in 1953, GOYA began a regular publication of a monthly newsletter, the *Neoleon* (Youth), which later was changed to *Tri-Unity* to encompass the entire Holy Trinity community.

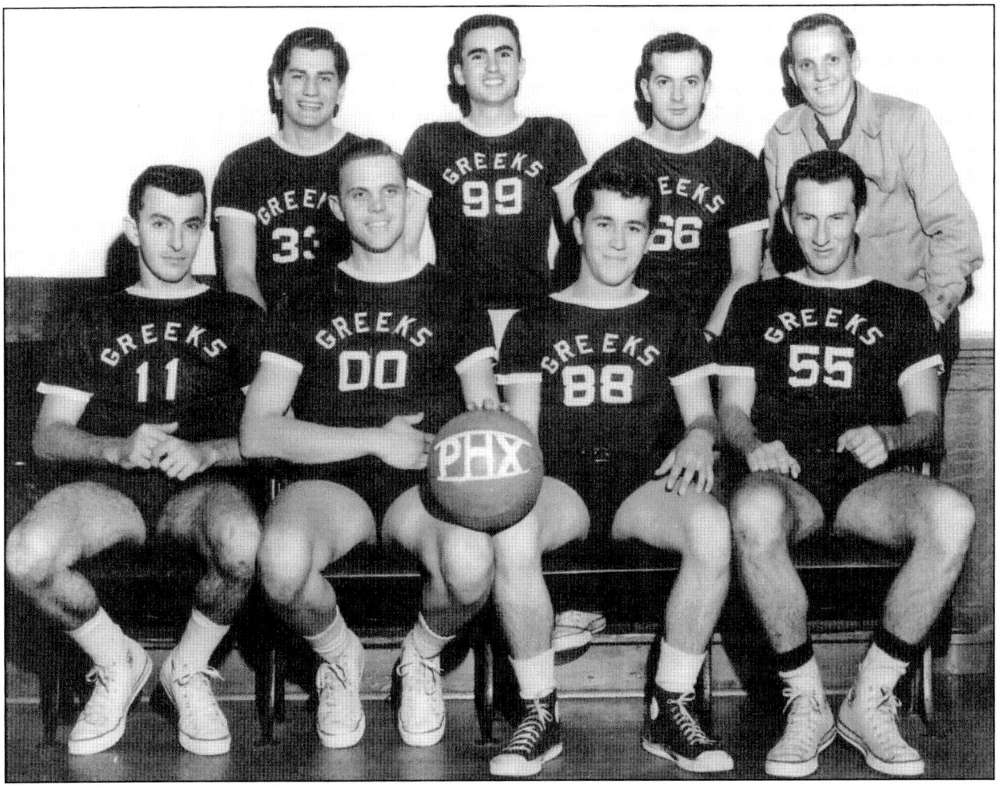


Pictured here is the basketball team of the 1960s. From left to right are (first row) George Zorbas, Nick Tountas, Pano Stephens, and Gus Diamond; (second row) Ari Pastis, Nick Baziotis, Louie Ketcios, and Louie Malamas (coach). The Greek basketball team of the 1930s YMCA church league played four years, from 1932 to 1936. They played a total of 123 games, winning 114, and compiled four division championships and three league titles. Members of the team were George, Tony, and Nick Thomas; Sam and Jimmy Stamatis; Gus Glitsos; Melvin Georgouses; George Xalis; Clements Ladas; and Angelo Falkedes.

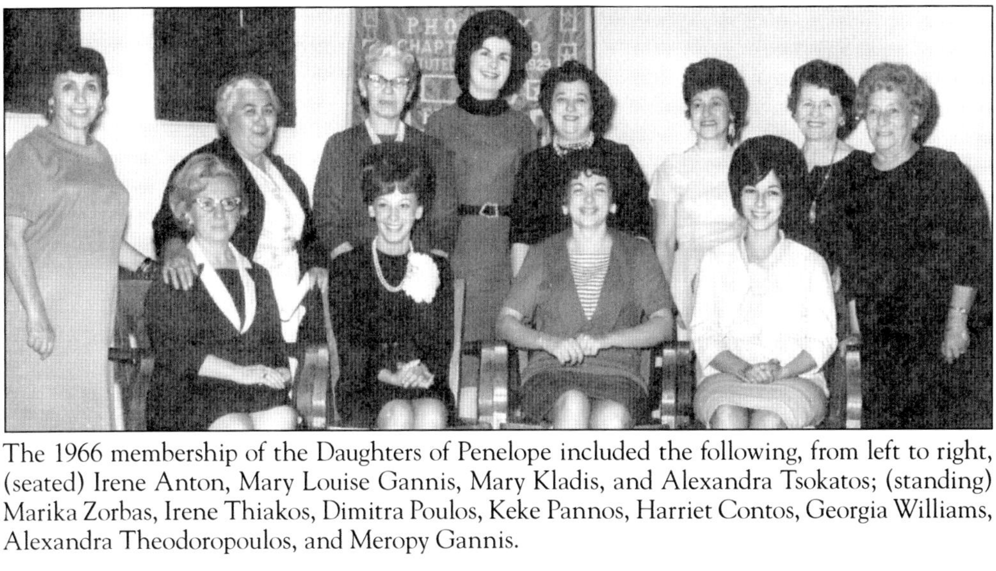

The 1966 membership of the Daughters of Penelope included the following, from left to right, (seated) Irene Anton, Mary Louise Gannis, Mary Kladis, and Alexandra Tsokatos; (standing) Marika Zorbas, Irene Thiakos, Dimitra Poulos, Keke Pannos, Harriet Contos, Georgia Williams, Alexandra Theodoropoulos, and Meropy Gannis.

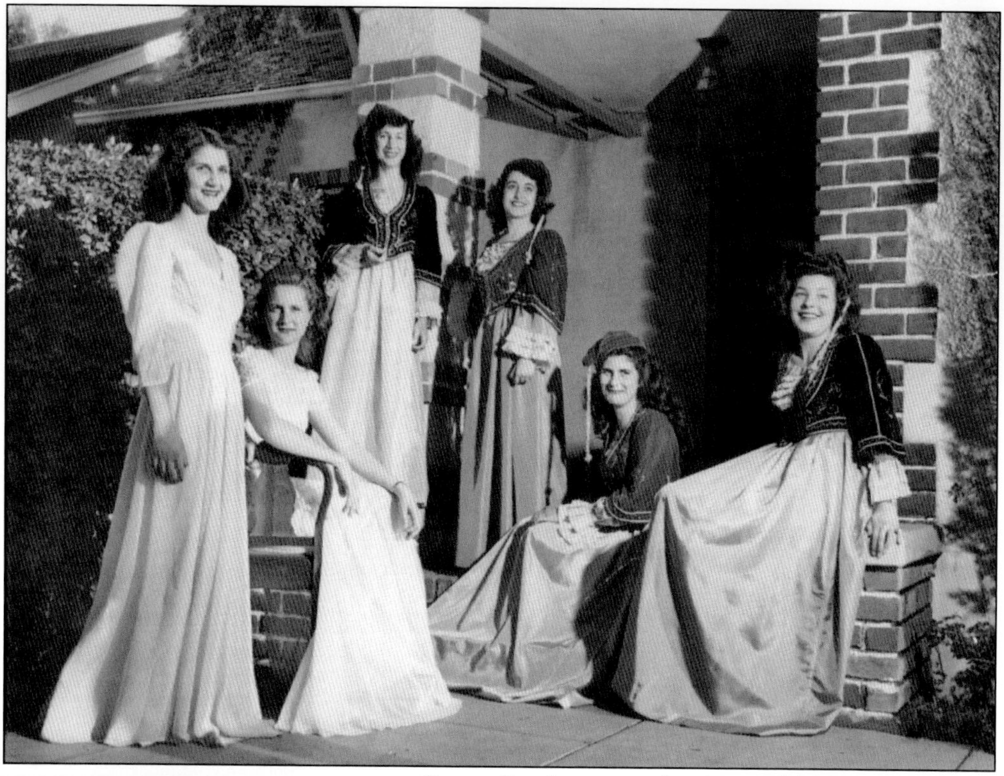

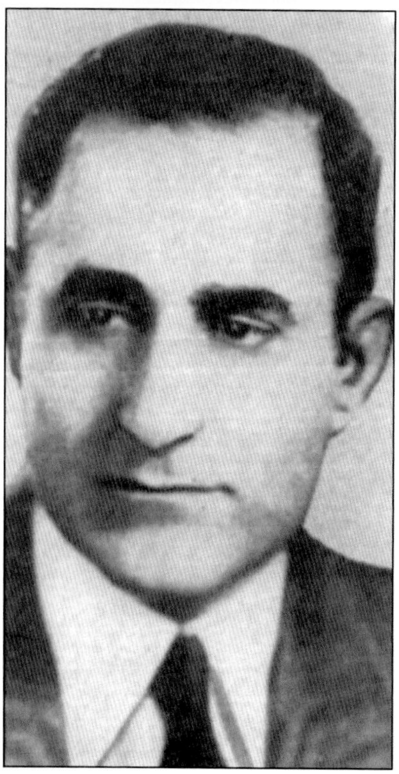

Young Greek women, daughters of AHEPA members, are pictured in costume prior to a 1945 event. The young ladies were preparing for the fund-raising event at the Shrine Auditorium for the Tubercular Hospital in Athens, Greece. From left to right, the young ladies are Mary Falkedes Scarla, Stella Ladas Glitsos, Tassie Ladas, Zella Zannis, Katherine Katsenes Nicholas, and Emily Gannis Kimmell.

John Contos was president of the Pan Messinian organization in the 1950s and 1960s. This group was organized by individuals residing in Phoenix originally from the province of Messinia, Greece. Contos was a promoter during the 1920s. He teamed up with Jim Londos, the heavyweight wrestling champion of the world, to raise money for many charitable events such as the Greek War Relief, the Tubercular Hospital in Greece, and to help youngsters with speech and hearing deficiencies.

# *Seven*

# Social Events

In the early years before the church was built, a visiting priest came to perform weddings and baptisms. Some of these events were held in homes, rented halls, and churches of other Christian denominations. The community was determined to celebrate weddings and baptisms, and the lack of a church did not deter them.

In Greek culture, children are usually named after Christian saints; consequently, a person's "Name Day," such as St. Demetrios Day on October 26, is cause for celebration, with a festive party at the celebrants' home open to all.

The largest such event, which became something of an annual institution, was held at the Theodoropoulos residence, 345 West Willetta Street, celebrating the January 1 name day of Vasiliki "Bessie" Theodoropoulos. The party was held on two levels, the upstairs for the adults and the decorated basement, complete with recorded dance music, for the youngsters.

There were also frequent picnics at which a dozen or more families would meet at the sprawling South Mountain Park to enjoy a generous amount of food and drink, along with the ever-present Greek folk dancing.

Through the years, the various church organizations performed dramatic plays and wrote variety shows that had the audiences falling off their chairs with laughter.

Whether a holiday or not, it is in the nature of Greeks to sing and dance as a matter of celebrating life.

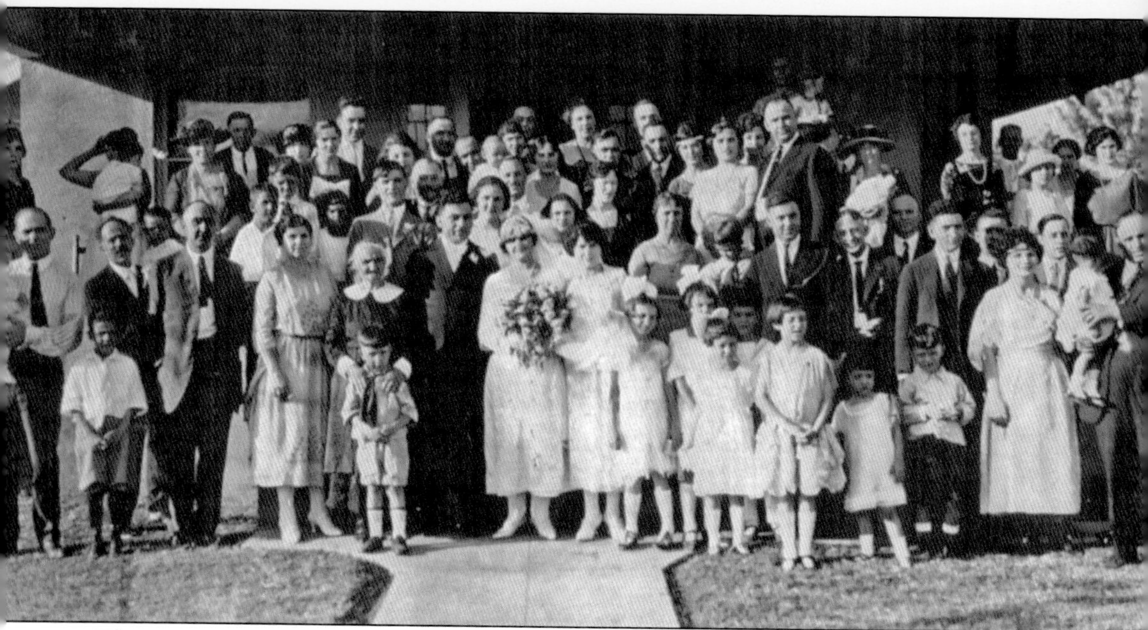

This is a Georgouses family wedding in 1922. Ceremonies were held in homes before the church was built. This home was north of Roosevelt Street on Second Street.

These young ladies attend a baptism at the Hellenic Community House. Until a new church was built in 1947, the community house was used as a church. Standing in the back row are Helen Stamatis Glitsos, Sylvia Georgouses, Mary Georgantos, and Aspacia Georgouses. The front row consists of three unidentified, Vaso Sanichas, Georgia Sanichas, and Florence Georgouses.

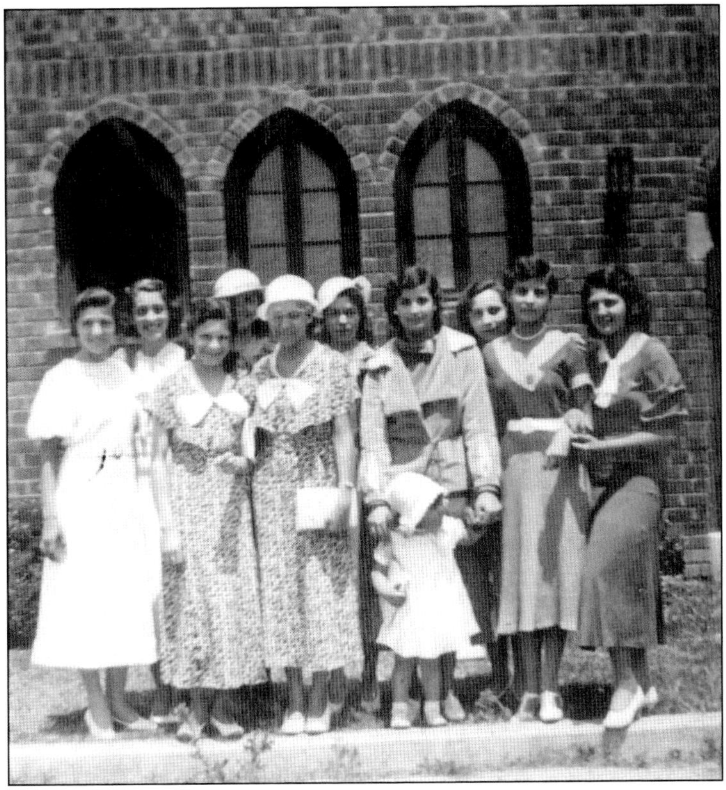

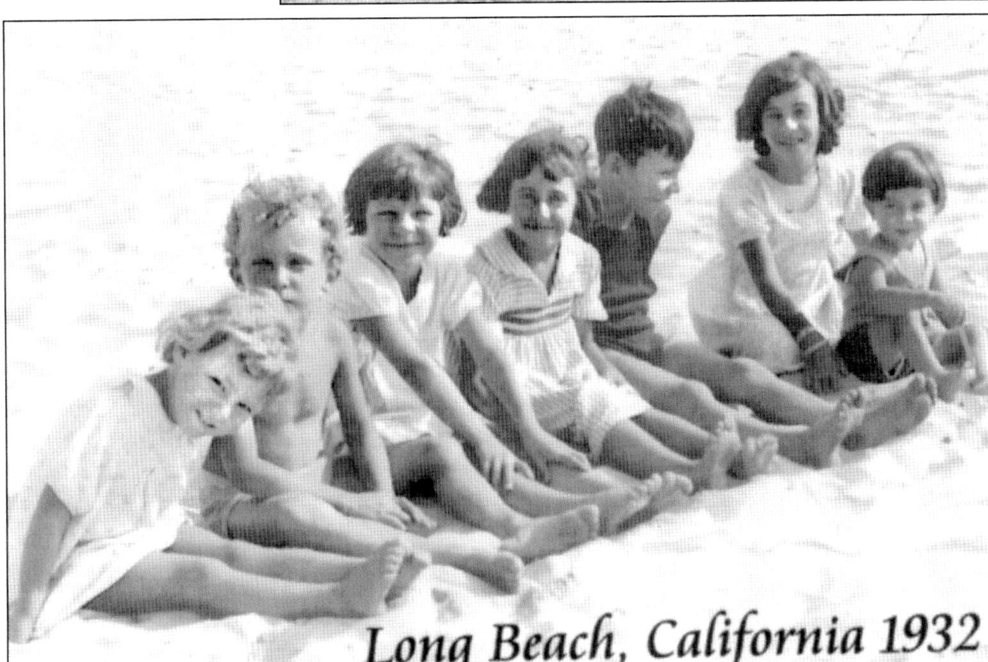


Many Greek families escaped from the Phoenix heat in the summer, and Long Beach was a popular destination. The children pictured, from left to right, are Fannie Gannis Pappas, Pete Zannis, Emily Gannis Kimmell, Zella Zannis, John Gannis, Harriet Manos Pappas, and Pete Manos.

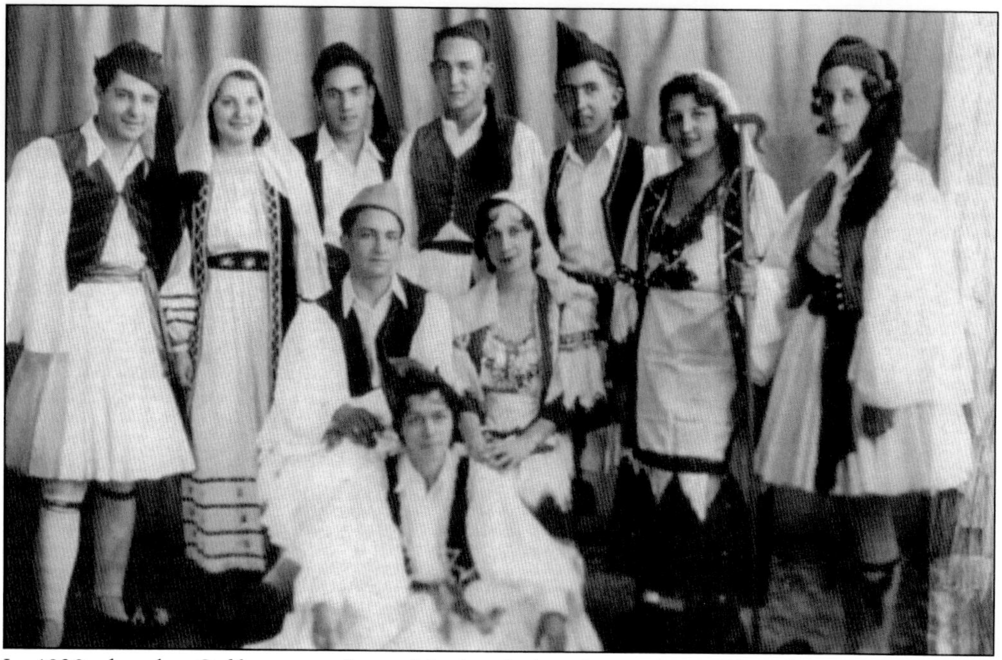

In 1930, the play *Golfo* was preformed by local church members. The play was directed by Chrysanthe Stamatis. From left to right are (first row) Mr. Contos, Aspacia Georgouses, and Mary Georgantos (front); (second row) Gus Georgouses, Sylvia Georgouses, George Thomas, Gus Glitsos, unidentified, Florence Georgouses, and Helen Stamatis Glitsos.

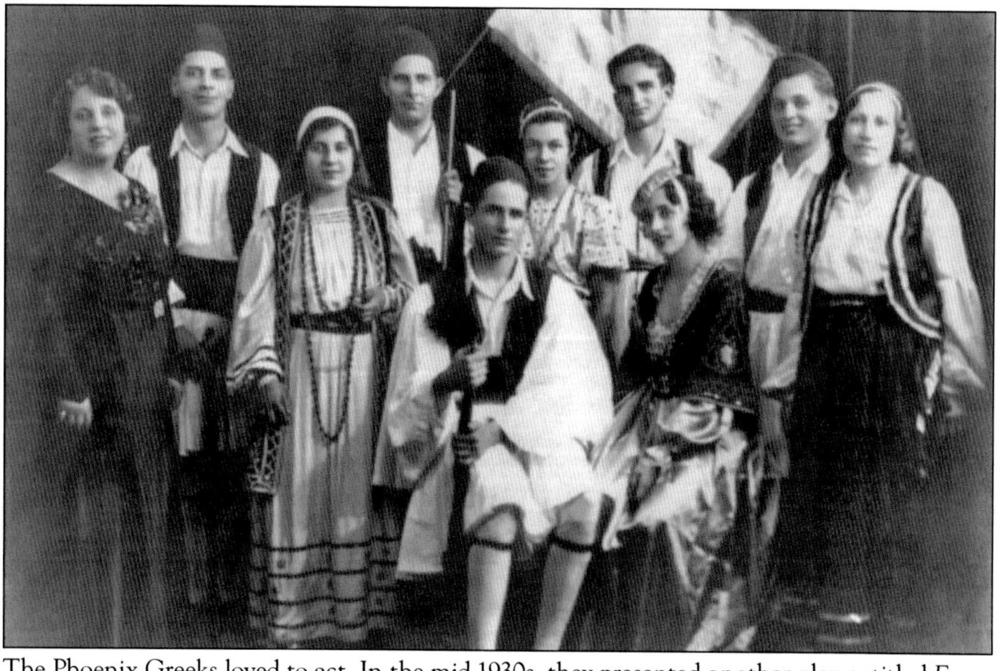

The Phoenix Greeks loved to act. In the mid-1930s, they presented another play entitled *Esme*. The actors and actresses are, from left to right, (first row) George Xalis and Helen Stamatis Glitsos; (second row) Chrysanthe Stamatis (director), Bill Bergman, Anna Fotinos, Tom Katsenes, Mary Georgantos, Nick Xalis, Jim Stamatis, and Kostantina Vlangos.

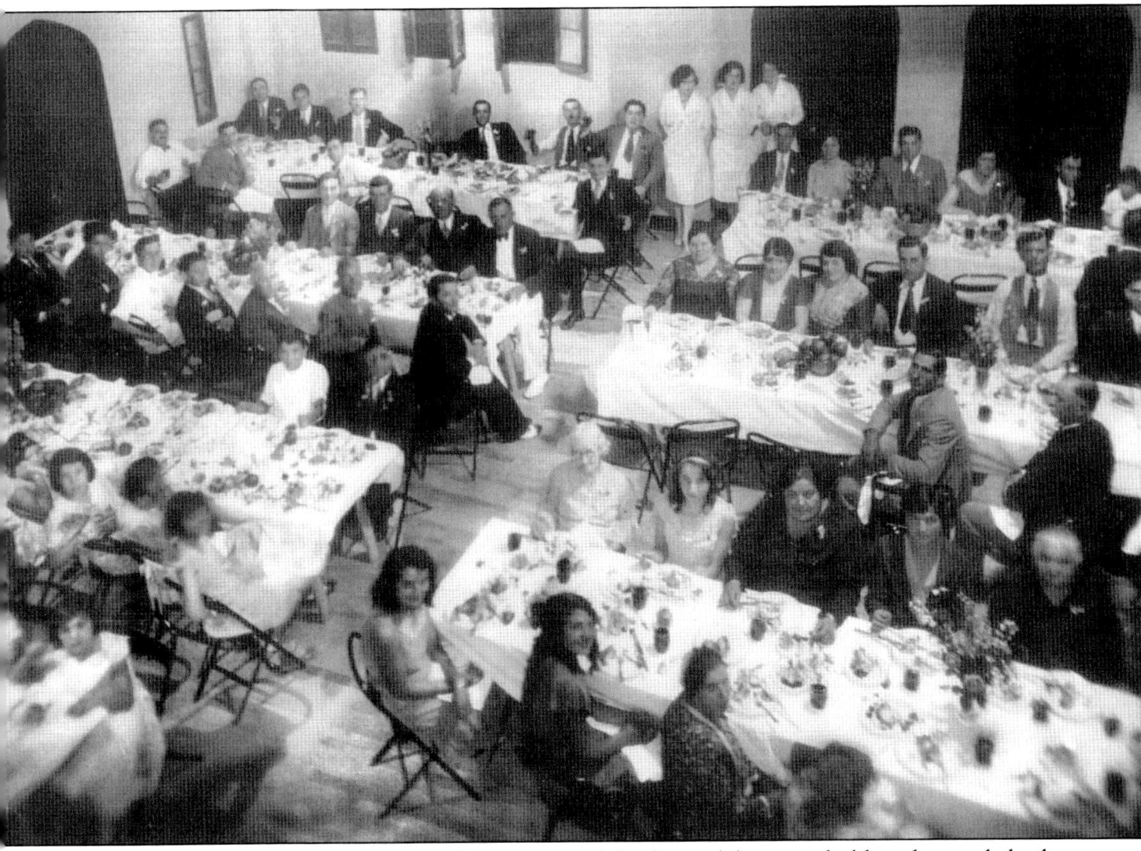

A baptism reception is held in 1931. This was one of the first celebrations held in the newly built Hellenic Orthodox Church Community House.

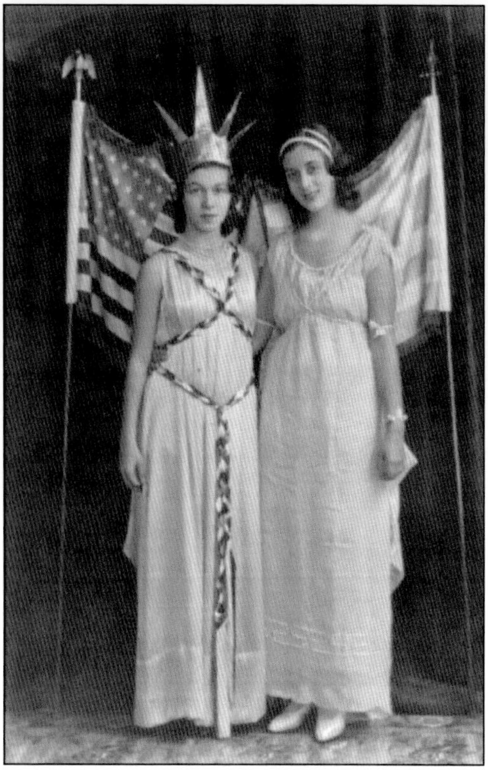

In 1931, a church event was held. The community selected Mary Georgantos (left) as Miss U.S.A. and Helen Stamatis (right) as Miss Greece.

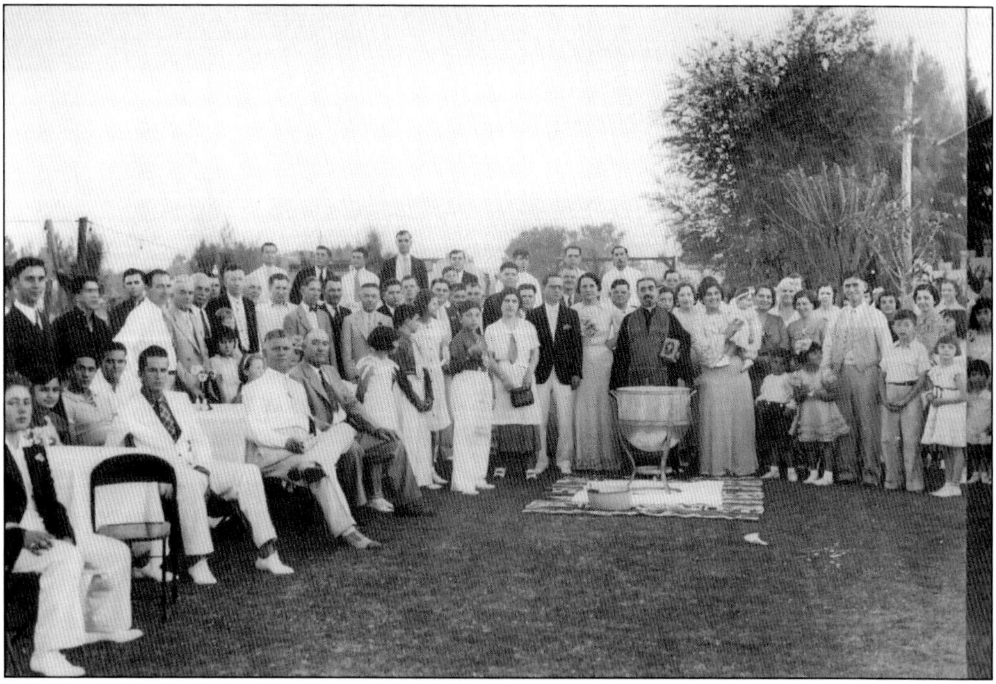

The baptism of Katherine Johnson (Pedersen) in 1935 was held at the Johnson home, located at 1601 East Tuckey Lane. The baptism ceremony was held in the yard by a visiting priest, who is standing behind the baptismal font.

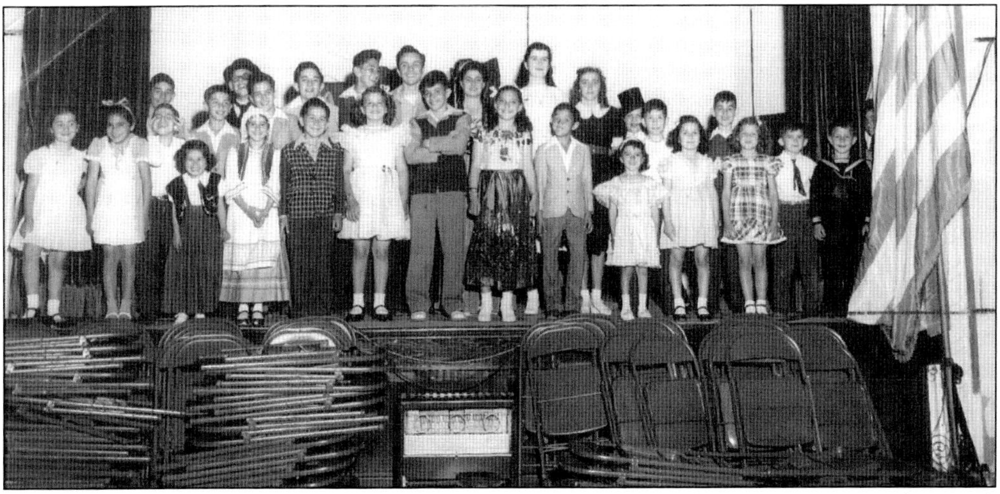

The end of the Greek school year was always celebrated with a graduation program or play. Look at all of those smiling faces.

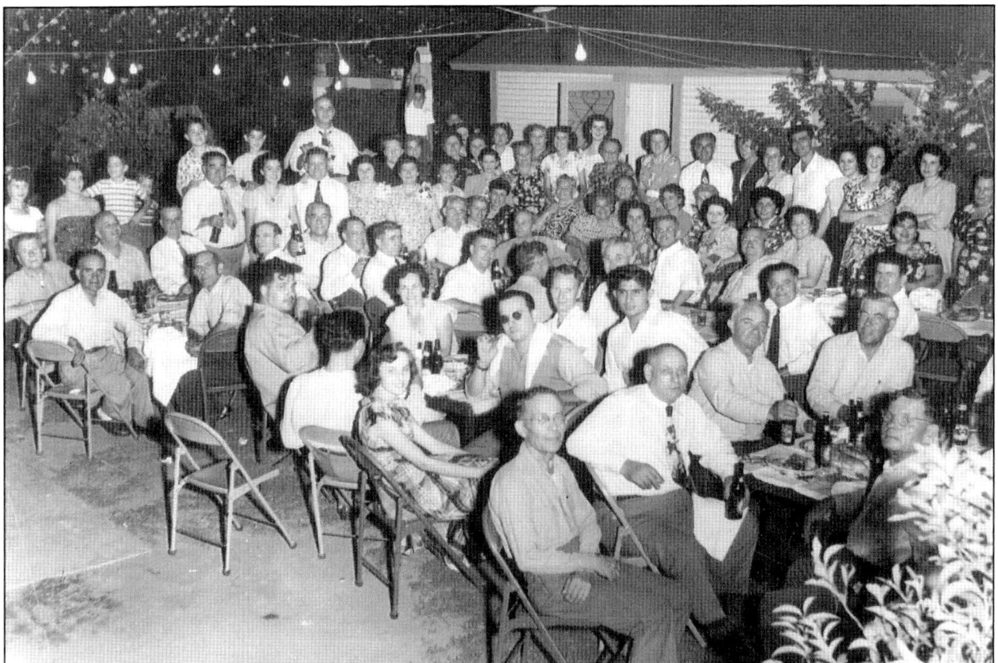

In 1949, a party was held at the residence of John and Katina Pappas at 420 East Roosevelt to welcome newlyweds Pete and Vasiliki (Zelios) Chotras. Pete Chotras was the brother of Katina Pappas.

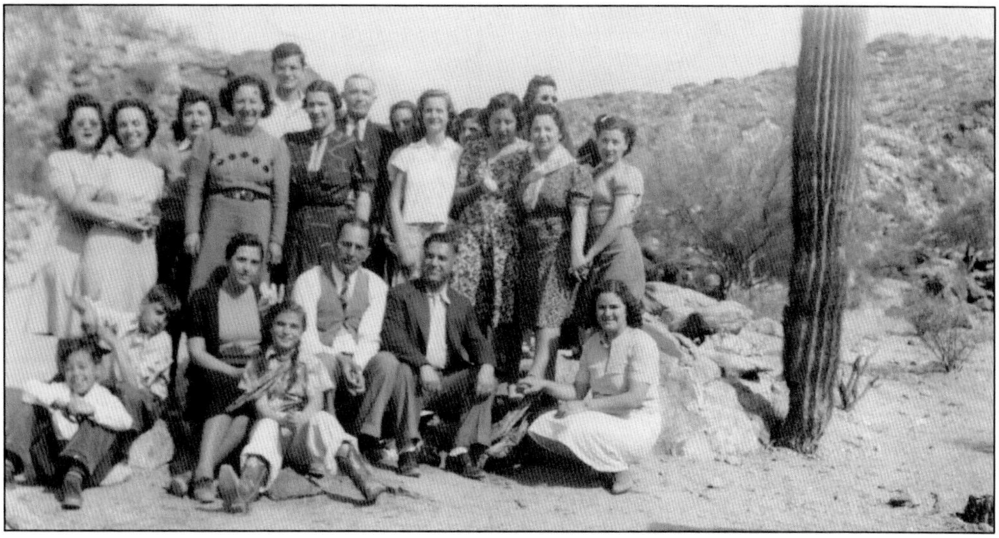

In the 1940s, the Greeks continue to picnic in all their finery. From left to right are (first row) two unidentified, Christina Pallas, Evangeline Diamos, Tom Katsenes, Sam Pritchard, and Christina Ioannou; (second row) unidentified, Tassie (Tsegouris) Renshaw, Connie Xalis, Meropy Gannis, John Xalis, Katina Diamos, Chris Pallas, unidentified, Stella (Ladas) Glitsos, three unidentified, Tasia Pritchard, and Mary Johnson.

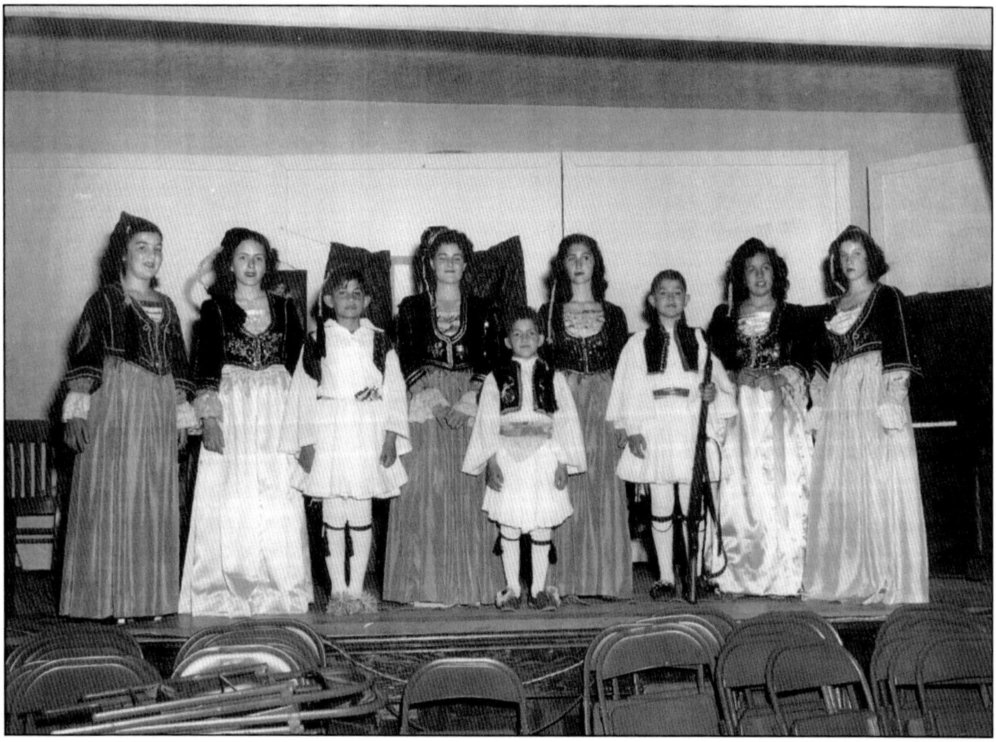

In the late 1940s, the Greek school traditionally held plays in celebration of Greek Independence Day, March 25. The young actors and actresses (in costume) are Jenny Pappas, Bessie Theodoropoulos, Nick Johnson, Alice Speropoulos, Gus Theodoropoulos, Katherine Johnson, Alex Pappas, Helen Metsopoulos, and Stella Dourbetakis.

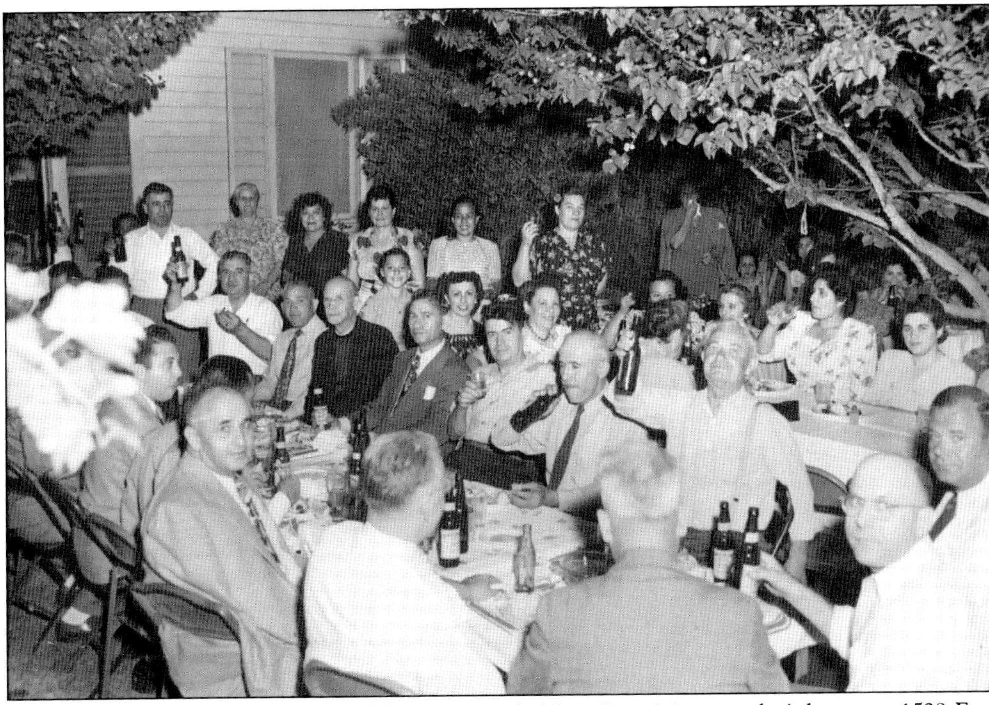

This St. Constantine name day celebration was held at Gust Metsopoulos's home at 1529 East Roosevelt Street in the 1940s. Name day celebrations were very important occasions and still are in Greece. This is the celebration of the saint's day whose name is given to an individual at the time of his or her baptism.

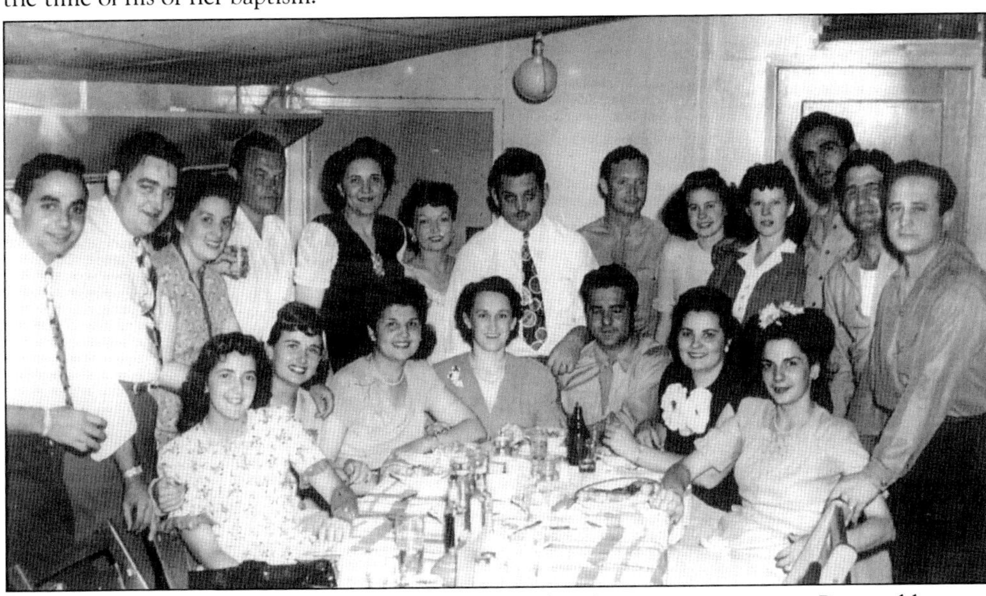

The young people in the community frequently gather for various occasions. Pictured here are (seated) Helen Beys, unidentified, Florence Georgouses, Hazel Stamatis, Gus Georgouses, Sylvia Georgouses, and Jenny Falkedes Prato; (standing) Mel Georgouses, Gus Glitsos, Helen Stamatis Glitsos, Jesse Herlyck, Katherine Georgouses Beys, unidentified, Jim Stamatis, two unidentified, Irma Thomas, Nick Thomas, Tony Thomas, and Charlie Stratton.

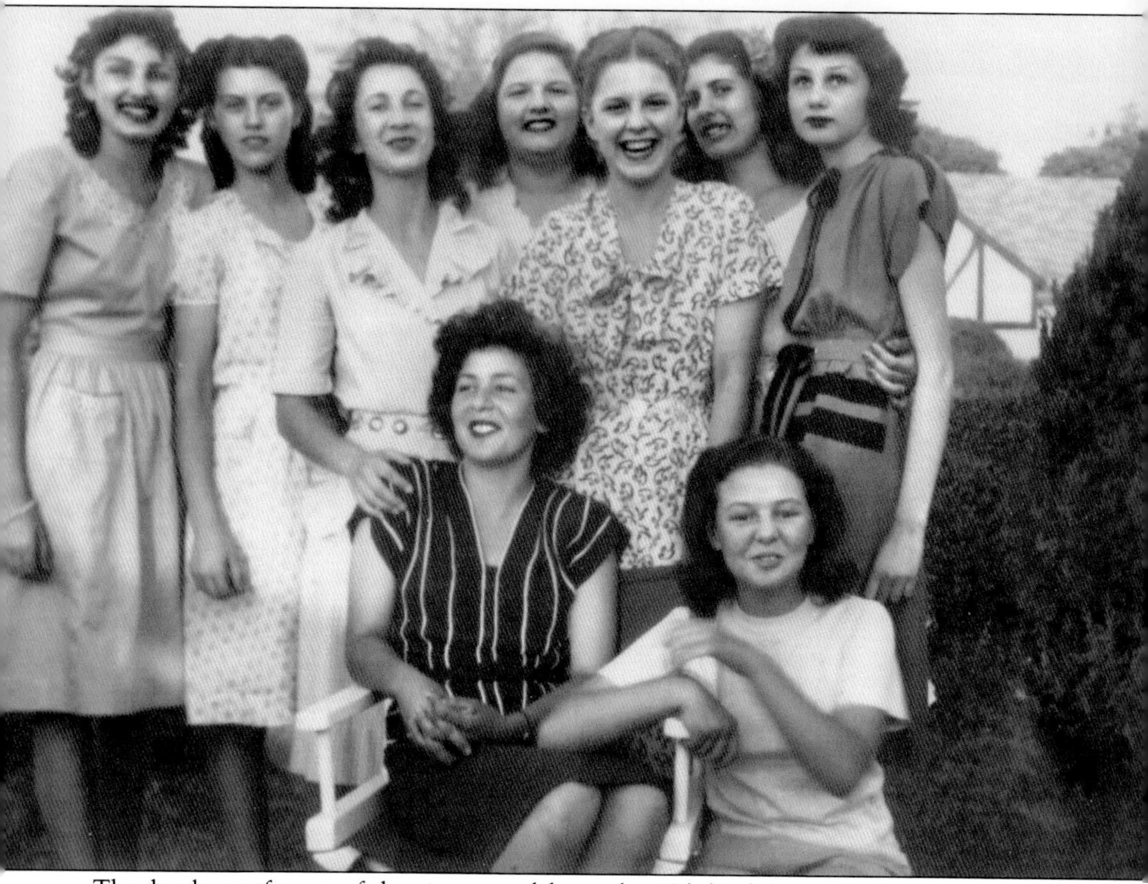

The daughters of many of the pioneers celebrate the 16th birthday of Emily Gannis Kimmell. From left to right are (first row) Emily Gannis Kimmell and Fannie Gannis Pappas; (second row) Pauline Annos Drew, Doris Kostopoulos, Tassie Ladas, Sophie Poulos, Agapi Poulos, Katherine Katsenes Nicholas, and Mary Annos Floor.

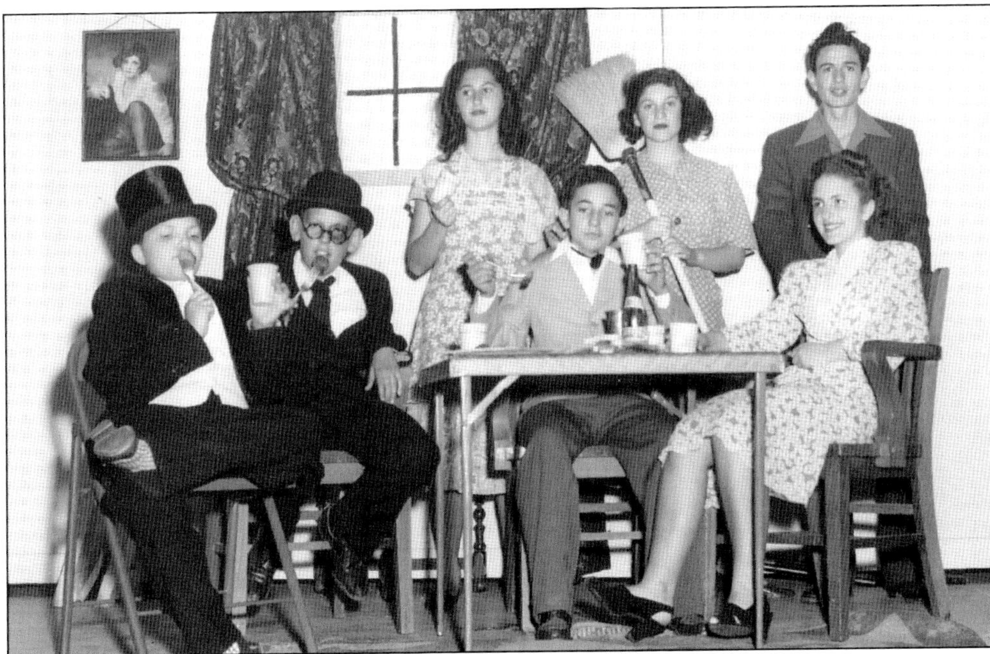

Carrying on the ancient tradition of Greek drama in the early 1950s are, from left to right, (first row) Diane Theodoropoulos, Andy Limber, George Manos, and Bessie Theodoropoulos; (second row) Katherine Johnson, Stella Dourbetakis, and Jimmy Metsopoulos. This was on stage in the big social hall at Holy Trinity Hellenic Orthodox Church, 333 East Virginia Avenue, in Phoenix.

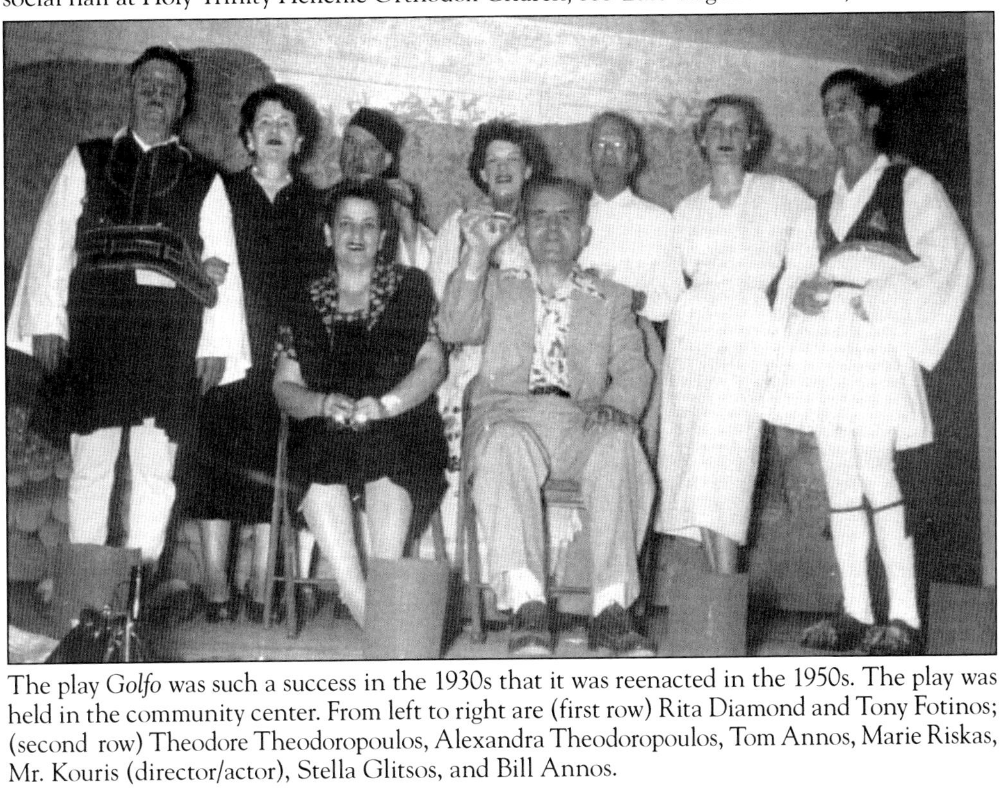

The play *Golfo* was such a success in the 1930s that it was reenacted in the 1950s. The play was held in the community center. From left to right are (first row) Rita Diamond and Tony Fotinos; (second row) Theodore Theodoropoulos, Alexandra Theodoropoulos, Tom Annos, Marie Riskas, Mr. Kouris (director/actor), Stella Glitsos, and Bill Annos.

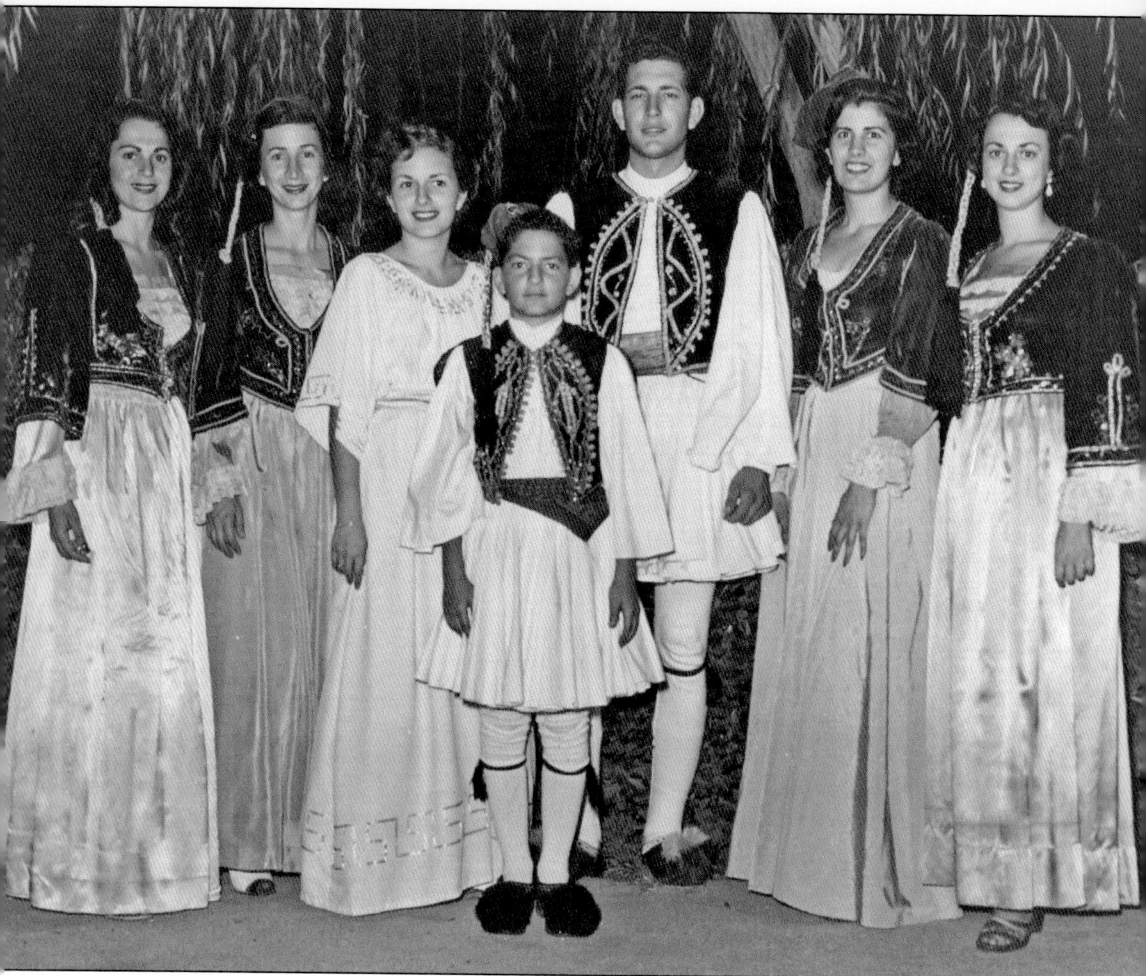

The Festival of Nations was held at the Encanto Park Bandshell in 1952. Pictured from left to right are Georgia Hotis Poulos, Tassie Ladas, Bessie Theodoropoulos Hotis, Gus Theodoropoulos, Stacy Hotis, Katherine Katsenes Nicholas, and Amelia Christakis.

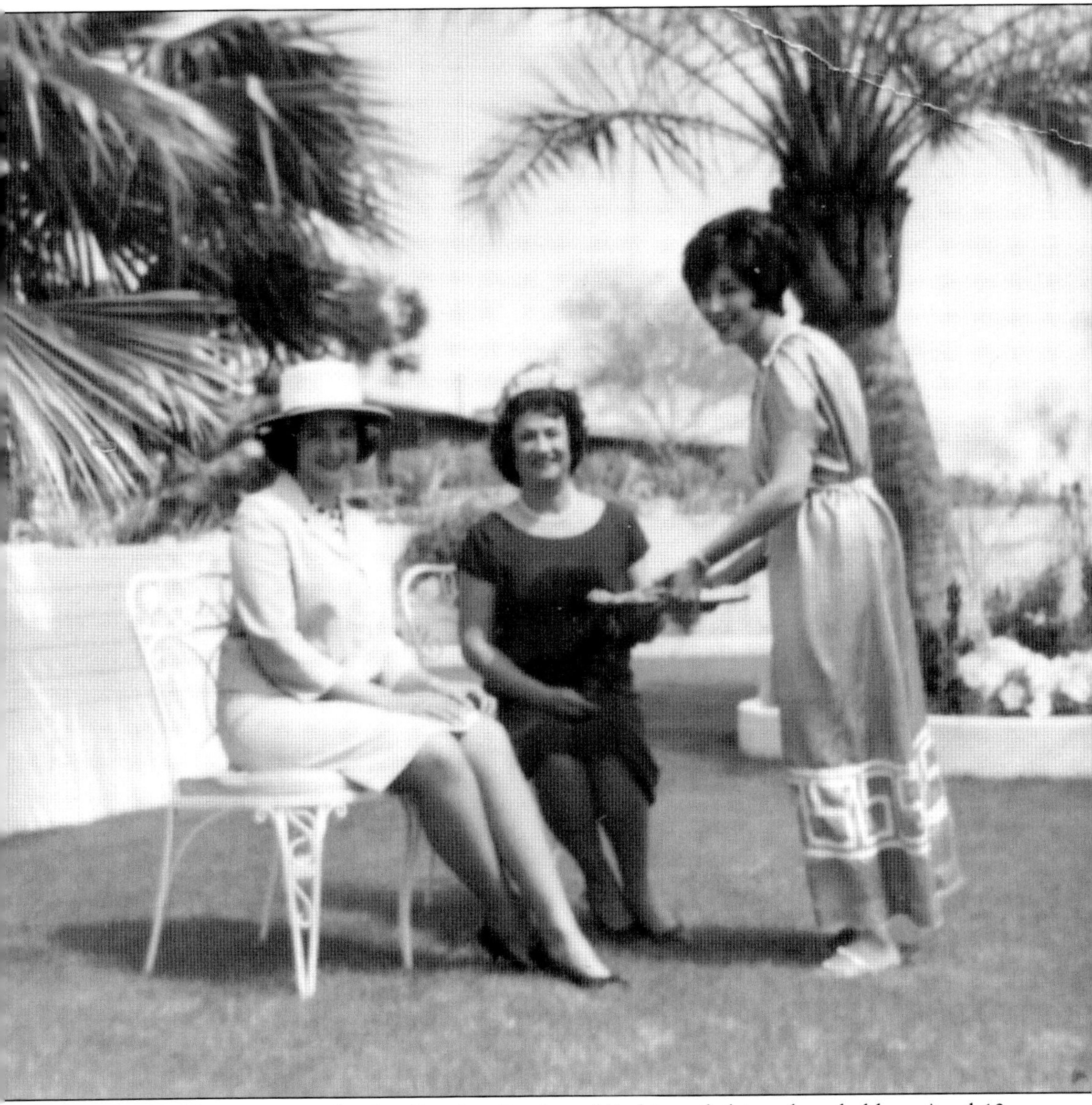

This is a publicity picture for the Grecian Garden of Fashions fashion show held on April 10, 1965. The picture was taken at Evelyn Kokalis's home. Alexandra Tsokatos Anagnopoulos is serving Greek coffee to Mae Ducas (left) and Evelyn Kokalis (right).

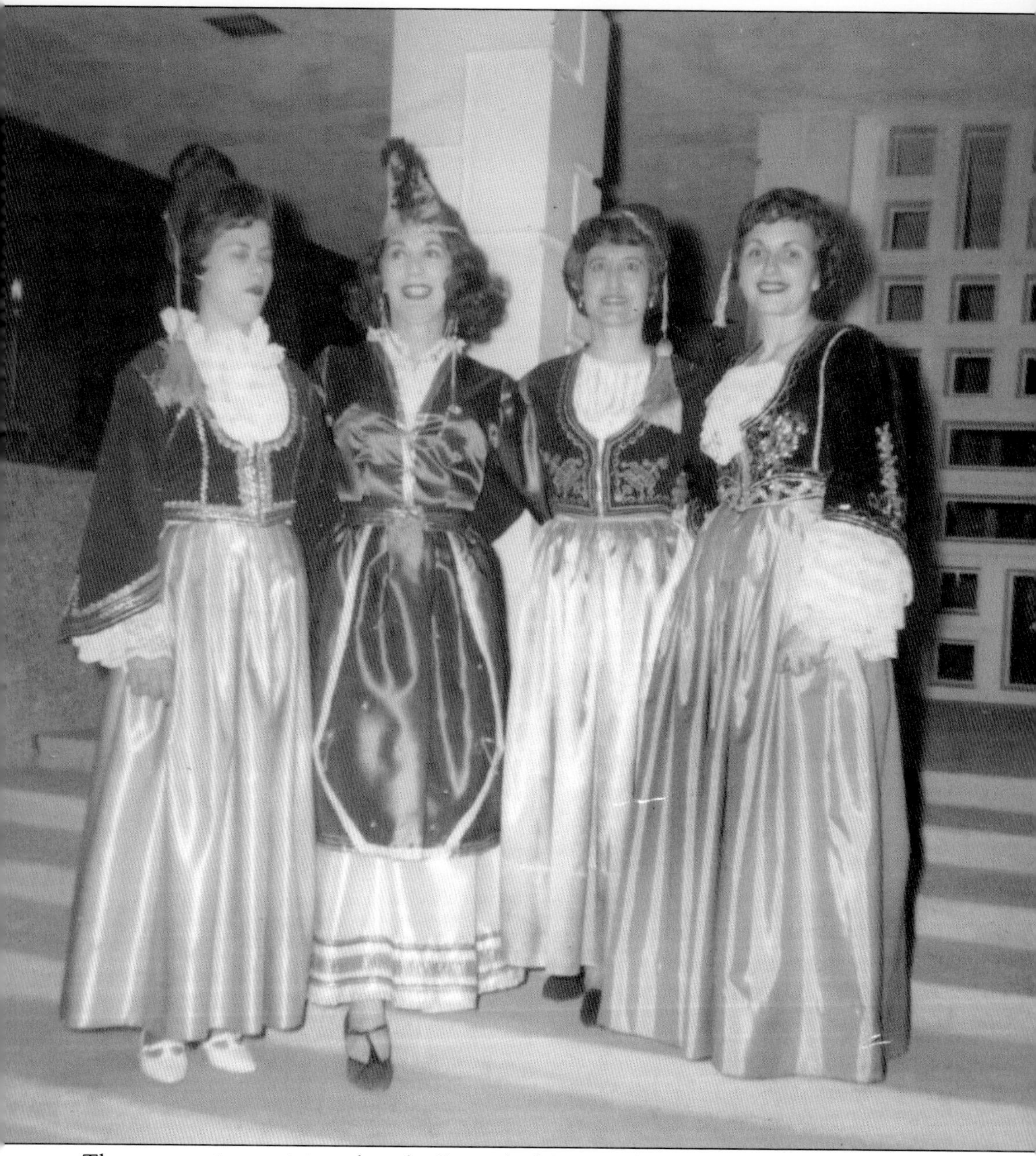

The community participated in the Festival of Arts at the Phoenix Center in March 1966. The participants, from left to right, are Maria Fakonas, Mary Contes, Zella Zannis, and Bessie Theodoropoulos Hotis.

In 1968, Tassos and Lucia Fakonas participated in the Maricopa County Festival of Nations. They are pictured in Greek costumes performing traditional Greek dances.

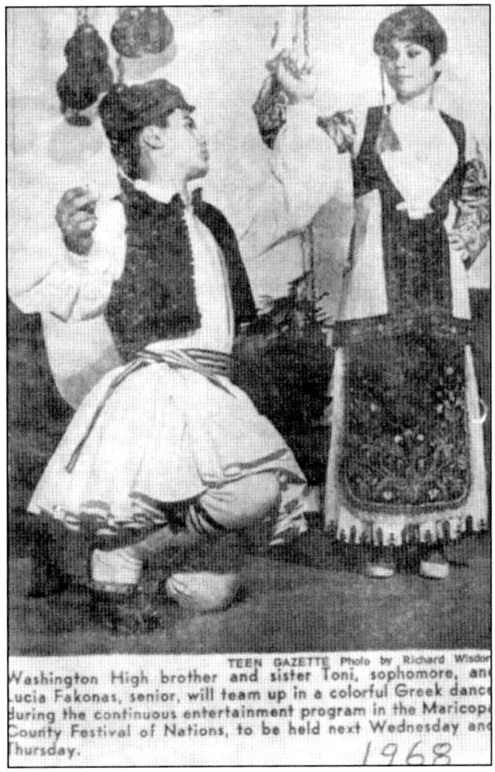

TEEN GAZETTE Photo by Richard Wisdom

Washington High brother and sister Toni, sophomore, and Lucia Fakonas, senior, will team up in a colorful Greek dance during the continuous entertainment program in the Maricopa County Festival of Nations, to be held next Wednesday and Thursday.

1968

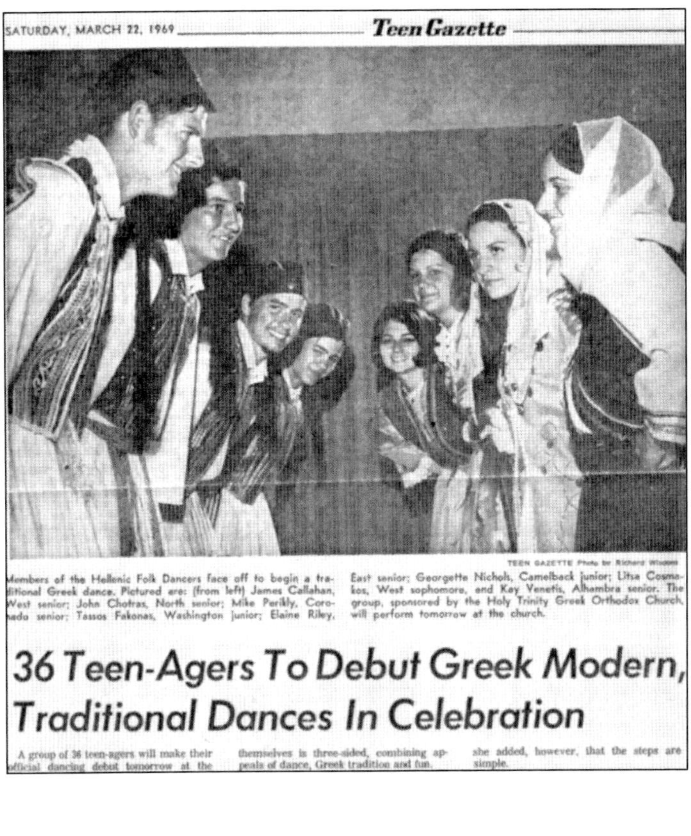

SATURDAY, MARCH 22, 1969 — Teen Gazette

TEEN GAZETTE Photo by Richard Wisdom

Members of the Hellenic Folk Dancers face off to begin a traditional Greek dance. Pictured are: (from left) James Callahan, West senior; John Chotras, North senior; Mike Perikly, Coronado senior; Tassos Fakonas, Washington junior; Elaine Riley, East senior; Georgette Nichols, Camelback junior; Litsa Cosmakos, West sophomore, and Kay Venetis, Alhambra senior. The group, sponsored by the Holy Trinity Greek Orthodox Church, will perform tomorrow at the church.

## 36 Teen-Agers To Debut Greek Modern, Traditional Dances In Celebration

A group of 36 teen-agers will make their official dancing debut tomorrow at the ... themselves is three-sided, combining appeals of dance, Greek tradition and fun. ... she added, however, that the steps are simple.

Members of the Hellenic Folk Dancers are preparing for the Greek Independence Day celebration at the community hall on March 25, 1969. The young men on the left are James Callahan, John Chotras, Mike Perikley, Tassos Fakonas, and the girls on the right are Elaine Riley, Georgette Nichols, Litsa Cosmakos, and Kay Venetis.

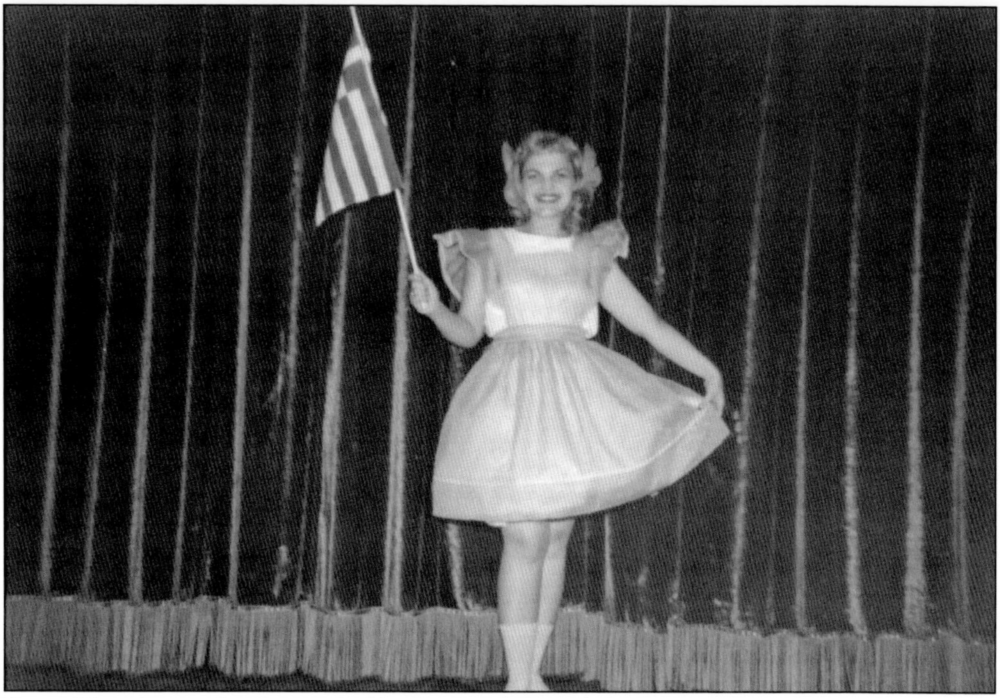

Diane Theodoropoulos Starros holds the Greek flag while reciting a Greek poem during the 1961 variety show.

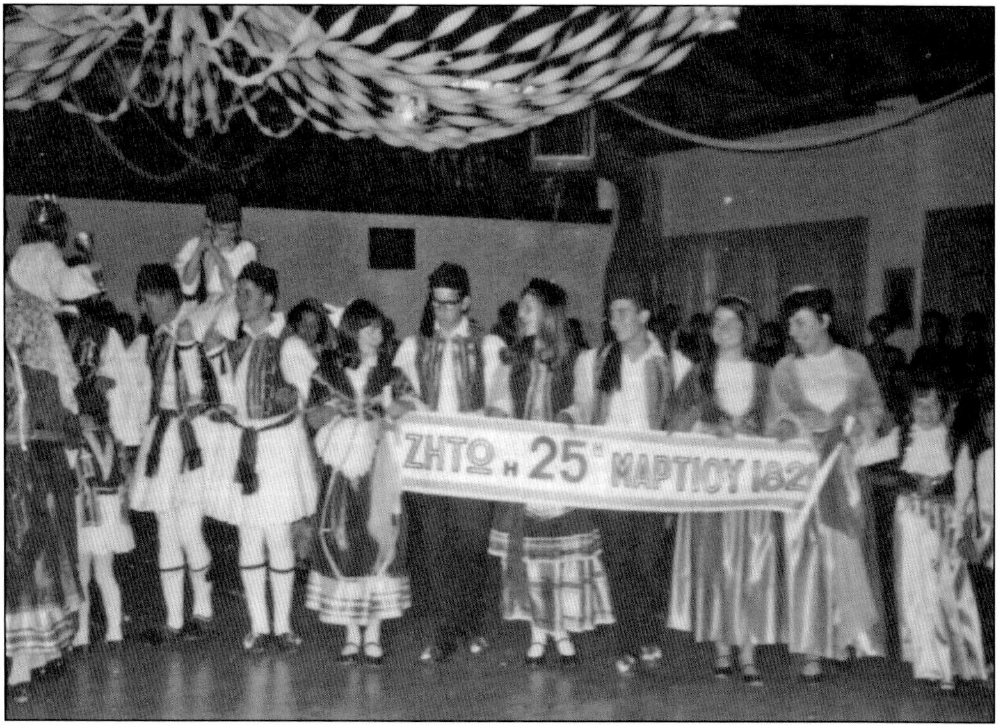


Thirty-six teenagers, directed by Mae Ducas and assisted by Mary Contes, danced at the community hall in celebration of Greek Independence Day, March 25, 1969.

# *Eight*

# Civic Leaders and Community Events

The founders of the Holy Trinity community were adamant that their children become good American citizens and receive higher education. Many of the first generation of Greek Americans in Phoenix went on to become doctors, judges, lawyers, business executives, and civic leaders.

The Greek community also participated in many community events. A few in the later years were a Greek War Relief Society fund-raiser on March 13, 1941; Hotel Westward Ho; Festival of Nations at Encanto Park in 1962; Phoenix Annual Festival of Arts in 1967; Festival of Nations in 1968; and Firebird Festival of Arts in April 1970.

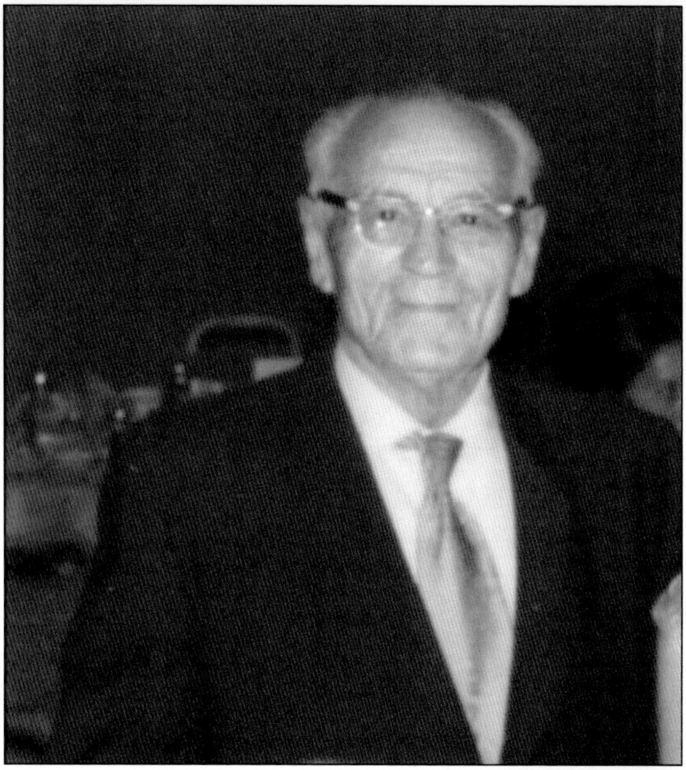

Sam Colachis was president of the Arizona Restaurant Association and a 30-year member of the Arizona Club. He was a 41-year member and supporter of the YMCA. He became the elder statesman in the Phoenix area for providing assistance to many Greek immigrants, helping them to receive American citizenship.

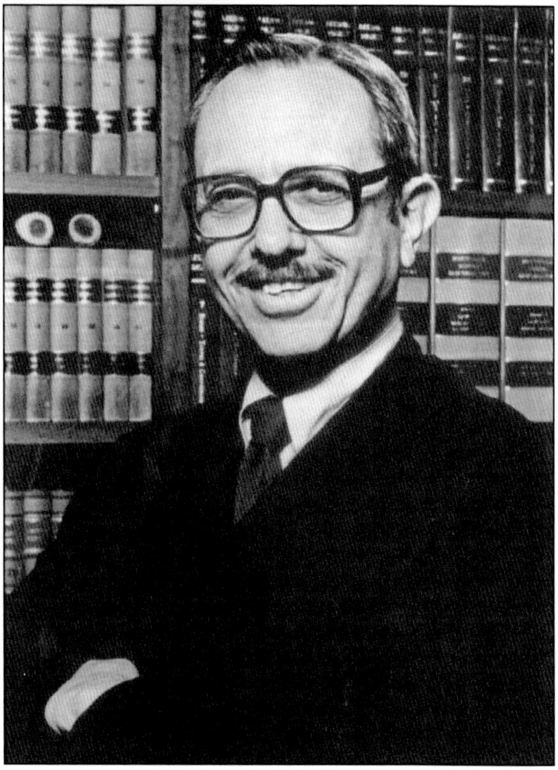

Chris Tountas served as Maricopa County court commissioner in the 1980s. Chris was an active attorney for many years prior to his post as court commissioner. Chris was also very active in the Holy Trinity community.

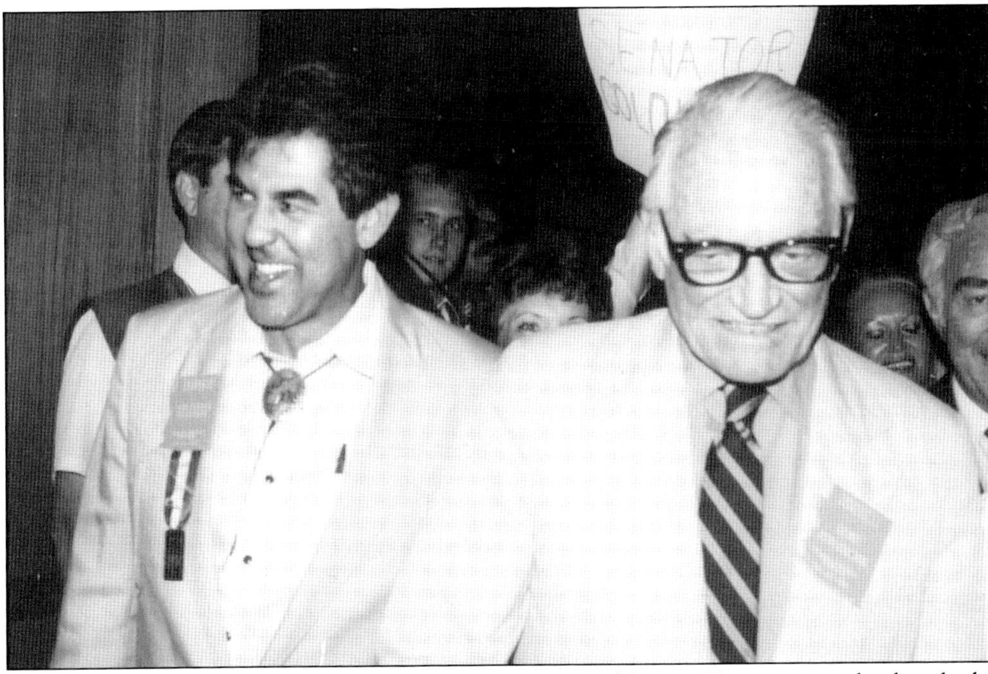

Shown here is Tom Pappas (left) with Sen. Barry M. Goldwater. Tom was involved with the Republican Party from the time he was a teenager. He later became the state chairman for the Republican Party. Tom founded the Young Republicans.

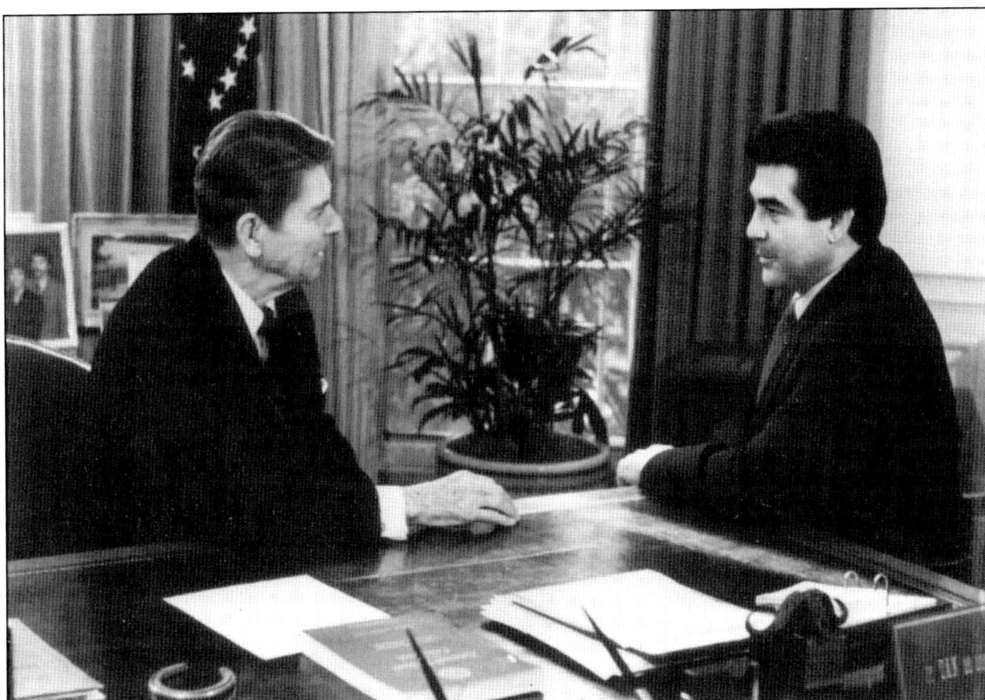

Tom Pappas poses with Pres. Ronald Reagan in the Oval Office in the 1980s as state chairman for the Republican Party.

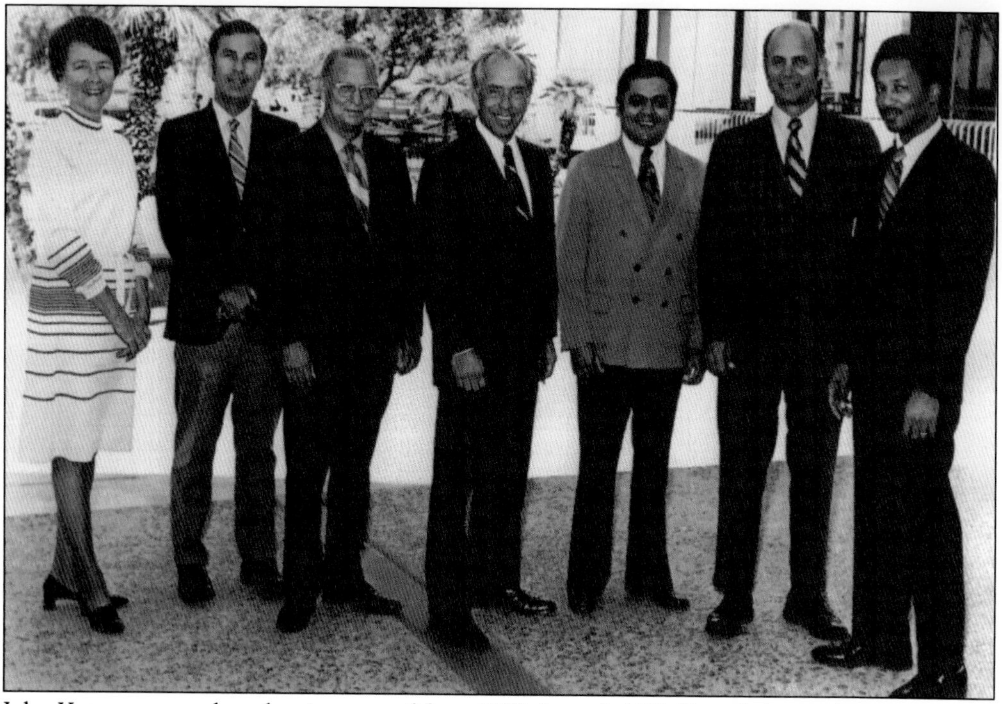

John Katsenes served on the city council from 1970 through 1974. From left to right are Margaret T. Hance, Ed Korrick, Henry E. Brodersen, Mayor John D. Driggs, and councilmen Armando de Leon, John T. Katsenes, and Calvin C. Goode.

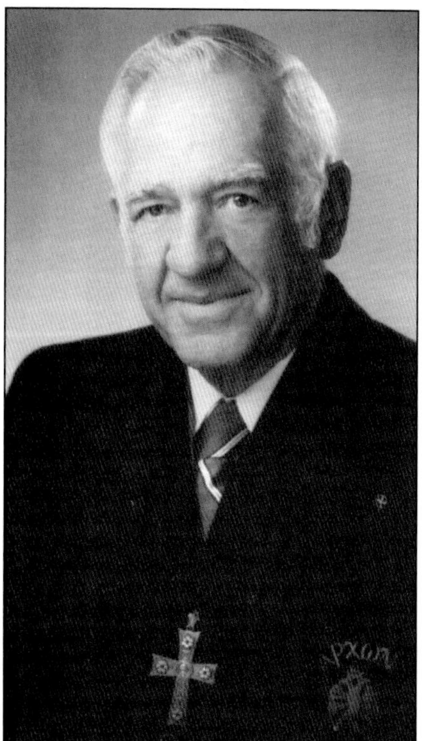

George Kokalis was active in the state Republican Party, where he chaired the Early Birds in 1972 and the Trunk and Tusk in 1973. He served on the board of directors of the Arizona Country Club for five years. He also served on the Samaritan Medical Foundation Board for 20 years. He has been honored many times for his civic and philanthropic activities.

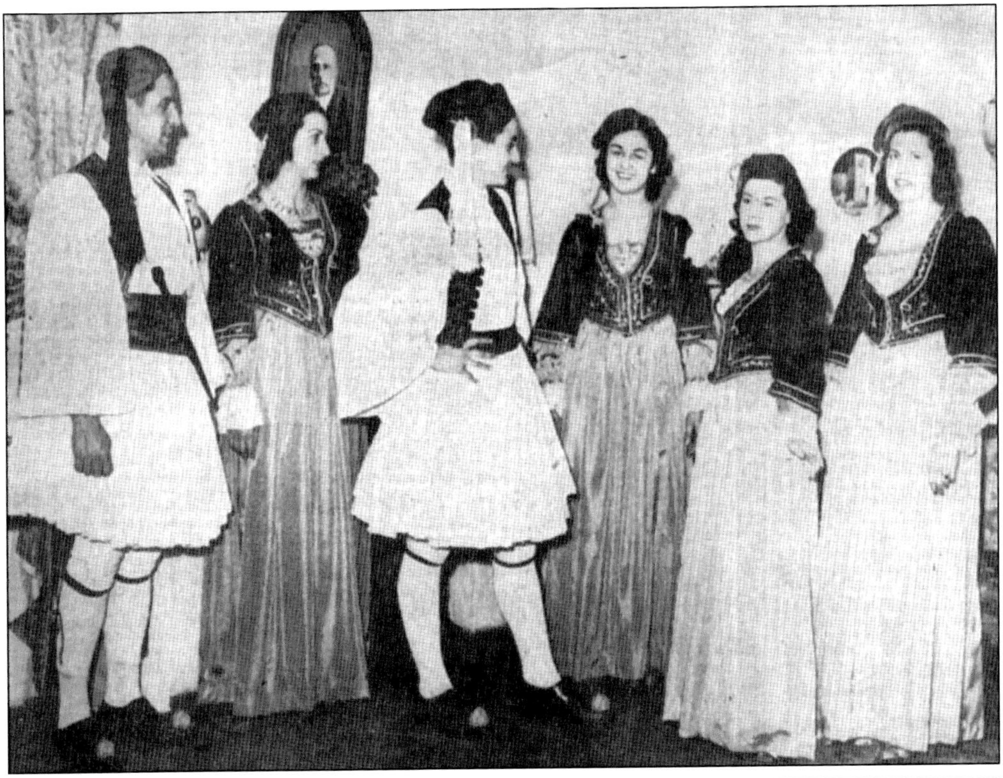

In 1941, a ball was held at the Hotel Westward Ho to benefit the Greek War Relief. From left to right are Paul Ladas, Sophie Herlyck, Harry Ladas, Lula Tamaras, Mary Ladas, and Angie Thomas, all in ethnic Greek costumes.

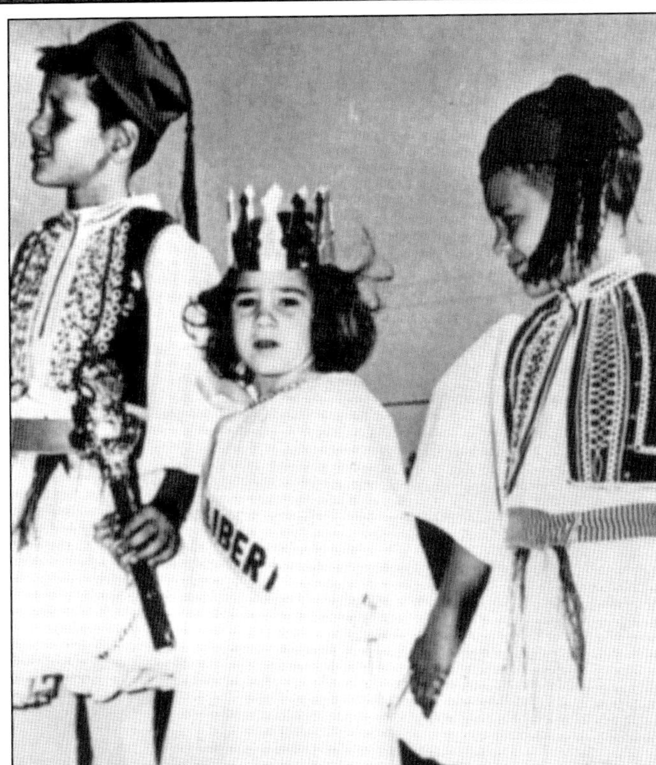

Shown here with Miss Liberty U.S.A., Kathy Pappas, are James Poulos, left, and Nick Gannis, right. They were at the airport to greet Spiro Agnew when he was campaigning for vice president in the 1960s.

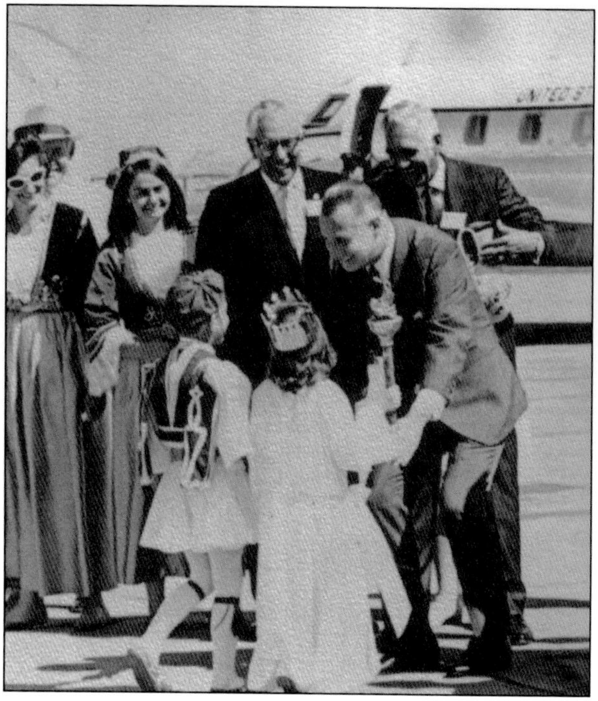

In 1960s, Spiro Agnew stopped in Phoenix during his campaign for the office of vice president. Because he was of Greek descent, he was greeted by a contingency of Greeks from Holy Trinity Church.

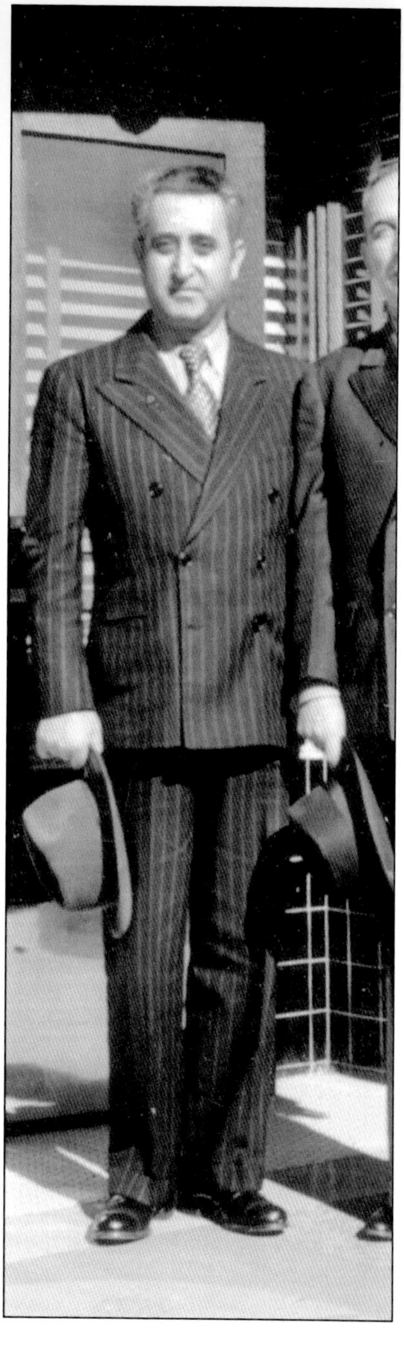

Milton Stamatis was in business beginning in 1917 when he moved to Phoenix. Stamatis was a highly regarded entrepreneur and was involved in many civic activities. He took time in his busy schedule to be involved in civic affairs and organizations such as the Benevolent Order of Elks, the Mooseheart Legion, the Arizona Club, president of the Phoenix AHEPA (American Hellenic Education Progressive Association) Chapter 219, the Phoenix Chamber of Commerce, chairman of the Greek War Relief, as well as his strong leadership and support of the Holy Trinity Greek Orthodox Church.

# *Nine*

# World Wars I and II

This chapter is dedicated to the young men from Phoenix who served during World Wars I and II. Of course, such monumental world events as the Great War (1914–1918) in Europe and elsewhere shaped the course of the American nation and its people for generations to come. What impact the war may have had on the Greek families at the time in Phoenix can only be determined by speculation.

According to the information provided to the authors, the following five men are the only World War I veterans from the Phoenix Greek community: Tony Georgouses, James N. Parros, William Tsokatos, Michael J. Zannis, and Harry Johnson.

World War II brought the Greek community in Phoenix closer into the mainstream of American life as the nation battled the Axis powers of Germany, Japan, and Italy. Most had a personal stake in the outcome of the war in Europe, as they had left behind relatives in Greece, which was invaded in 1940 by the Italians and followed by the Germans.

The following pages contain photographs of veterans of the world wars. The authors were unable to locate photographs of the following World War II veterans: Chris Abaramas (army), William Georgantos (navy), Gus Georgouses (army), John Georgouses (army air corps), Milton Georgouses (army), Art Haritos (army), Peter Kanton (navy), James Manos (army), Louis Pappas (army), and Louie Vlangos (navy).

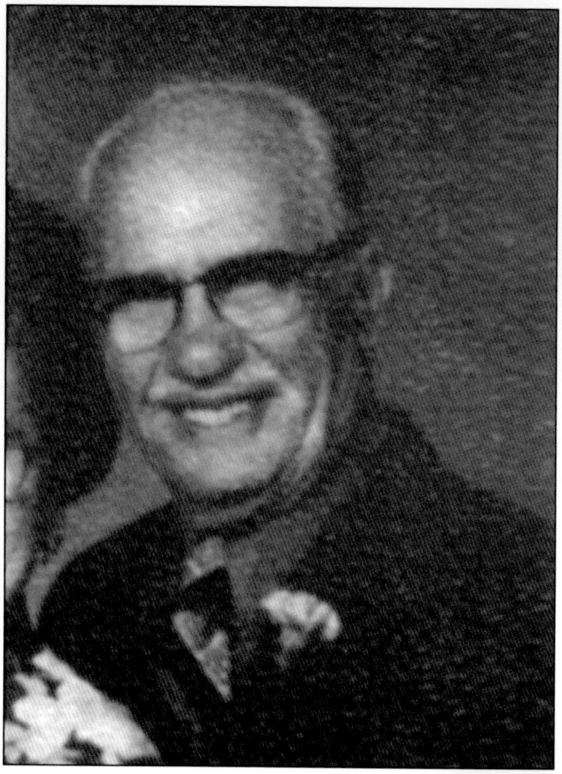

James Parros served in the army during World War I. He was a manager at Madison Square Garden in Phoenix. He later married Toula (Limber) Parros.

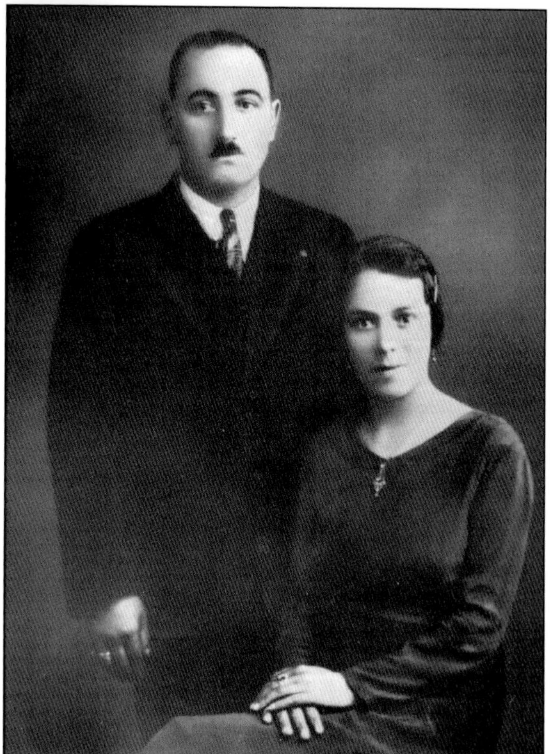

William G. Tsogatos (also spelled Tsokatos) came to the United States as a teenager in 1910. He served in the army in World War I aboard a ship, as a fireman. He worked in the merchant marines and then returned to Phoenix. He married Evangelia Laskari in 1931 in Leonidion, Greece, and returned to Phoenix.

Jim Anton (Antonopolos) served in World War II. He served in Company E, 158th Infantry at Cap Parajeo in the Panama Canal Zone and was then sent to England, France, Germany, and Australia as a private first class. He spent seven months in Manchester, England, where he met his future wife, Jean Sedgley. Jim was the nephew of Chris and Christina Pallas. He lived with his aunt and uncle at a young age after the early death of his parents.

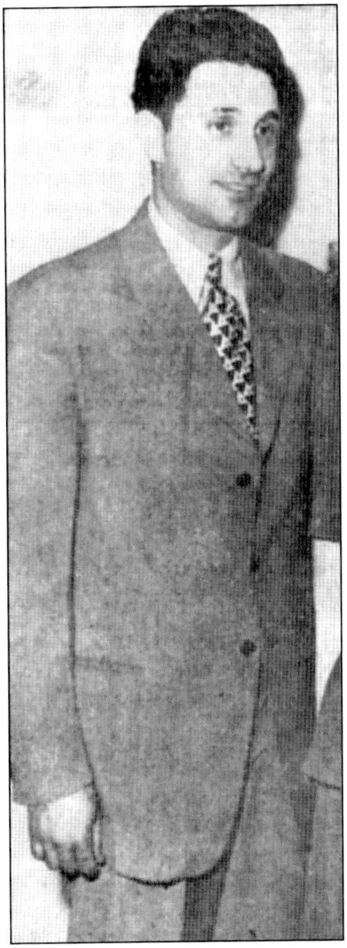

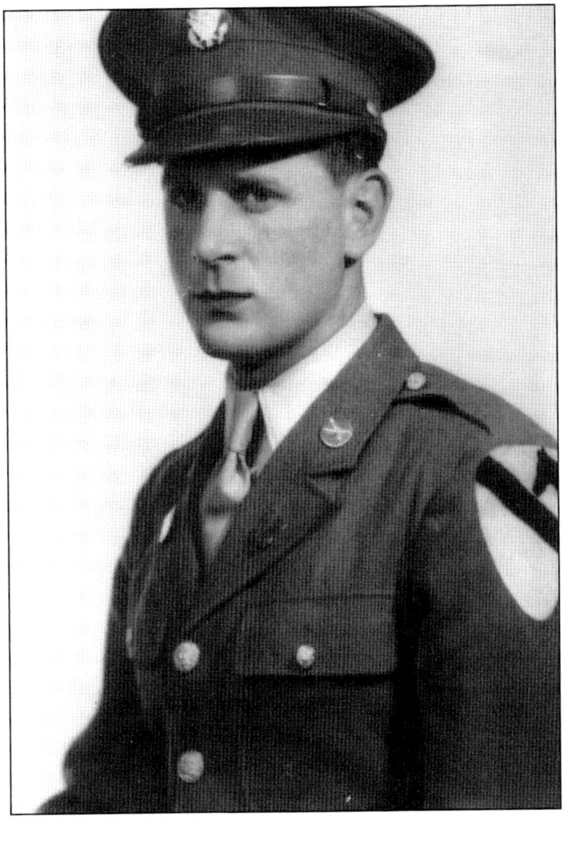

Clements Ladas served in the army from 1940 to 1945. Staff Sergeant Ladas served in the South Pacific. He was killed during the liberation of the Santa Tomas Prison Camp outside of Manila in the Philippines. He was the son of Charles and Pitsa Ladas. His brothers, James, Paul, and Harry, served in the navy and army.

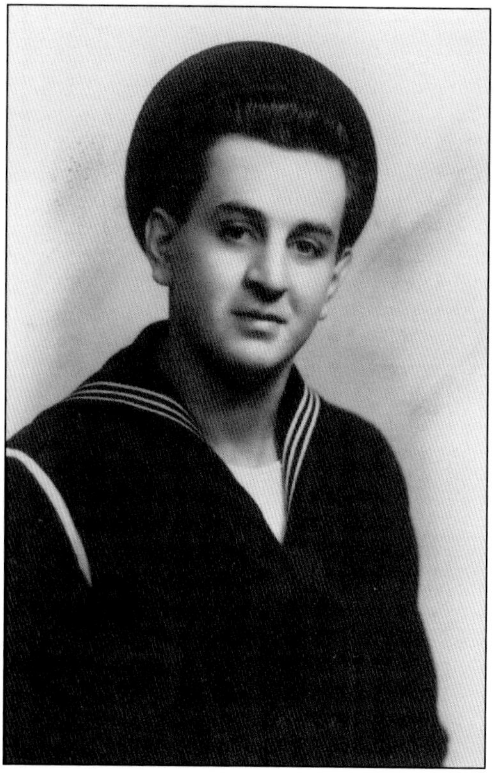

Harry Ladas served in the U.S. Navy from 1941 to 1945. Harry was a fire controlman third class. He served in the South Pacific on the destroyer USS *Mertz*. He was the son of Charles and Pitsa Ladas. His three brothers, Clements, Paul, and James, also served at that time.

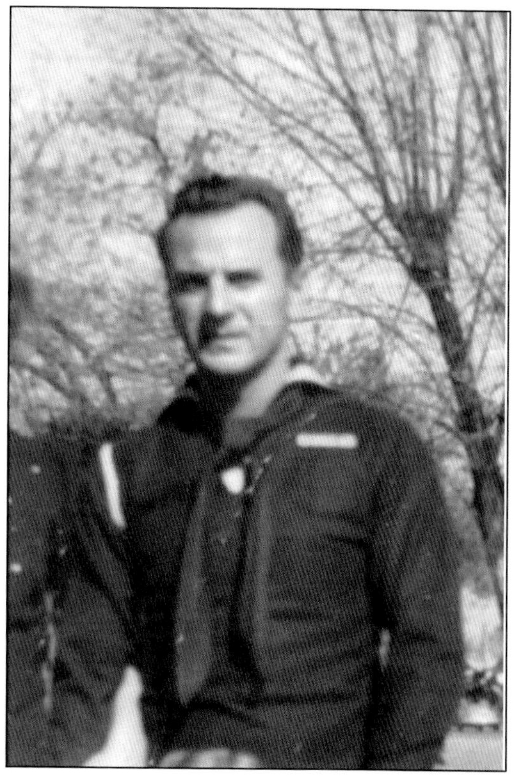

James C. Ladas was a seaman first class in the navy from 1942 to 1945. He served in the South Pacific aboard the USS *Intrepid*, an aircraft carrier of the Essex class. His three brothers, Clements (army), Paul (army), and Harry (navy), also served during World War II.

Paul C. Ladas was in the army from 1942 to 1945. Corporal Ladas served in the Aleutian Islands and in the War Department in Washington, D.C.

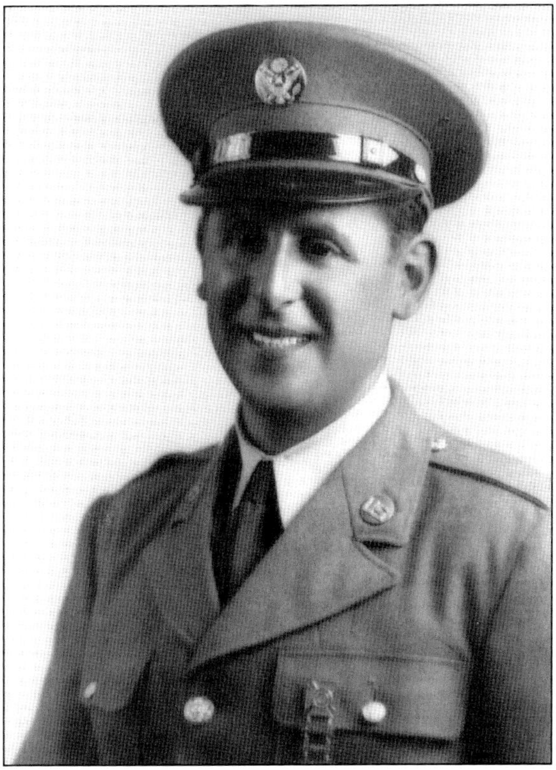

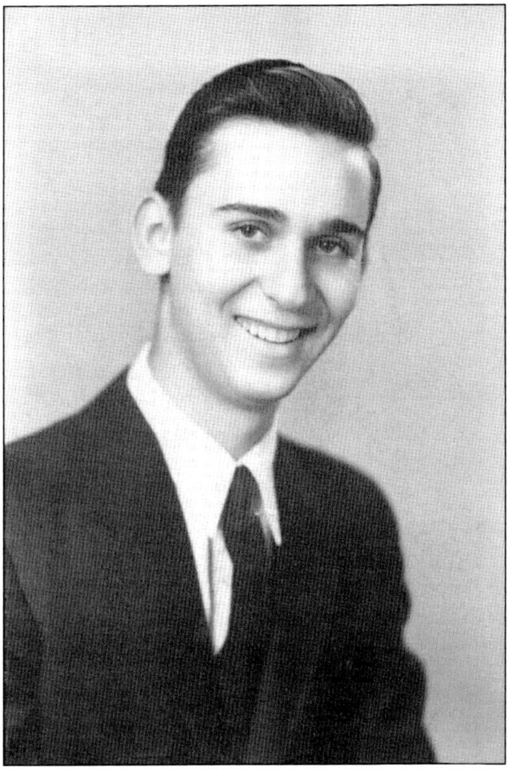

Angelo Falkedes served in World War II. He was the son of George and Katherine Falkedes. Angelo entered the service attending the 368th Squadron Technical School in Scofield, Illinois, in 1942.

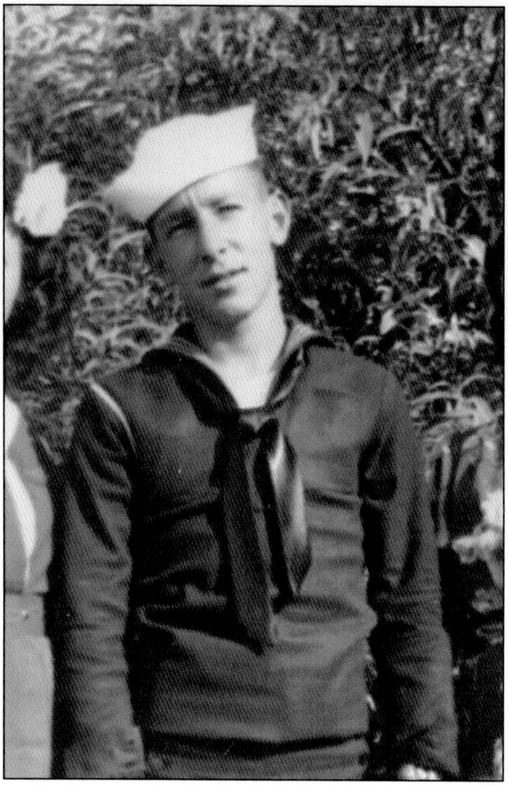

John Gannis served in the U.S. Navy from 1942 to 1945. He served in Hawaii and on Midway Island as a radioman. He was one of the first radio operators to receive the message from Admiral Nimitz that the Japanese had surrendered on August 15, 1945, at 8:35 a.m. John is the son of Nick and Meropy Gannis.

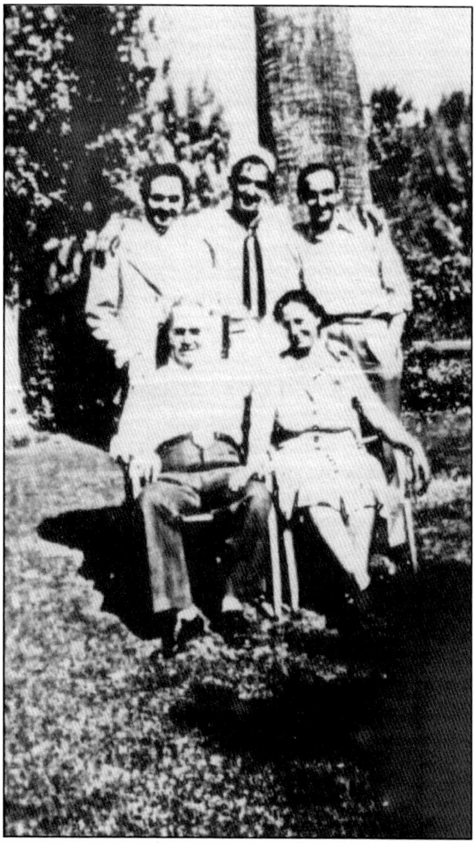

Jim Georgouses served in the navy in World War II. He was the son of Nick and Panayiota Georgouses. Jim's father died at a young age, and his mother then married Chris Petoumenos.

Paul Glitsos served in the U.S. Navy from 1941 to 1945 as a special artificer first class. He served on the naval base at Pacific Beach, California. He was the son of John and Rena Glitsos.

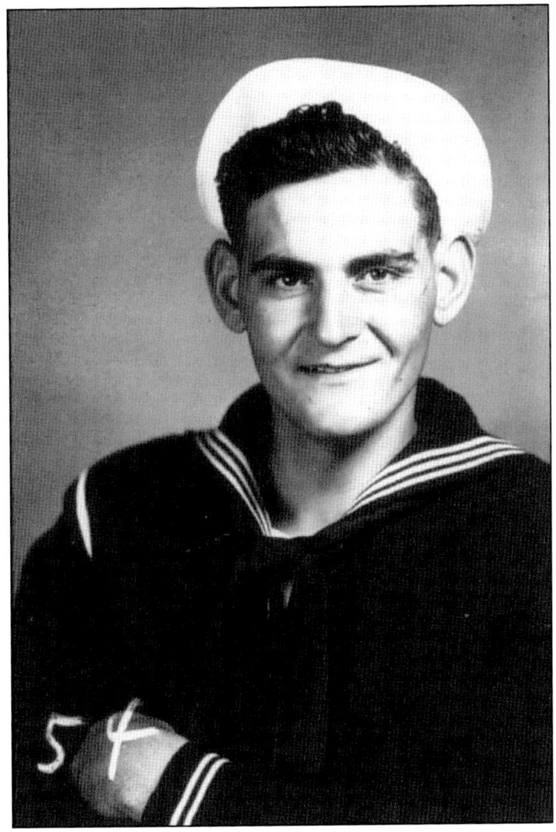

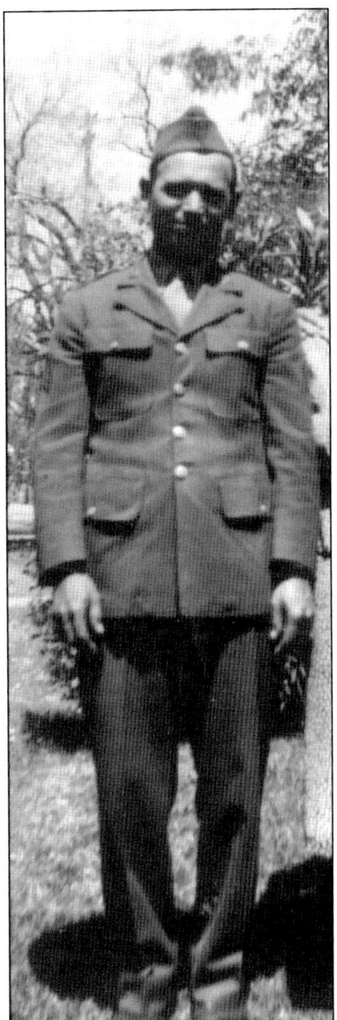

Michael J. Ioannou served in the air force from 1941 to 1945. He was the nephew of Floros and Eftihia Mitchell.

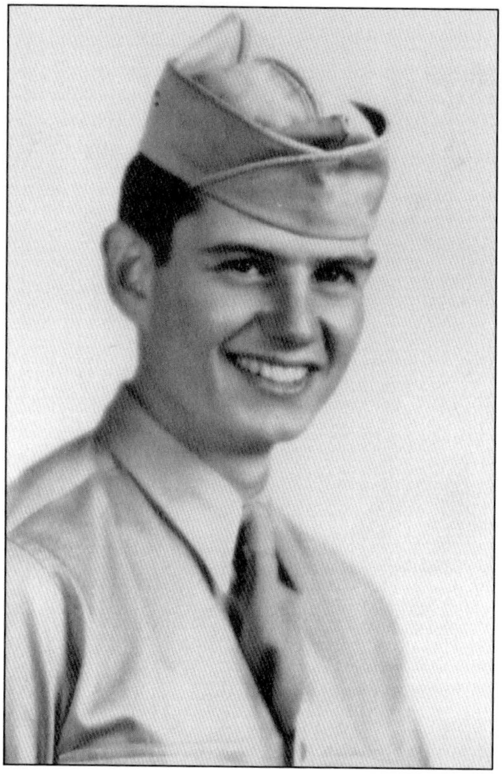

George Poulos served in the U.S. Army in Europe during the height of World War II. He was the son of Despo and James Poulos.

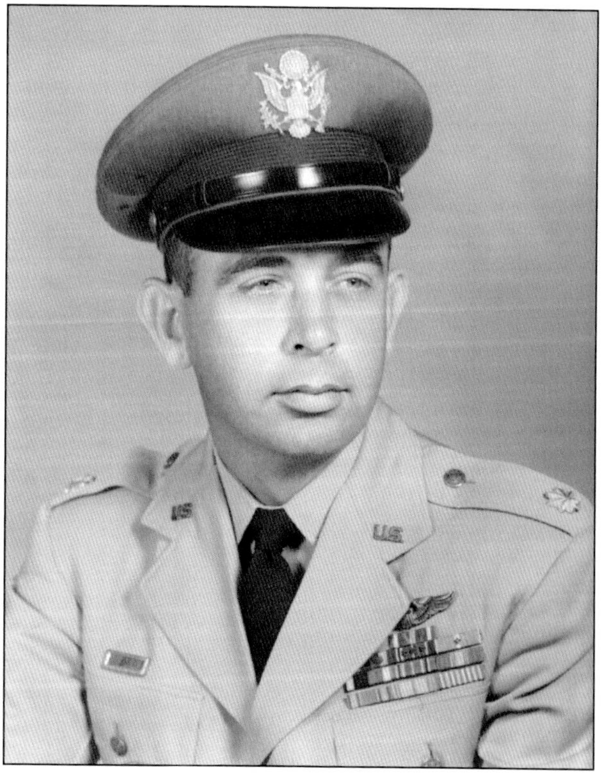

Milton "Pete" Stamatis Jr. was an air force colonel stationed in England during World War II. He and his crew bombed Germany every night for 30 days. Pete is the son of Milton and Chrysanthe Stamatis.

Sam Stamatis was a lieutenant colonel in the Adjutant General's Department in Washington, D.C., during World War II. He was the son of Milton and Chrysanthe Stamatis.

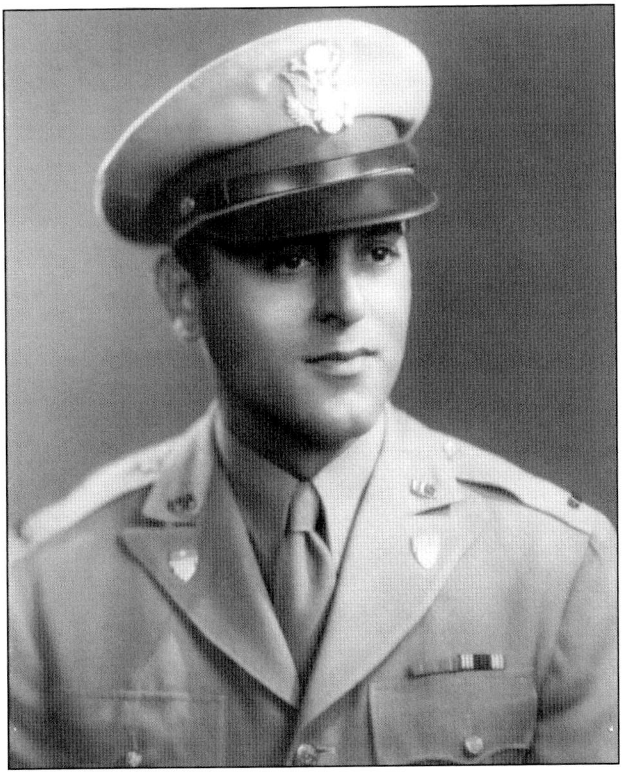

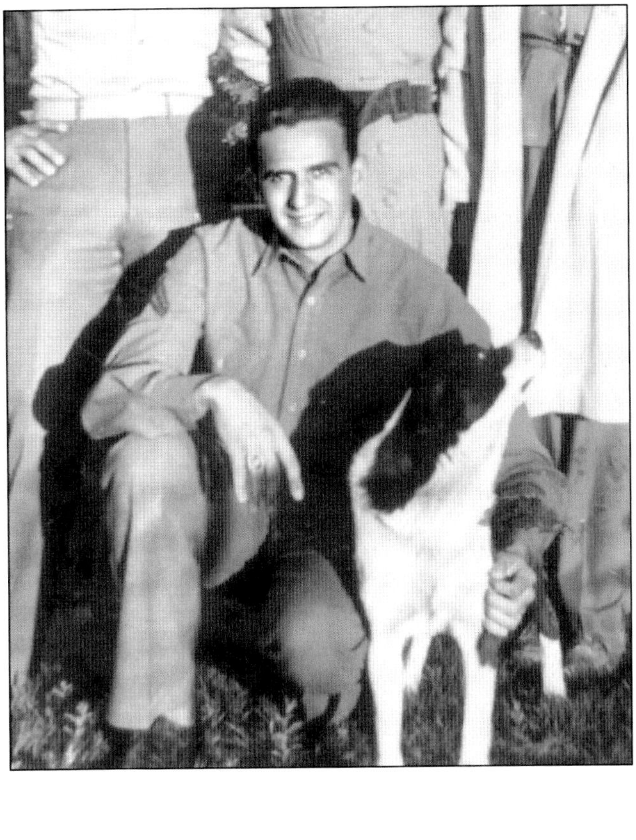

S.Sgt. Nick Thomas served in the army as a medic during World War II. He was in the invasion of North Africa, the Tunisian campaign, and the invasion of Sicily. He saved many lives during his time as a medic. His brother, Tony, also served in World War II. They were the sons of John and Olga Thomas.

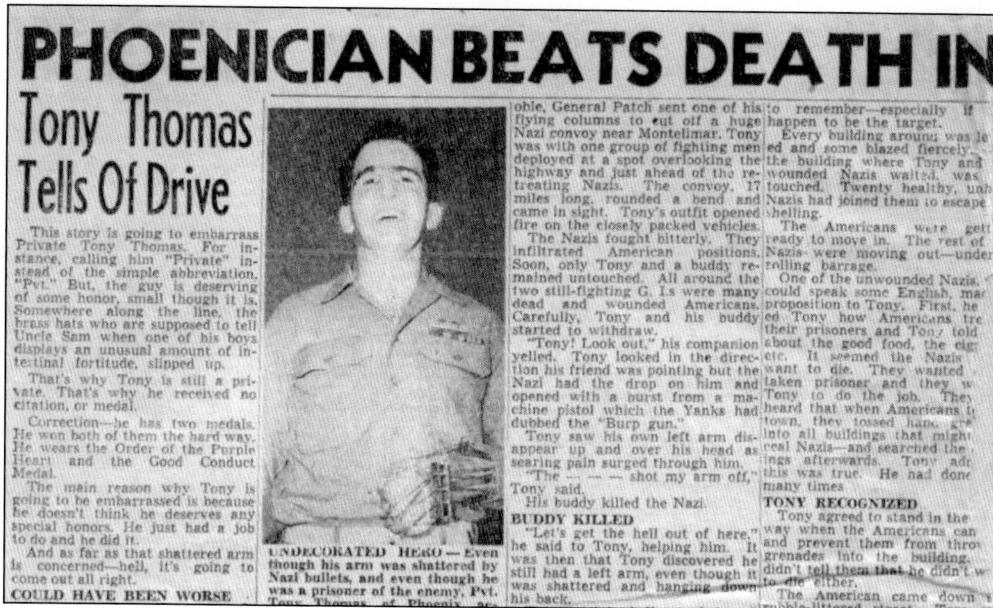

# PHOENICIAN BEATS DEATH IN

## Tony Thomas Tells Of Drive

This story is going to embarrass Private Tony Thomas. For instance, calling him "Private" instead of the simple abbreviation, "Pvt." But, the guy is deserving of some honor, small though it is. Somewhere along the line, the brass hats who are supposed to tell Uncle Sam when one of his boys displays an unusual amount of intestinal fortitude, slipped up.

That's why Tony is still a private. That's why he received no citation, or medal.

Correction—he has two medals. He won both of them the hard way. He wears the Order of the Purple Heart and the Good Conduct Medal.

The main reason why Tony is going to be embarrassed is because he doesn't think he deserves any special honors. He just had a job to do and he did it.

And as far as that shattered arm is concerned—hell, it's going to come out all right.

**COULD HAVE BEEN WORSE**

UNDECORATED HERO — Even though his arm was shattered by Nazi bullets, and even though he was a prisoner of the enemy, Pvt.

oble, General Patch sent one of his flying columns to cut off a huge Nazi convoy near Montelimar. Tony was with one group of fighting men deployed at a spot overlooking the highway and just ahead of the retreating Nazis. The convoy, 17 miles long, rounded a bend and came in sight. Tony's outfit opened fire on the closely packed vehicles.

The Nazis fought bitterly. They infiltrated American positions. Soon, only Tony and a buddy remained untouched. All around the two still-fighting G. I.s were many dead and wounded Americans. Carefully, Tony and his buddy started to withdraw.

"Tony! Look out," his companion yelled. Tony looked in the direction his friend was pointing but the Nazi had the drop on him and opened with a burst from a machine pistol which the Yanks had dubbed the "Burp gun."

Tony saw his own left arm disappear up and over his head as searing pain surged through him.

"The — — — shot my arm off," Tony said.

His buddy killed the Nazi.

**BUDDY KILLED**

"Let's get the hell out of here," he said to Tony, helping him. It was then that Tony discovered he still had a left arm, even though it was shattered and hanging down his back.

to remember—especially if happen to be the target.

Every building around was le ed and some blazed fiercely. the building where Tony and wounded Nazis waited, was touched. Twenty healthy, unh Nazis had joined them to escape shelling.

The Americans were gett ready to move in. The rest of Nazis were moving out—under rolling barrage.

One of the unwounded Nazis, could speak some English, ma proposition to Tony. First, he ed Tony how Americans tre their prisoners and Tony told about the good food, the cig etc. It seemed the Nazis want to die. They wanted taken prisoner and they w Tony to do the job. They heard that when Americans t town, they tossed hand gre into all buildings that might ceal Nazis—and searched the ings afterwards. Tony adr this was true. He had done many times.

**TONY RECOGNIZED**

Tony agreed to stand in the way when the Americans can and prevent them from thro grenades into the building. didn't tell them that he didn't w to die either.

The American came down

Tony Thomas was in the army in 1943. Private Thomas received a Purple Heart—his left arm was shattered by Nazi bullets. In 1944, he landed in Naples, Italy, in Lt. Gen. Mark Clark's Fifth Army. Tony was taken prisoner for a short time. He then in turn took Nazis prisoner (15 plus a "bunch" more) without a gun.

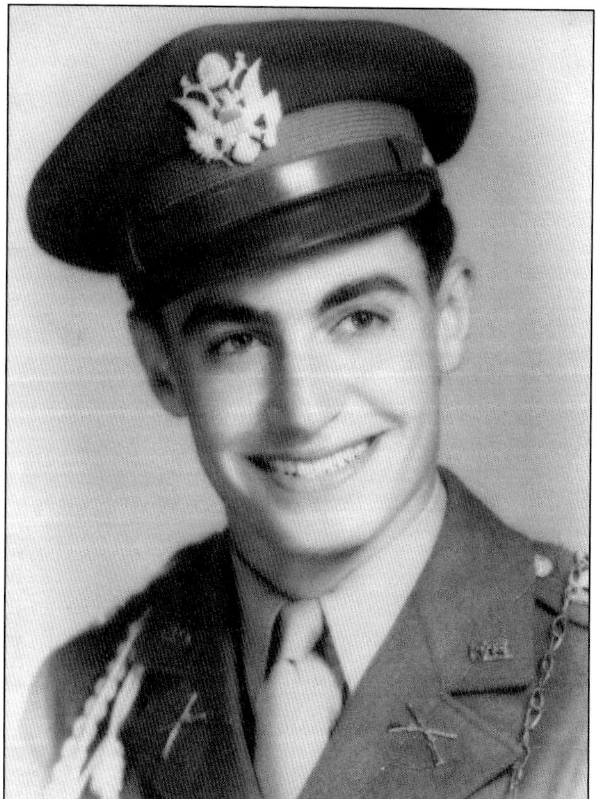

John M. Zannis served in the army from 1944 to 1948. He served in General Patton's Third Army and received a Purple Heart. At one point, he was hospitalized with injuries. He remained in the reserves until retiring as a lieutenant colonel. He was the son of Michael and Joan Zannis.

# *Ten*

# NEW CHURCH

George Kokalis, who served as president of the community at the new church from 1970 to 1982, was the catalyst that sparked the 1973 move of Holy Trinity from the aged facilities at 333 East Virginia Avenue to a community center and cathedral at 1973 East Maryland Avenue.

In 1972, the community sold the church at 333 East Virginia Avenue and used the proceeds to purchase 17.5 acres at 1973 East Maryland Avenue for a new church, community center, education building, and chapel. The property on Maryland Avenue was developed in three phases. The first phase was the ground-breaking for the community center (the first building to be constructed and to serve as the church), which was held in 1973.

Phase two began with the ground-breaking for the church on February 16, 1975, with Archbishop Iakovos of North and South America officiating. The first church service in the building was held on Palm Sunday, April 18, 1976, with a procession to the new edifice from the community center. The Holy Trinity Greek Orthodox Church of Phoenix contains the largest installation of faceted glass in the southwestern United States. The brilliantly colored glass is designed in patterns of exquisite Byzantine iconography. The church has often been referred to as the "Jewel of the Desert."

The third phase was the construction of the education building and office building; the Zeotopoulos Library and the St. George Chapel were built concurrently.

The rest, as they say, is history.

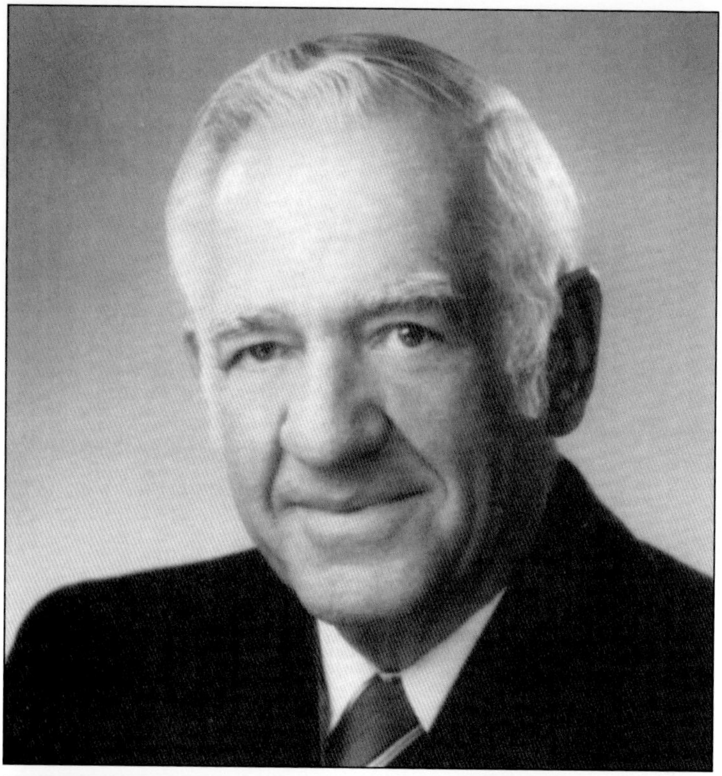

George Kokalia (left) and Milton Soiles (below) were archons of the Ecumenical Patriarchate of Constantinople. The title *archon* is bestowed upon individuals in recognition of their service, support, and dedication to the ecumenical patriarchate throughout the world. Both men's investiture into the order was on July 4, 1982, during the Clergy-Laity Congress.

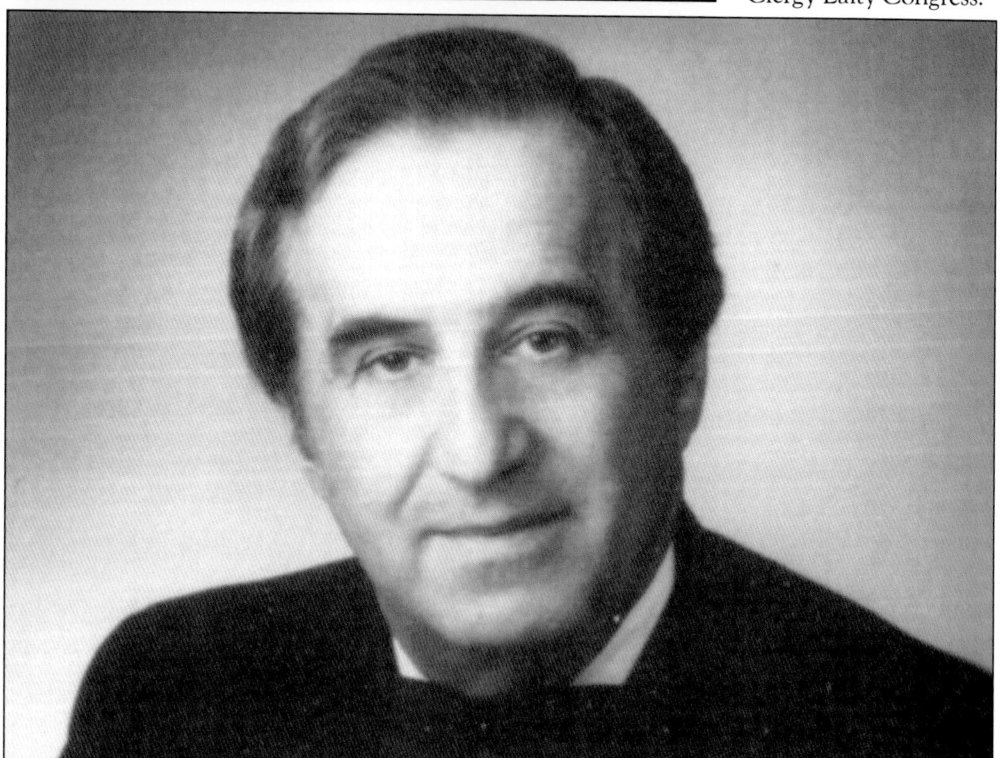

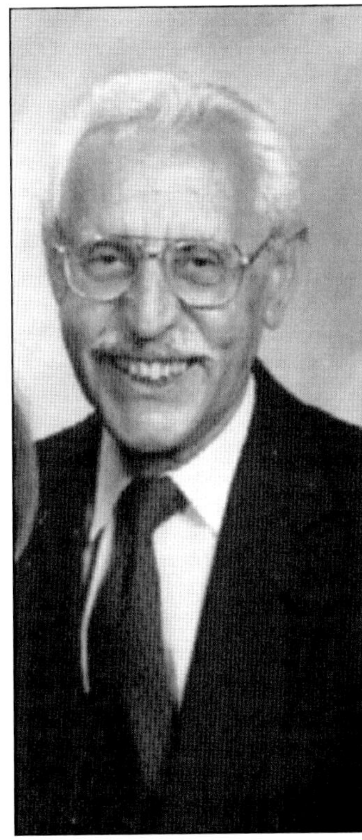

George Souvall (right) and Danny Speros (below) were also archons of the Ecumenical Patriarchate of Constantinople, and their investiture also occurred on July 4, 1982, during the Clergy-Laity Congress.

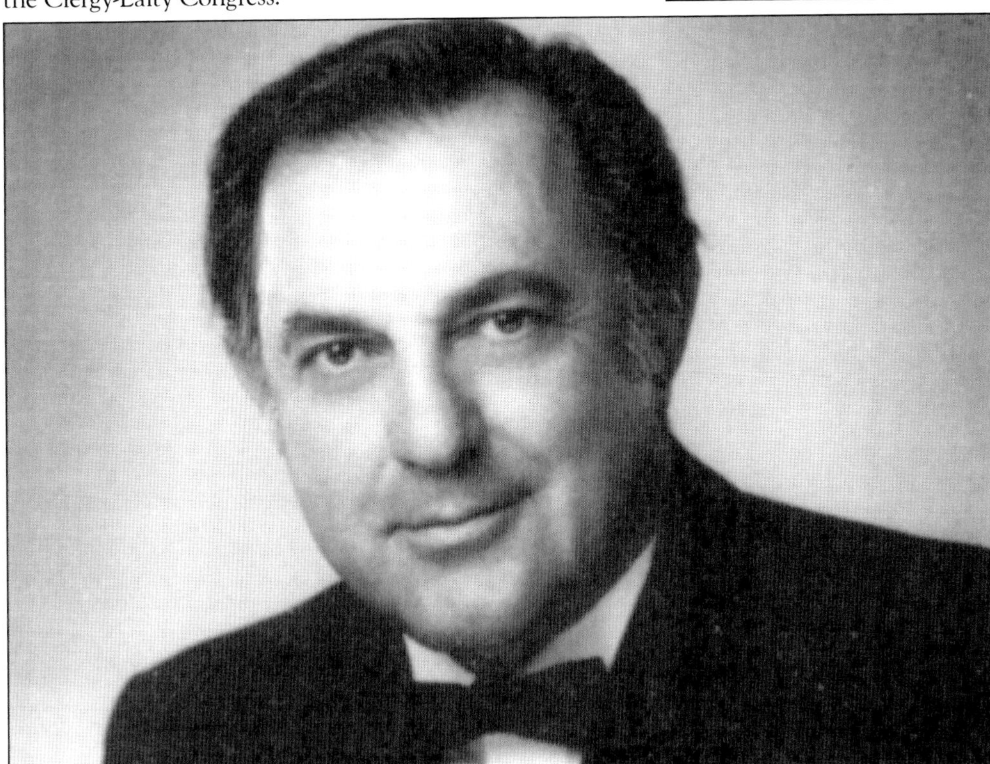

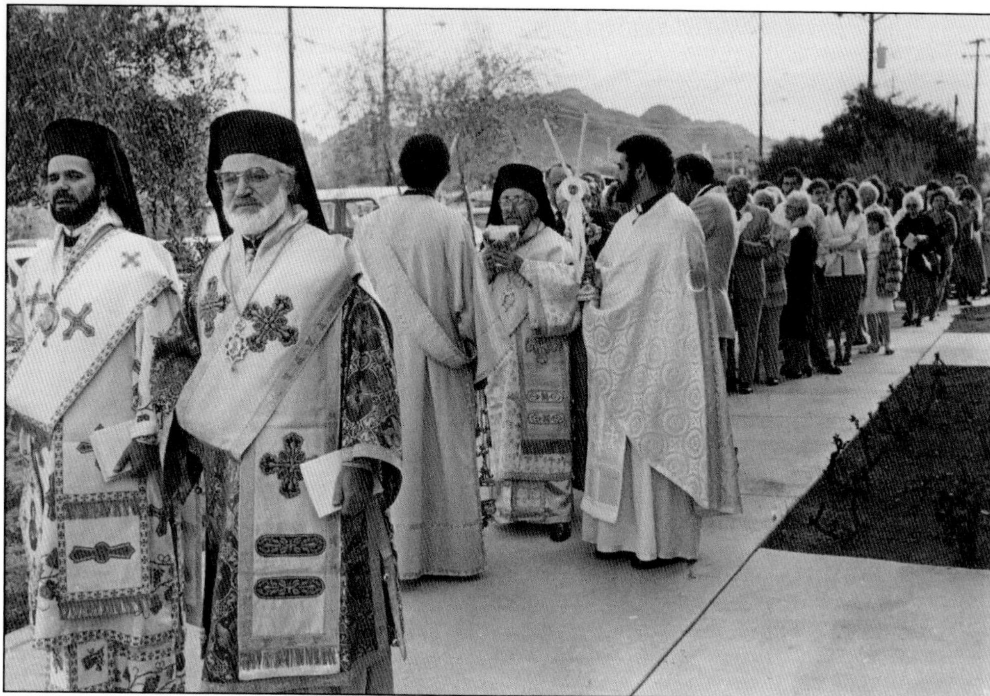

Shown here is the procession of bishops, priests, and parishioners during the consecration ceremony on February 27, 1983, for the new church at 1973 East Maryland Avenue.

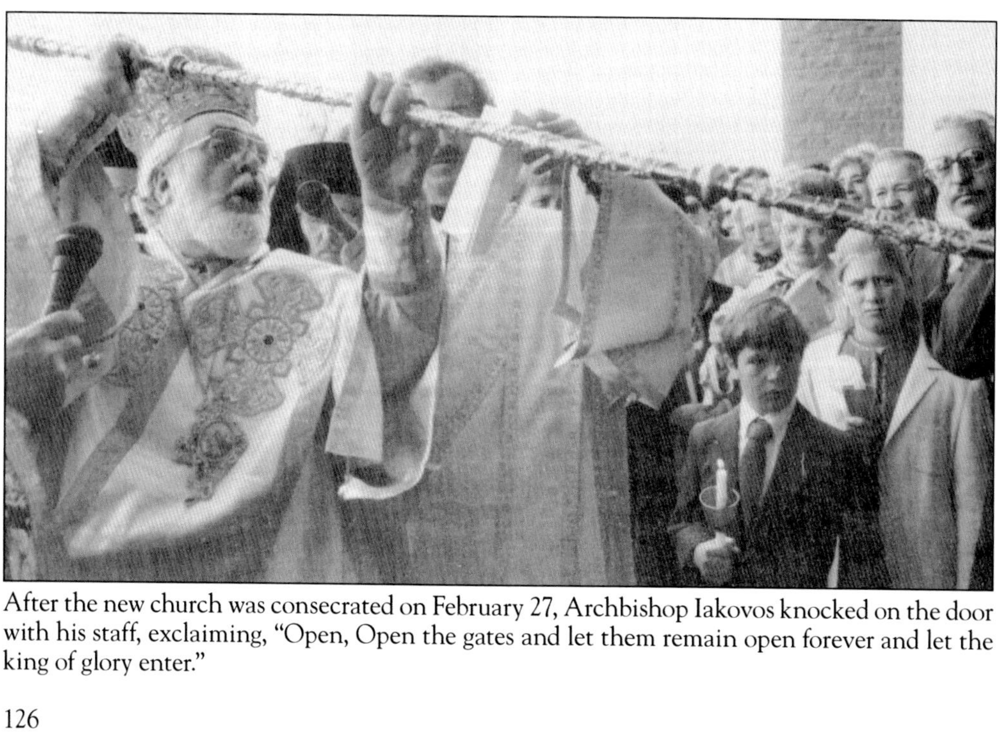

After the new church was consecrated on February 27, Archbishop Iakovos knocked on the door with his staff, exclaiming, "Open, Open the gates and let them remain open forever and let the king of glory enter."

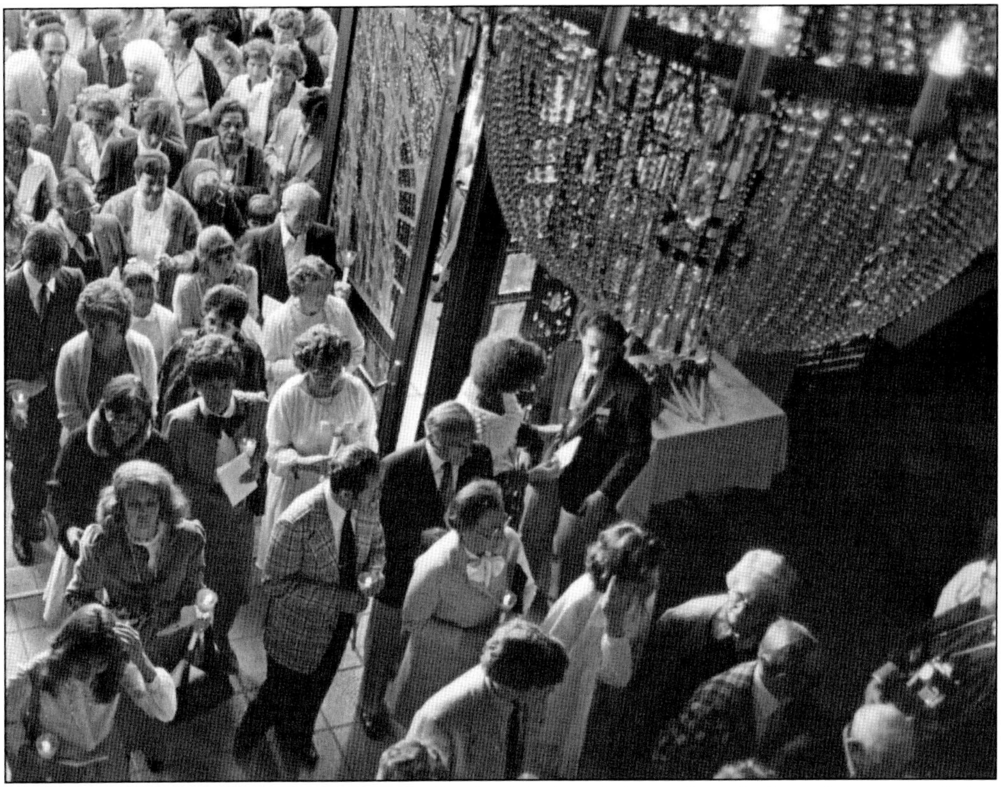

Parishioners enter the new church after the Archbishop Iakovos knocked on the door with his staff claiming the building for Christ.

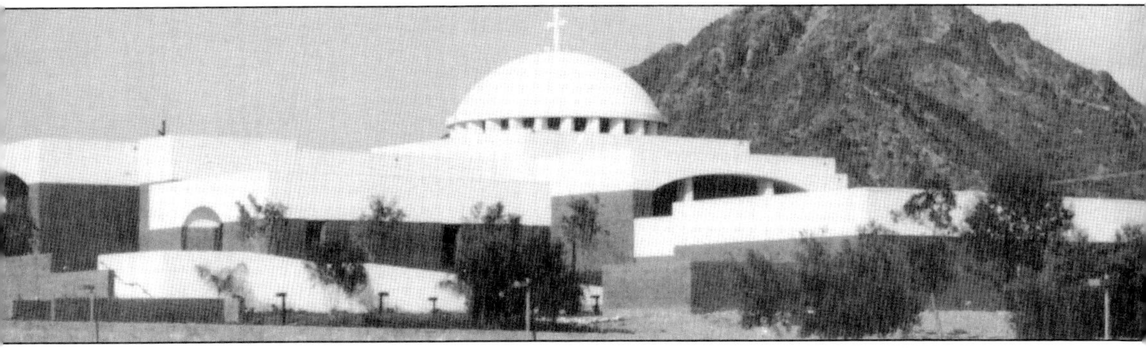

There were 60 years of intervening struggle between the 1923 assembly of 10 to the consecration of the present Holy Trinity in 1983. This remarkable accomplishment and fulfillment of a dream are a tribute to the spirit and dedication of parishioners.